RUSSIA AND THE NIS IN THE WORLD ECONOMY

RUSSIA AND THE NIS IN THE WORLD ECONOMY

East-West Investment, Financing, and Trade

Edited by
Deborah Anne Palmieri

Westport, Connecticut
London

Library of Congress Cataloging-in-Publication Data

Russia and the NIS in the world economy : east-west investment,
    financing, and trade / edited by Deborah Anne Palmieri.
        p.   cm.
    Includes bibliographical references and index.
    ISBN 0–275–94531–6 (alk. paper)
    1. Former Soviet republics—Foreign economic relations. 2. Russia
(Federation)—Foreign economic relations. I. Palmieri, Deborah
Anne.
HF1557.R87   1994
337.47—dc20   93–48213

British Library Cataloguing in Publication Data is available.

Library of Congress Catalog Card Number: 93–48213
ISBN 0–275–94531–6

First published in 1994

Praeger Publishers, 88 Post Road West, Westport, CT 06881
An imprint of Greenwood Publishing Group, Inc.

Printed in the United States of America

♾™

The paper used in this book complies with the
Permanent Paper Standard issued by the National
Information Standards Organization (Z39.48–1984).
10 9 8 7 6 5 4 3 2 1

Contents

Contents

Preface

When I invited contributors to write about specific topics pertaining to their areas of expertise, I wanted to match key issues concerning Russia's role in the world economy with individuals conducting innovative research in these areas. The goal of this book is to conjoin vital issue areas with research by scholars that can genuinely shed light on Russia's domestic economic developments and its international economic relations with the West.

Scholars today are naturally reluctant to put pen to paper amid rapidly changing events, one contradictory to that of the day before. Many feel it is highly risky to commit to paper information and analysis that may become instantaneously obsolete. They are right to have these concerns. However, the rapid pace of change is unlikely to cease in the near future, and it is my strong belief that we need to capture this remarkable process as it unfolds by writing about all of the newly changed policies, institutions, varying casts of economic and political decision makers, and so on.

There is inevitably a degree of imperfection that comes into play as we attempt to write about and understand such variable and volatile circumstances. Despite this, the book aims to provide the scholarly and policy community with material of relevance in understanding the present and future role of Russia in the world economy.

Introduction

This volume brings together scholarly writings that illuminate our understanding of the rapidly changing contemporary role of Russia and the newly independent states (NIS) in the world economy, with special reference to the industrialized West. Many questions and issues need to be addressed to enhance a greater understanding of Russian global economic integration. These encompass conceptual, theoretical, practical, and empirical themes.

The first set pertains to investment-related questions. What opportunities and problems are associated with foreign investment as a vehicle of economic development for the former Soviet Union (FSU)? Russian and Western officials wax euphoric that such investment will stimulate critical economic growth, but this hypothesis should not be taken for granted, and in examining the question it is useful to look at Third World foreign investment experience and its impact on domestic economies. Is there a discernible pattern of foreign investment in the FSU? If so, what are its features and likely effects? Understanding the conceptual side of investment issues is complemented by an actual case study of an investment joint venture. A case study can help illustrate the defining features of a joint venture, the major aspects of its business structure, and its operations. An investigation into the microoperations of one firm's experience with the FSU can shed light on the pros and cons of the FSU/Western investment relationship.

The second set of questions centers on financing, money, and banking issues. Financial issues are a complicated, obscure, and difficult dimension of FSU global economic involvement, not only for Westerners, but also for Russians themselves. What are the perimeters of Russia's domestic banking crisis? How are its domestic finances organized, including the microeconomics of the traditional government-enterprise relationship and other issues pertaining to the Central Bank and ruble convertibility? Another major financial question centers on commodity exchanges, a phenomenon little understood in the West. What role did these exchanges play in market transformation and integration into the world economy? How are these exchanges now developing and what is their future role in the Russian economy?

The third set of questions centers on trade-related issues. What are domestic trade policies and how do NIS view the role of foreign trade? What types of regulatory systems for imports and exports are evolving? Can an export strategy be identified? Are there any particularly noteworthy regional or sectoral trade developments that require more in-depth investigation to illustrate the importance of changing commercial trends to the global economy?

Finally, I wanted to enrich conceptual aspects of the volume with a case study example of a Western firm working in Russia. This should shed light on a number of interesting questions. What will the microlevel experience of the firm tell us about patterns of Soviet/Russian interaction with Western companies? What successes and problems or difficulties did these companies meet when doing business in Russia? What lessons can be learned from their experiences? I felt it would also be useful to include a policy-related paper on addressing defense conversion in the marketization process. That way, the reader could have writings on Russia and the NIS in the world economy that intersected the spectrum of conceptual, empirical, case-study, and policy issues in one volume.

The book thus shaped up in the following way. Chapter 1, "Russia's Foreign Economic Relations with the West," provides an introduction to a broad spectrum of dimensions that should be considered in understanding Russia's evolving relationship with the West. This includes a conceptualization of Russia's foreign economic policy toward the West and Yeltsin's developmental strategy, which is derived from a belief and philosophy that Russia will benefit by building a Western style economy based on market driven economic principles. It includes a discussion of the profound change in attitude that the West now has adopted toward Russia. This thinking, from the corporate boardroom to the halls of Congress and public opinion, has led to the embracing of Russia with an almost messianic obligation to ensure that democracy and economic transformation succeed to approximate that of Western civilization. According to the new ethic, foreigners see the tool of foreign investment and a quasi–"open-door" policy in Russia as fundamental to the ability of Yeltsin to guarantee economic reform. International economic institutions like the International Monetary Fund (IMF), the World Bank, and the International Bank for Reconstruction and Development (IBRD), once hostile and discriminatory toward East-bloc economies, now embrace admission of Russia, other NIS, and Eastern

European states to their organizations and support them through huge aid and recovery packages.

Chapter 2, "Foreign Investment, Economic Growth, and Market Transition" by Eileen M. Crumm, provides unique analysis and insight into issues of NIS global economic integration through joint venture vehicles and foreign direct investment (FDI). She scrutinizes the common assumption, espoused both by the West and Russia's reformers, that foreign investment and FDI guarantee domestic prosperity, increased productivity, and economic stabilization. After conducting an extensive factual review of the extent and distribution of foreign investment activity among NIS, including a sectoral analysis of investment dollars, Professor Crumm determines that the only states that are likely to benefit from FDI in stimulating growth are Russia, Kazakhstan, Turkmenistan, Azerbaijan, and, to some extent, Uzbekistan. These states also possess scarce natural resources, particularly oil and natural gas.

What is particularly intriguing about Crumm's analysis is a discussion of the effects of foreign investment on economic development in Third World states, a comparison curiously absent in current debates over Russian modernization questions. Based on Third World experience, she concludes that states that are in a most favorable position to take advantage of foreign investment have enhanced regulatory capacities, possess an infrastructure for technological research facilities, and are endowed with generous natural resources. For the NIS, Crumm concludes that the most beneficial foreign investment is in the concentrated, monopolistic industries and manufacturing sectors producing consumer goods for domestic consumption rather than investment producing manufactures geared for export sales.

Chapter 3, "Russian Banking and Finance: A Crisis of Credibility" by Eric A. Stubbs, analyzes the current crisis in Russian banking and other finance-related matters. Stubbs evaluates the difficulties and challenges faced by Russia while making the transition to a modern commercial banking and financial system. He highlights the nature and extent of the present Russian banking crisis, including a synopsis of the history of banking institutions under the old Soviet system. Stubbs also analyzes several key issues and problems, including the relationship between the Russian government and enterprises, the politicization of the role of the Central Bank of Russia, and the valuation of the ruble and its convertibility. He ends the chapter by discussing the difficult choices and strategies available to the Russian government as it struggles with the reform process in banking and finance, particularly as defined by the rapid reform favored by Gaidar and others versus a gradualist model.

Chapter 4, "The Yeltsin Revolution and Russian Export Protectionism" by William E. Schmickle, analyzes Yeltsin's trade policy, starting with its origins in Gorbachev's trade reform strategy that criticized conventional protectionist policies. He analyzes this important aspect of Russia's foreign economic policy, including a vivid portrayal of the leading personalities and institutions in the debate. Professor Schmickle argues that essentially three foreign trade scenarios emerged from the months following the August coup. Under the first, price reform, fiscal restraint, privatization, and demonopolization of state property would engender a modernized tariff and nontariff system committed to long-term openness. Under the second, reforms were less likely to succeed and instead inflation, unemployment, speculation, and chaotic privatization with increasing corruption would create conditions whereby "predatory" traders would drain domestic resources for private gain through unofficial or black market transactions, thus avoiding taxes and regular procedures. Finally, the third scenario, under conditions of Russian state disintegration, meant that local authorities (from autonomous republics, oblasts, and krais) would erect barriers and set their own policies according to regional interests.

Chapter 5, "Breaking with Moscow: The Rise of Trade and Economic Activity in Former Soviet Border Regions" by James Clay Moltz, argues that an important trade development has emerged, the growth of "transborder economic ties." At the peripheral border regions of the FSU, countries are setting up strong ties with foreign partners on their borders. Moltz discerns two trends in the development pattern of the linkages between the old Soviet Union and its foreign neighbors, those that are culturally and historically based, and those that are economic in origin. He uses the example of growing ties between Central Asia and adjacent Muslim states to illustrate the first trend, specifically between Azerbaijan, Turkmenistan and Iran; Kazakhstan and China; and Kyrgyzstan and China. Similarly, the creation of the Black Sea Economic Cooperation Region (joining Turkey, Russia, Ukraine, Moldova, Romania, Bulgaria, Georgia, Armenia, and Azerbaijan) illustrates this trend. The economic ties that the Kaliningrad region is developing with Poland and Germany and the Karelian region with Finland are examples of the second trend. A development that seems to fit both patterns, argues Moltz, are the ties now being forged across the Bering Sea by the Kamchatka, Chukotka, and Magadan oblasts with the American and Canadian Pacific Northwest. For each of these case examples, Moltz draws on a wealth of carefully detailed and documented sources.

Moltz pays particular attention to the south border region, observing the opening of the Russian Far East to its Pacific Rim neighbors, especially China, South Korea, and Japan. He analyzes in detail policies that this region has implemented to make accessible its "Far Eastern frontiers." Moltz ends the chapter by assessing unique types of problems faced by foreign investors in border regions. One of these is the communication gap between Moscow and local officials, which often sends conflicting messages to potential investors. The constantly changing state role in governing joint ventures and other business transactions results in inconsistent laws and center-regional conflicts within state ministeries. Moltz concludes that many areas that were marginal or peripheral to the old Soviet Union may now become thriving, independent economic centers and important sources of new export-led growth.

Chapter 6, "Commodity Exchanges and the Post-Soviet Market" by Ariel Cohen, offers a rare insight into the evolution of commodity exchange networks in Russia. Piecing together original Russian source material on this subject, about which little is known in the West, Cohen analyzes the role of exchanges as key institutions in the marketization process and evaluates their strengths and shortcomings. He places special emphasis on their crucial period of development from early 1991 to early 1992, but also looks at their roots in the Russian prerevolutionary exchanges.

Cohen examines the origins of the principal Russian commodities exchange, Rossiyskaya Tovarno-Syryevaya Birzha (RTSB) and the processes and procedures by which it functioned. He includes an insight into the world of Russian commodity exchange brokers and reviews competing exchanges in Moscow, including RTSB's major competitor, the Moscow Commodities Exchange, Moskovskaya Tovarnaya Birzha (MTB), whose origins evolved from the old Soviet bureaucracy. Regional exchanges outside of Moscow also played an important role. Siberian exchanges specializing in oil developed. Another, the Asian Exchange, played a key role in developing trade ties with the Pacific Rim region. Other regional exchanges include one in Vorkuta to trade in lumber, coals, and other raw materials; the Altai Commodities Exchange (ATB) in Barnaul; the Southern Universal Exchange (Yu.U.B.) in Nikolayev, Ukraine; the Tbilisi Universal Exchange in Georgia; and others in Kiev, Gomel, Odessa, Perm, Ryazan, Duzbass, Volgograd, and Dnepropetrovsk. Moscow also faced stiff competition upon the founding of the Leningrad Stock Exchange, or Leningradskaya Fondovaya Birzha (LFB), in early 1991.

Cohen reviews problems and obstacles the exchanges faced, including shortages of qualified brokers and staff to administer the exchanges, and a lack of cooperation early on from government ministries to secure necessary licenses. He helps the reader comprehend how these commodity exchanges are instrumental in the reform process as distribution channels and price-setting mechanisms. Cohen also provides insights into deficiencies of the emerging commodities system, including lack of computerized information systems to set prices among the different regional exchanges; lack of specialization and focus by commodities markets; and lack of a code of business conduct, or business ethics. He ends the chapter on a solemn note, by illustrating many examples of how undesirable business conduct threatens to undermine the whole system (for example, demands for up-front payments for goods that later are never delivered, and the belated return of funds or nonreporting of large numbers of transactions). Cohen concludes that while commodities exchanges are not a panacea, combined with other market institutions, including systems of civil and private property law, exchanges will serve as Russian "windows to the world" and facilitate its global economic integration.

Chapter 7, "Monsanto's Operations in the Former Soviet Union: A Case-Study" by Paula M. Ross, offers a fascinating inside view of a company whose operations have not been extensively publicly chronicled in the FSU. The multibillion dollar Monsanto Company, specializing not only in chemicals and pharmaceuticals but also agricultural products, synthetic fibers, plastics, and food products including NutraSweet, has been doing business with the Soviet Union since the 1950s. Ross offers readers a perspective on Monsanto's business structure and operations in the Soviet Union, and how Monsanto worked to develop its Soviet market niche. In an unusually detailed way, Ross covers a range of Monsanto's business dealings, including sales of chemicals, agricultural herbicides, and pharmaceuticals, and the spawning of technology agreements to help the Soviets develop advanced production methods in polymers and diamondlike coatings and the upgrading of phosphate facilities. Agricultural operations were a key component of Monsanto's Russian portfolio. Not only did Monsanto experience increased sales of their *Roundup* herbicide but they also became involved in demonstration farms and other agricultural operations, as in Sumy, Ukraine, to promote advanced farming technology.

Ross goes on to detail other aspects of Monsanto's business operations in the FSU, including research and development, communications, employees, how the company worked through the Soviet foreign (and now FSU) trade system, and how they developed other appropriate business channels such as methods of product delivery, contracts, and product and trade financing. She includes an assessment of how Monsanto viewed the issue of ruble inconvertibility (not a problem) and analyzes what they perceived as trade barriers to business, including disregard for intellectual property rights, patent stealing, and unfavorable U.S. export trade policy.

Chapter 8, "Marketization through Defense Conversion: A Policy Perspective on the Ukrainian Case" written by Margaret B. McLean and Deborah Anne Palmieri, is a policy position statement on Ukrainian prospects for defense conversion. While few disagree that defense conversion is a vital component of the reform process for the NIS, few agree on specifically how this can be done. The complexities are enormous. This chapter evaluates the Ukrainian case by looking at the issue both philosophically and operationally. It points out some of the difficult trade-offs faced by countries like Ukraine, whose economies under Soviet rule were heavily defense-based. While conversion can conceivably provide avenues for the technological upgrading of outdated manufacturing equipment, new supply and distribution networks, and increased productivity to modern sectors of Ukraine's economy, there is also a downside. Who will absorb the shortrun, start-up costs of such a massive retooling of basic industrial structure, one that is likely to be substantially less profitable than lucrative defense industries, not to mention other spinoff effects including unemployment, employee retraining, enterprise bankruptcies, and the political and economic instability caused by it all?

McLean and Palmieri address these issues and others central to the conversion process. They evaluate the pros and cons of several conversion strategies, including the domestic regrouping, joint efforts, compensation, public finance, Western credits, and foreign manufacturing strategies. The chapter ends with a discussion of four critical steps that Ukraine must take to ensure a successful conversion process, including appropriate business, tax, and legal incentives that protect intellectual property rights, avoiding double taxation and streamlining the investment process.

In summary, inevitably this book has not been able to cover every topic of interest on Russian and NIS integration into the global economy. Each essay may not have perfectly or comprehensively covered all that it should have. But it is hoped that the volume will provide some unique insights; display the vivid complexities of Russia and the NIS's past, present, and future involvement in the world economy; and stimulate further research in this area.

1

Russia's Foreign Economic Relations with the West

Deborah Anne Palmieri

There is one thing stronger than all the armies in the world, and that is an idea whose time has come.

— Victor Hugo

After an almost 76-year hiatus, during which economic relations following the Russian Revolution between the Soviet Union and the nations of the industrialized West were either minimal or underutilized at best, the idea and the time has come for a symbiotic relationship. There is no doubt, as Samuel P. Huntington put it, that globally "the most torn country is Russia." Torn in the sense that it grapples with the question most fundamental to its modern identity, that of whether "Russia is a part of the West, or a leader of a distinct Slavic-Orthodox civilization."[1] But since 1991, independent Russia, under the leadership of Boris Yeltsin, has distinctly chosen to favor, at least for the time being, the path of liberalization and Westernization.[2] Despite strong opposing forces, it has chosen to emphasize market principles and global economic integration over other alternatives, including paths of communism, Russification, Slavic nationalism, and other inwardly looking isolationist policies.

YELTSIN'S STRATEGY

Yeltsin was unambiguous about casting Russia's lot with the West. This was clear in a statement he made at the Group of 7 (G-7) Economic Summit in July 1992. "Russia . . . is returning and will return to Europe, in which it was for a thousand years, for thousands of years."[3] The new Russian strategy is predicated on the foreign policy belief that

Russia and the West need each other to guarantee "a stable world order," with Russia a member of the "civilized democratic community," with a stake in serving as an "equilibrium force" in Europe and Asia.[4] Likewise, Western nations have adopted an economics-based strategy to bring Russia into the fold, and to gain this country's confidence as a foreign policy associate and a long-term industrial partner. As one observer put it, the "old power game of geopolitics is giving way to a new strategic era of geofinance."[5] Many echo the view of former Federal Republic of Germany (FRG) (now Germany) Minister Hans-Dietrich Genscher that Russia should become the eighth member of the G-7.[6]

Yeltsin's cooperative strategy in the realm of foreign economic relations embraces five critical components that will be discussed in this chapter.[7] The first is to integrate into the global economic system by increasing trade and investment with Western countries, with the expectation to modernize the Russian infrastructure with the aid of American, European, and Japanese expertise and technical know-how. The second component is to solicit extensive economic aid from the West to underwrite the reform process. The third component is to successfully manage the Russian debt problem by a combination of methods, including holding off creditors, rescheduling Russian debt to more favorable terms, such as spreading them out over a long period of time, and improving loan terms. The fourth is to gain membership or access to key Western international economic institutions including the International Monetary Fund (IMF), World Bank, International Bank for Reconstruction and Development (IBRD), and General Agreement on Tariffs and Trade (GATT). Finally, the last element in Yeltsin's strategy is to target the United States more so than other G-7 nations in order to gain access to American capital to build a strategic economic and foreign policy partnership.

Yeltsin's foreign economic strategy is predicated on his ability to maintain and sustain a stable domestic economy. He is charged with the unenviable task of transforming a formerly command economy to an open market system with a democratic political system.[8] He needs to create a whole new administrative apparatus and a legal and business environment conducive to implementing market reforms. According to his "Russian Government Program for Deepening Economic Reforms to 1995-6," the main aspects the reform program needs to concentrate on for the next three years include liberalization of the economy; monetary and financial stabilization; privatization or the creation of private ownership of the vast resources now in state hands; the implementation of structural changes in the economy (for example, military conversion and emphasis on consumer production); the creation of a competitive market environment; and the introduction of appropriate social policies.[9]

All of these changes must be implemented amid a deteriorating economy whose gross national product (GNP) is dropping precipitously

(2 percent in 1990, 9 percent in 1991, 20 percent in 1992, and a similar decrease for 1993), and an annual inflation rate that had reached over 1,000 percent by 1993.[10] Yet Yeltsin expects to hit bottom in 1993 and then gradually pull out of the slump during 1994 and beyond.

NEW TRADE AND INVESTMENT PATTERNS

The first component of Yeltsin's strategy is to fully integrate into the global economic system by increasing trade and investment with Western countries and improve the structure of Russian foreign trade.[11] This contrasts with the conventional Soviet trading pattern in the past, which relied on intra-CMEA (Council for Mutual Economic Assistance) trade and disregarded the need for trade with "developed capitalist countries." What trade there was with the West was characterized by the exchange of Soviet raw materials and unadvanced products for manufactured goods and advanced technology from the West. Under this traditional pattern, Soviet exports included mainly raw materials such as wood, fuels, and lubricants (including coal, coke, oil, and oil products), gas, chemicals, base metals, iron and steel, and machinery (especially transportation equipment). Imports included general categories of machinery and equipment, consumer goods, and food.[12]

By the 1980s, Soviet trade, especially under Gorbachev, began to increase in favor of advanced industrialized nations. This trend was evident even by 1980. For example, in 1960, 49.7 percent of Soviet imports came from Eastern Europe. They declined to 42.9 percent by 1980. Reciprocally, in 1960, 19.5 percent of imports were from developed countries. By 1980, this figure had increased to 35.4 percent. In terms of Soviet exports, in 1960, 55.3 percent went to Eastern Europe; by 1980, this figure had declined to 42.1 percent. Soviet exports comprised 17.9 percent of foreign trade to developed countries in 1960, and by 1980, the figure had jumped to 31.9 percent. Exports and imports to and from the West continued to increase throughout the 1980s until the demise of the Soviet Union in December 1991.[13] Russia under Yeltsin continued this policy as a major cornerstone of the reform strategy.

Russia's foreign trade turnover in 1992 increased substantially with developed capitalist countries, and decreased with ex-CMEA and "other socialist" countries, as the statistics in Table 1.1 indicate.[14]

Nonetheless, as PlanEcon reports, this trade turnover, which amounted to $45.3 billion (or 62 percent of total trade) decreased 17 percent from the year before.[15]

Yeltsin wants more trade with the West for basic reasons. Russia needs hard currency and better market prices for its exports to the West. By importing Western technology and products, Yeltsin is continuing a strategy that dates back to the Brezhnev years: the hope that trade with the West, specifically imports of capital equipment and

TABLE 1.1
Direction of Trade

(percentage of total 1992)

	Exports	Imports
Ex-CMEA	19.7	15.7
Other Socialist	9.7	7.7
Developed Capitalist Countries	60.1	64.0
Developing Capitalist Countries	10.5	12.6

Source: *Financial Times*, 27 May 1993, sec. 3, p. 3.

technology, will speed up economic development. Similar to a
quasi–import-led strategy, Yeltsin hopes that trade and investment can
serve as important vehicles whereby Russia can acquire necessary
goods and services to spark economic development. Yeltsin also continued Gorbachev's strategy of expanding industrial cooperation with the
West, especially through joint venturing activity.[16]

Russian joint ventures with foreign countries increased substantially by 1992, as the data in Table 1.2 suggest.

According to the data displayed by Table 1.2, the greatest number of
joint ventures registered with the League of Joint Ventures and
International Associations and Organizations by April 1992 included
the United States, Germany, Finland, and Italy as the top investors. In
terms of ruble volume of authorized capital, the greatest support came
from the United States, Italy, Germany, and Austria.[17] Joint venture
activity is expected to increase, despite the associated risks of doing
business with Russia.[18] Yeltsin has consistently favored lenient policies

TABLE 1.2
Russian Joint Ventures by Foreign Country Partner

Country	Number Joint Ventures	Total Authorized Capital (million rubles)
Austria	164	606
Finland	208	391
France	90	501
Germany	373	781
Great Britain	122	228
Italy	198	1,038
Japan	43	138
Spain	34	66
Sweden	212	519
United States	398	11,034

Source: *Interflo*, July 1992, FBIS-SOV, 19 June 1992, 35:2.

for foreign investors and has produced legislation and decrees toward this end. Two of the most important sections of this legislation include "On the Liberalization of Foreign Economic Activity in RSFSR," (November 1991, also referred to as Presidential Decree No. 213), and the Russian law on foreign investment of July 1991, which permits 100 percent foreign ownership of enterprises and other favorable provisions on profit repatriation, preferential tax rates, and tax holidays for projects in certain industrial or agricultural sectors of the economy. The result of such legislation was that by early 1993, almost $2 billion in foreign investment was directed into the Russian marketplace.[19]

FOREIGN AID PACKAGES

A key component of Yeltsin's foreign economic policy strategy is to use economic aid from the West to rebuild Russia. His goal is to pump in as much aid and loan money as possible to complement foreign investment in order to liberalize the economy, privatize state-led enterprises, create a competitive market environment, and finance other government initiatives and programs.[20] He hopes to use aid money to stimulate private sector growth, promote defense conversion, and fight hyperinflation. Yeltsin and other members of his government have called for three kinds of economic assistance: humanitarian; funds to deal with the balance of payments and debt servicing crisis; and funds to contribute to a ruble stabilization fund.[21]

Western countries approved two major aid packages in 1993. The Vancouver Summit Assistance Package from the United States totalled $1.6 billion in grants and credits. See Table 1.3.

TABLE 1.3
Vancouver Summit Assistance Package

	Million $
Grants	
Grant Food Assistance	194.0
Technical Cooperation	281.9
Nunn-Lugar	215.0
Subtotal Grants	690.9
Credits	
Food for Progress Credit Sales	700.0
Eximbank Credits	82.0
OPIC Credits	150.0
Subtotal Credits	932.0
Total Package	1,622.9

Source: "Vancouver Summit Assistance Package," Press Release from White House, 4 April 1993, Office of the Press Secretary.

At the G-7 meeting in April 1993, G-7 leaders announced a $44 billion aid program from the IMF, World Bank, and other sources of bilateral aid.[22] See Table 1.4 for a breakdown of the aid package.

G-7 officials continued to demand stringent conditions before the funds could be released. These included limits on central bank credit creation, increased interest rates from Russia's banks, a reduction in state subsidies to enterprises, and a solid budget program.[23]

U.S. loan activity is especially supportive of financing Russian oil and gas transactions. As one oil and gas executive heading up a well drilling equipment company about to invest in the Tyumen region commented, "If we can get them the technology to get the oil out, they can generate the hard currency needed to help pull out of the current crisis."[24] In April 1993, Eximbank signed an $82 million loan agreement with GAZPROM, the Russian natural gas production and distribution organization.[25]

TABLE 1.4
G-7 Aid Package

	Billion $
Bilateral Governments	
Public Debt Restructuring	15.00
Export Credits and Guarantees	10.00
IMF	
Systemic Transformation Facility	3.00
Stand-by-Loan	4.10
Currency Stabilization Fund	6.00
World Bank	
World Bank Loan Commitments	3.40
Import Rehabilitation Loans	1.10
Oil Sector Loan	.05
European Bank for Reconstruction and Development	
Small- and Medium-Enterprise Fund	.30

Source: Financial Times, 27 May 1993, Special Section on Russia, p. 2.

RUSSIA'S DEBT TRAP

A key component of Yeltsin's foreign economic strategy toward the West is the successful management of Russia's pressing foreign debt, which by mid-1993 was estimated at approximately $80 billion.[26] Most of this debt was carried over from the former Soviet Union.[27] As debt specialist Paul Gardiner commented, "quantifying the external debt is difficult. Figures from different sources are inconsistent, both for the total owed and for breakdown by type of claims, maturity, and creditor."[28] Approximately $33 billion is owed to official creditors, $35 billion to commercial banks, and approximately $10 billion to suppliers.[29] While the debt burden is not greatly out of proportion for a country with the size, resources, and capabilities of Russia, Yeltsin's problem is that the country does not have the cash flow to secure the interest, let alone the principal, of its outstanding loans. An increasingly poor credit rating has disastrous consequences including a diminished ability by Russia to secure more loans and plummeting confidence in Russia's creditworthiness and trustworthiness by international creditors.

Another problem Russia faces is that poor loan planning over the past decade or two resulted in having many medium-term obligations come due simultaneously. For example, Russia was expected to pay $10 billion in 1992 and $12 billion in 1993.[30] Another problem was that of settling the debts between Russia and ex-Soviet republics. After a great deal of complicated negotiations, Yeltsin proposed to take responsibility for Soviet foreign debt, in exchange for an agreement by other republics to relinquish their claims on Soviet foreign assets. All agreed except Ukraine, which believes that its portion of assets exceeds its 16.4 percent of the debt.[31] The pressing payment obligations and inheritance of all former Soviet debt coincided with a drastic reduction in foreign currency earnings from oil sales to the West, which fell from $22 billion in 1986 to $6 billion in 1992. Consequently, Russia experienced an escalation of payment defaults, including a $149 million capital repayment on a European Community food credit and $897 million in U.S.-backed agricultural loans.

As a result of these factors, the debt servicing crisis, which began to mount in 1990 and compounded during 1991, came to a head in early 1992, when Russia was unable to pay either principal or interest (except payments on certain U.S. food loans and all bond repayments). Yeltsin appealed to Western creditors to try and gain more time by reducing immediate payments and rescheduling loan payments over a longer period of time. Yeltsin and his finance minister, Boris Fyodorov, approached their major creditors consisting of the Paris Club, the London Club, and other creditors outside these circles from Saudi Arabia, United Arab Emirates, Kuwait, and South Korea, to strike a rescheduling deal with each one.[32]

Russian officials successfully convinced creditors not only of their intent to pay and determination to succeed in their reform efforts but also that they faced a short-term liquidity problem and not a long-term solvency problem.[33] The Paris Club agreed to allow Russia to pay $1.9 billion, while the London Club agreed to accept $500 million in back interest for the fourth quarter 1993.[34]

Other rescheduling talks were conducted bilaterally, for example, between Russia and the United States albeit under the umbrella of the Paris Club.[35] The Russian government fared well through the negotiations. Much of the official debt was rescheduled over ten years, with a five year grace period and partial capitalization of interest payments.[36] Settlement of debt issues was important for Russia, since it now opens the door to new borrowing and access to additional grain credits from the United States. Western strategy in granting the debt relief was clear. It was more of a political than an economic gesture, designed to show support for the democratic and reform movement. As Jacque Attali, former President of the European Bank for Reconstruction and Development (EBRD) stated, "deferment of debt payments is a key element of a package of measures essential to saving democracy in Russia."[37]

INSTITUTIONAL LEGITIMIZATION

The fourth component of Yeltsin's strategy toward the West has been to gain membership in the major Western international economic institutions, a continuation of efforts that began in the late 1980s under Gorbachev. Most of the international economic organizations, including IMF, World Bank, and GATT, formed shortly after World War II in the midst of Cold War tensions excluded the Soviet Union either through a deliberate plan, indifference, or lack of desire on the part of the Soviets.[38] Nikita Khrushchev, Leonid Brezhnev, and even Mikhail Gorbachev would envy what Yeltsin has been able to accomplish in a few short years. Determined to break out of isolationism and economic autarky and put Russia on a path of integration, one of Yeltsin's main priorities has been to express his desire for a new Russian role in the global economic order. While in the past many argued that the structure of a centrally planned economy was incompatible with membership in these market institutions, Yeltsin, through his reform program, promised to comply with the rules of the game in part by privatizing the economy, setting up market institutions, and totally revamping the banking and foreign trade systems. Yeltsin calculated that in order to change Russia's structure of foreign trade (namely the export of raw materials and energy and import of manufactures) and to modernize the Russian industrial infrastructure, he needed the benefits of lower tariffs, membership in the world's major trading organizations, and financing of his reform programs. He indicated he would change his system in order to fit into the existing international system and its code of conduct.

Following an extensive period of debate and study, the IMF and World Bank opened their doors to Russia in June 1992.[39] The IMF had been preparing for some time to accommodate Russia and other newly independent states. In early 1992, it created a new FSU division, headed by former British Treasury economist John Odling-Smee. It assigned

130–150 staff members to Russian and former Soviet matters, with the hope that more staff additions would soon be forthcoming.[40] By July 1992 the World Bank had approved a credit line of $1 billion for Russian stabilization programs.[41] Several months after joining the World Bank, Russia was granted a $600 million rehabilitation loan to finance imports essential to the economic reform program. An affiliate organization of the World Bank, the International Finance Corporation was responsible for speeding up the privatization process by working with medium- to large-sized organizations.[42]

Russia is still not a member of the GATT, the 108-member multilateral organization that provides a code of conduct for international trade among its members and acts as a forum for dispute settlement.[43] Russia has, nonetheless, held observer status in GATT since May 1990. The Clinton Administration has indicated it will support Russian membership when Russia submits a formal application.[44] Another organization, the EBRD, now provides technical assistance, loans, and debt guarantees for Russia. Its special emphasis is to develop the private sector, increase direct foreign investment, and strengthen financial institutions. EBRD focuses on projects mainly in the following sectors: military conversion, energy, nuclear safety, and agriculture and agribusiness.

RUSSIAN-AMERICAN CONNECTIONS

While Yeltsin has cultivated strong ties with all Western nations, he exhibits an especially high degree of interest in the United States. Yeltsin heralds America's economic developmental experience as "a great example for today's Russian reformers and entrepreneurs."[45] And with the wave of summit meetings and collapse of the old Cold War economic institutional structures, the United States has found its own set of advantages and benefits in pursuing an economic association with Russia.[46] George Bush articulated the belief held on both sides that a U.S.-Russian partnership "will become one of the largest two-way trading relationships in the entire world."[47] His secretary of commerce at the time echoed this view: "The United States wants to be Russia's number one trading partner and investor."[48]

Americans have several reasons for a newly reassessed interest in Russia. With communism's collapse, the former "enemy state" provided a novel challenge and a new "cause celebre," and "the historical transformation of the Russian economy is one of the greatest challenges of our time."[49] The United States began to view Russia's economic potential in a different light with the passing of the Cold War period. Before, such potential was looked at mainly from the perspective of how the Soviet Union's resources could fuel defense capabilities and outstrip the United States in the arms race. Estimates of Soviet and Russian economic potential, which were previously interpreted from a mindset of hostility, coupled with the expectation of adversarial relations, began to acquire rejuvenated meaning when viewed with an expectation of economic cooperation. Americans started to see Russia as a land of new economic opportunity and began searching for trade and investment outlets complementary to its own growth needs.[50]

U.S.-Russian business and commercial ties expanded significantly over previous levels during the early 1990s. Two of the most significant developments in the U.S.-Russian commercial relationship were the agreements that came out of the summit talks between President George Bush and President Boris Yeltsin in June 1992, including the United States-Russia Business Summit and the April 1993 Vancouver Summit initiatives between President Bill Clinton and President Boris Yeltsin. U.S. economic policy toward the Soviet Union and Russia had begun to soften before these summits. In September 1991, a revised Commerce Control List eliminated many commodities formerly banned for sale to Russia as national security risks, many of them commonly available high-tech items on U.S. retail shelves. On February 27, 1992, the Export-Import Bank initiated new programs to finance U.S. exports to Russia. On April 1, 1992, House Joint Resolution 465 officially repealed the Stevenson-Byrd Amendments, which effectively removed a $300 million limit on financing U.S. exports to Russia.

The U.S.-Russian economic agreements that evolved from the June 1992 summit were the most important economic developments since the Nixon-Brezhnev Summit of 1972, and probably the most significant developments in U.S. foreign economic policy toward Russia and the Soviet Union since 1945, if not the entire century. The United States-Russia Trade Agreement provided for reciprocal most favored nation (MFN) tariff treatment (an objective that Khrushchev first set in 1956) and improved market access for both sides, and enacted strong intellectual property rights protection for foreign companies.[51] According to the Trade Agreement, Russia was accorded nondiscriminatory trade treatment. The Bilateral Investment Treaty created a legal framework to enhance expanded business relations between both countries, including guarantees for profit repatriation, dispute arbitration, and compensation under circumstances of expropriation. The treaty also minimized screening procedures through the Council of Ministers, expedited investment-related currency transfers, and prevented Russian interference in the hiring process for foreign joint ventures.[52] The Treaty for the Avoidance of Double Taxation of Income (that replaced the 1973 Convention on Matters of Taxation) guaranteed favorable tax laws by eliminating or reducing investment tax liabilities.[53]

Besides these treaties, the United States-Russia Business Development Committee was formed.[54] The purpose of this committee is to resolve obstacles to business relations, to encourage project cooperation and the expansion of all commercial linkages, and to establish a separate Subcommittee of Defense Conversion.[55] Its other working groups included the Foreign Trade Regulation Group, Investment and Commercial Projects Group, and the Industrial Cooperation and Trade Promotion Group.[56]

The second major milestone in the development of U.S.-Russian economic relations was the signing of protocols at the early April 1993 summit meetings between President Bill Clinton and President Boris Yeltsin in Vancouver, Canada.

In the Vancouver Declaration, Yeltsin and Clinton concluded a new round of bilateral economic programs and declared "their firm commitment to a dynamic and effective U.S.-Russian partnership."[57] The United States committed to a $1.6 billion aid package to Russia. Clinton explained his administration's rationale for this assistance, partially on the basis that a prosperous Russia "could add untold billions in new growth to the global economy" resulting in "new jobs and new investment opportunities for Americans."[58] The agreement contained not only provisions for special solicitations for U.S. investment but also an emphasis on developing Russia's oil and gas sectors.[59] Yeltsin commented that the summit "was the first economically oriented meeting of the two great powers" and that it "signals a shift from general assurances of support to Russia to pragmatic, specific, nitty-gritty projects."[60]

The Clinton Administration announced it would support eliminating Russian exclusion from the Generalized System of Preferences (GSP) in order to increase trade volume between both countries.[61] Through a variety of U.S. government agencies, numerous other initiatives developed during 1992 and 1993 to facilitate trade, financing, and investment, as the following examples illustrate. The Commodity Credit Corporation, through the United States Department of Agriculture, provides credit guarantees to encourage NIS purchases of agricultural commodities.[62] The United States Trade and Development Agency by May 1993 had approved $5.7 million for U.S. firms to conduct feasibility studies and other plans related to industrial projects for the Russian government. The United States Export-Import Bank opened its programs to support exports to Russia and by early 1993 had issued guarantees and insurance totaling $230 million.[63] Other government efforts through the Overseas Private Investment Corporation (OPIC) provide loans, guarantees, and insurance, and through Peace Corps programs they also provide project assistance and business counseling.

The United States Department of Commerce has been especially active in building and expanding business development projects with Russia, particularly in light of the vote of confidence given to the reform movement with Yeltsin's successful showing at the April 1993 referendum. Secretary of Commerce Ronald H. Brown advocated that "one of the most effective contributions we in government can make is to help bring about the rapid expansion of U.S.-Russian trade and investment."[64] Toward this end, the Commerce Department set up Business Information Services for the Newly Independent States (BISNIS), an up-to-date information service on trade regulations, legislation, and market data.[65] The Consortia of American Businesses in the NIS is another pilot program enabling small- and medium-sized companies to pool joint resources to enter NIS marketplaces. The Commerce Department is establishing American Business Centers in Russia and the NIS is to provide business services (phone, fax, office space, translation, business information, etc.) and by 1993 had offices in cities including St. Petersburg, Nizhni Novgorod, Tyumen, and Vladivostok.[66] The Commerce Department is expanding its U.S. and Foreign Commercial Service network in Russia and the NIS. Other programs include Special American Business Intern Training, which brings executives and scientists from the FSU for three- to six-month internships with U.S. companies. The Commerce Department sponsors numerous trade promotion events, including trade missions and exhibits in the NIS.[67]

CONCLUDING REMARKS

In sum, Russia has unquestionably embarked upon a path of relying on the development of its foreign economic relations with the West, almost with the expectation that it will perform miracles for future domestic economic development. As this chapter has argued, Russia's economic strategy toward the West rests on the foreign policy premise that Russia and the West need to work together to guarantee international stability. Former enemies now turned allies, both Russia and the West hope to join economic forces and avoid the politics of confrontation of the past and the military and defense spending that went along with them that drained the economies of both. Yeltsin's strategy of global economic integration is a go-for-broke attempt to quickly normalize trade and economic ties with industrially advanced nations and secure large amounts of money from them at the same time to underwrite the reform process. Yeltsin has incorporated into this plan staving off the Russian debt crisis and gaining membership into major Western economic institutions. He particularly desires to cement an economic alliance with the United States.

It is too early to tell whether Yeltsin's strategy will succeed or fail. The question is intertwined with the broader issue of Russia's centuries long quest for economic modernization and its struggle to overcome isolation, backwardness, and underdevelopment. Yeltsin's attempt to serve as catalyst for Russia's transformation may finally, after hundreds of years of historical attempts and failures, deliver a beacon of brightness for Russia in the twenty-first century. If his strategy succeeds, Russia can look forward to the economic prosperity, stability, and growth it has long dreamed of. If his strategy fails, Russia can expect more of the same hardship, deprivation, pessimism, and harshness of daily existence to which it has long been accustomed.

NOTES

1. Samuel P. Huntington, "The Clash of Civilizations?" *Foreign Affairs*, vol. 72, no. 3 (Summer 1993): 43.

2. The Supreme Soviet voted to change the name of the Russian Socialist Federation of the Soviet Republic to the Russian Federation in December 1991. With the establishment of the Commonwealth of Independent States on December 26, 1991, the Union of Soviet Socialist Republics (USSR) ceased to exist as a state. Soviet head of state Mikhail Gorbachev resigned at the same time.

3. Federal News Service, July 8, 1992, "News Conference with Chancellor Helmut Kohl and President Boris Yeltsin at the Group of Seven Economic Summit." Statement by President Yeltsin to Chancellor Kohl in interview. (On-line)

4. Vladimir Lukin, "Our Security Predicament," *Foreign Policy*, no. 88 (Fall 1992): 67, 75. As of this writing, Vladimir Lukin is the Russian Ambassador to the United States.

5. Martin Walker, *Europe*, April 1992, p. 18.

6. Foreign Broadcast Information Service-East Asia (September 17, 1992): 2:1

7. For more on the historical origins of Yeltsin's strategy dating from the Gorbachev period and prior, see Deborah Anne Palmieri, "The Origins of Gorbachev's Foreign Economic Policy," *The U.S.S.R. and the World Economy: Challenges for the Global Integration of Soviet Markets Under Perestroika* (Westport, Conn.: Praeger, 1992). For discussion of historical origins of Gorbachev's reforms and relationship between domestic reform and international change, see Valerie Bunce, "Domestic Reform and International Change: The Gorbachev Reforms in Historical Perspective," *International Organization*, vol. 47, no. 1 (Winter 1993).

8. For background on issues pertaining to economic transformation, see Anders Aslund, ed., *The Post-Soviet Economy: Soviet and Western Perspectives* (New York: St. Martin's Press, 1992), especially chapters therein by Grigorii Khanin, "The Soviet Economy from Crisis to Catastrophe"; Anders Aslund, "A Critique of Soviet Reform Plans"; and Jeffrey Sachs, "The Grand Bargain." For a Soviet perspective circa 1990 and 1991, see Boris Z. Milner and Dimitry S. Lvov, eds., *Soviet Market Economy: Challenges and Reality* (Netherlands: North-Holland, 1991), especially chapters therein by Leonard Abalkin, Nikolai Petrakov, and Stanislav Shatalin. For more on economics under Gorbachev, see Reiner Weichhardt, ed., *The Soviet Economy Under Gorbachev* (Brussels: NATO, 1991). See also Reiner Weichhardt, ed., *Soviet Economic Reforms: Implementation Under Way* (Brussels: NATO, 1989).

9. See Foreign Broadcast Information Service-SOV (July 1, 1992): 26:2. For more on economic reform, see Richard Portes, "From Central Planning to a Market Economy," and Robert W. Campbell, "Economic Reform in the USSR and Its Successor States," both in Shafiqul Islam and Michael Mandelbaum, eds., *Making Markets: Economic Transformation in Eastern Europe and the Post-Soviet States* (New York: Council on Foreign Relations Press, 1993). See also Dimitri Simes, "Reform Reaffirmed," *Foreign Policy*, no. 90 (Spring 1993). For emphasis on privatization and ownership issues, see Jozef M. van Brabant, *Privatizing Eastern Europe: The Role of Markets and Ownership in the Transition* (Dordrecht, Netherlands: Kluwer Academic Publishers, 1992).

10. Figures on Russia's economic indicators will vary according to analysts. For figures just quoted, see "Commercial Overview," Business Information Service for Newly Independent States, U.S. Commerce Department, May 25, 1993. See also

"Selected Economic Indicators for Russia, 1991-6," *PlanEcon Business Report*, vol. 3, no. 5 (March 3, 1993).

11.   For discussion on the problems Russia faces, especially pertaining to foreign trade reform and problems of integration, see Alan Smith, *Russia and the World Economy: Problems of Integration* (London: Routledge, 1993).

12.   Central Intelligence Agency, *Handbook of Economic Indicators*, (Washington, D.C.: National Foreign Assessment Center, 1983), pp. 94–5, Tables 64 and 65.

13.   Source of data derived from Hedija H. Kravalis, "USSR: An Assessment of U.S. and Western Trade Potential with the Soviet Union Through 1985," in U.S. Joint Economic Committee, *East-West Trade: The Prospects to 1985* (Washington, D.C.: U.S. Government Printing Office, 1982), p. 306, Table A-1. See also William H. Cooper, "Soviet-Western Trade," in U.S. Joint Economic Committee, *The Soviet Economy in the 1980's: Problems and Prospects*, Part 2 (Washington, D.C.: U.S. Government Printing Office, 1982), and R. E. Hebden, "Trends in Soviet Trade Since 1960," *Geography* (London), vol. 65, no. 286 (January 1980): Part 1.

14.   This development has occurred in the context of a Russian foreign trade turnover that declined about 30 percent in 1992 from the previous year. Causes for this deterioration include political and economic instability, including decreasing national production, problems in trade financing, chaotic Russian trade laws, and a constantly changing trade ministerial system.

15.   *PlanEcon Business Report*, Special Issue, vol. 9, no. 5-5 (March 10, 1993): 35. PlanEcon argues that Russian statistics showing high levels of exports to foreign countries are distorted by official current price ruble statistics, and that Goskomstat data really shows sustained Russian trade with other FSU republics and a "turning inward" of trade direction with them rather than a "turning outward" to the West (p. 34). Their data also provides revealing statistics about changing patterns between Russia and its Western trading partners. In 1992, for example, trade volume decreased by 7 percent with Germany (conventionally the Soviet Union and Russia's leading Western trade partner), and decreased by 25 percent with Japan. Trade volume increased by 80 percent with the United Kingdom, 56 percent with the United States, 27 percent with Italy, 22 percent with France, and 14 percent with Netherlands and Finland (p. 35). PlanEcon presents an interesting question about the anomaly presented by seemingly conflicting bits of data. "With so many Western countries reported to have increased trade turnover with Russia in dollar terms, what caused an overall decline of 17 percent in trade with this group of countries?"

16.   Industrial cooperation is an umbrella term that refers to various types of Russian-Western economic activity including coproduction arrangements, technology transfers, joint venturing, and the delivery of complete plants and other types of activity. For more background on such activity over recent decades, see James L. Hecht, ed., *Rubles and Dollars: Strategies for Doing Business in the Soviet Union* (New York: HarperCollins, 1991); Alan Scherr, *Foreign Direct Investment in the Soviet Union: Status and Trends*, Briefing Paper No. 5 (Providence, R.I.: Brown University Center for Foreign Policy Development, 1991). For earlier works, see F. Levcik and Jan Stankovsky, *Industrial Cooperation Between East and West* (White Plains, N.Y.: M. E. Sharpe, 1979); Jozef Wilczynski, *The Multinationals and East-West Relations* (Boulder, Colo.: Westview, 1976); and Albert Masnata, *East-West Economic Cooperation: Problems and Solutions* (Lexington, Mass.: Lexington Books, 1974).

17.   It is interesting to note that one of the most important features of Russian industrial development from 1861 to 1917 was the steady investment of foreign capital in all branches of industry. By 1914, foreigners owned 47 percent of all joint stock of Russian industrial companies and over 75 percent of bank assets. Investor capital came from France (32.6 percent), Great Britain (22.6 percent), Germany (19.7 per-

cent), Belgium (14.3 percent), and the United States (5.2 percent). The greatest percentage of foreign capital was invested in mining, followed by chemical industries, metal fabrications, woodworking, and textiles. See Vinad Mehta, *Soviet Economic Development and Structure* (New Delhi: Sterling Publications, PVT, LTD, 1978), pp. 31–33. For more historical background, see also Maurice Dobb, *Soviet Economic Development Since 1917*, 6th ed. (New York: International Publishers, 1967); P. I. Lyashchenko, *Istoriya Narodnogo Khozyaistva SSSR*, vol. II (Moscow, 1950); and Alec Nove, *An Economic History of the USSR* (Middlesex: Penguin, 1982).

18. These risks include political and economic instability, difficulties in guaranteeing contract enforcement, undefined property rights, indiscriminate and unannounced taxation, arbitrary and unauthorized confiscation of funds from bank Western accounts, disregard for intellectual property rights and copyright laws, a nascent legal system unaccustomed to Western principles and practices, theft of shipments, and many more.

19. Quoted from Russian Daily Newswire, September 30, 1993. Most of these joint ventures were concentrated in Central Russia (about 80 percent), with a small number in Western Siberia and the Far East. Wholly owned foreign subsidiaries increased from 4.3 percent in March 1992 to 21 percent by early 1993.

20. For background, see Jeffrey Sachs, "Western Financial Assistance and Russia's Reforms," in *Making Markets: Economic Transformation in Eastern Europe and the Post-Soviet States*, eds. Shafiqul Islam and Michael Mandelbaum (New York: Council on Foreign Relations, 1993).

21. *Financial Times* (January 22, 1991): 11:1.

22. In 1992, the G-7 had promised a $24 billion aid package, but most of the aid could not be disbursed because Russia could not satisfy conditionality requirements.

23. *Financial Times*, special section on Russia, May 27, 1993, p. 3. The proper use of funds is a major concern in the West, especially in light of widespread corruption among Russian government ministerial officials and previous misspending in the past. A delegation from the U.S. Department of Treasury, headed by Lloyd Bentsen, visited Moscow in June 1993 to hold talks with Russian Finance Minister Boris Fyodorov to address these issues. See "Lloyd Bentsen to Persuade the G-7 to Backup Reform," *Financial and Business News* (Moscow), No. 25 (103), June 18–24, 1993.

24. Author interview with president of an international well drilling company planning to invest in Tyumen region.

25. See Eximbank News Press Release, April 5, 1993. The loan is a financed portion of a $96.5 million sale through Mitsui & Co., USA to GAZPROM of 295 Caterpillar tractors.

26. Russian gross inter-enterprise debt has increased significantly as well, from R43 billion in January 1992 to R1 trillion by mid-1992. See *The Economist* (May 2, 1992): 99:1.

27. At the beginning of 1993, Russia's foreign debt was estimated at $77.7 billion. In 1992, Russia experienced a payment delay for $23 billion. Russian analysts estimate that in 1993 Russia will pay $40 billion in principal and interest to foreign creditors. Y. Mikhailov, "Russia: Foreign Debt Report," Reuter Textline, Novecon, June 7, 1993. Accessed through Lexis-Nexis.

28. Paul Gardiner, "Ex-Soviet Debt: A Riddle in a Mystery in an Enigma," *Euromoney Supplement*, April 1992, p. 63. It is difficult to form an accurate picture of the exact amount and composition of debt, and data may vary among various banks, Russian ministries, and international financial institutions.

29. David Fairlamb, "Russia: The Deal That Had To Be Done — Debt Rescheduling," *Institutional Investor*, May 28, 1993. Accessed through Lexis-Nexis.

30. Ibid. Russia actually paid $1.8 billion to creditors in 1992, and expects to pay $3 billion in 1993, according to First Deputy Finance Minister Andrei Vavilov.

"Russian Debt Servicing Improving — Deputy Minister," *The Reuter European Business Report*, August 3, 1993. Accessed through Lexis-Nexis.

31.   For more on the debt settlement, refer to the Treaty on Secession with Respect to the Soviet Foreign Debt and the USSR Assets. See also *ECOTASS*, May 21, 1993, p. 3. Prior to the Treaty, Russia and seven republics had signed a memorandum of understanding on October 28, 1991, on the division of responsibilities for payment and servicing of USSR external debt and division of USSR assets.

32.   The Paris Club is comprised of 600 commercial and government creditors in 19 countries, and has a Russian debt rescheduling committee (Bank Advisory Committee) headed by the German Deutsche Bank. Other bank members include Credit Lyonnais, Industrial Bank of Japan, Dresdner Bank, Commerzbank, Creditanstatt Bankverein, Banque Nationale de Paris, Banca Commerciale de Paris, Bank of Tokyo, Dai-Ichi Kangyo Bank, Midland Bank, and Bank of America. The London Club refers to Western commercial bank creditors.

33.   Yeltsin placed the Russian Bank for Foreign Economic Affairs and the Russian Finance Ministry in charge of debt negotiations and repayment procedures.

34.   "Russian Debt Servicing Improving," *The Reuter European Business Report*, August 3, 1993. Accessed through Lexis-Nexis. Russia owes $3.5 billion in back interest to the London Club for 1993. Total debt owed to the London Club is approximately $24 billion. First Deputy Finance Minister Andrei Vavilov commented about this debt: "We haven't reached a compromise on interest repayments but the delayed portion of the arrears will be converted into bonds and securities and paid over the next five years." Russia owes the Paris Club $17 billion for debt servicing for 1993. The terms for settlement are not yet clear.

35.   See "U.S., Russia To Begin Bilateral Debt Talks Soon," *The Reuter European Business Report*, July 7, 1993. Accessed through Lexis-Nexis.

36.   David Fairlamb, "Russia." See also "Stepped Up Western Aid: Will It Help?" *Current Digest of the Post-Soviet Press*, vol. 45, no. 14 (May 5, 1993). Accessed through Lexis-Nexis.

37.   "Stepped Up Western Aid." Attali resigned from his position in July 1993 after an audit committee concluded that EBRD spending on its headquarters was excessive.

38.   For more background, see Catherine M. Sokil, "Issues of Soviet Participation in International Economic Institutions," in *Soviet Foreign Economic Policy and International Security*, ed. Eric A. Stubbs (New York: M. E. Sharpe, 1991); Catherine M. Sokil, "Soviet Participation in the GATT, IMF and World Bank," *Global Economic Policy*, vol. 1, no. 1 (Spring 1989); Paul Marer, "Centrally Planned Economies in the IMF, World Bank, and the GATT," in *Economic Adjustment and Reform in Eastern Europe and the Soviet Union*, Josef C. Brada, Ed A. Hewett, and Thomas A. Wolf, eds. (Durham, N.C.: Duke University Press, 1988); Vladimir Sobell, "The USSR and the Western Economic Order: Time for Cooperation?" *Radio Free Europe Research Report*, No. 128, September 15, 1986. See also Valerie J. Assetto, *The Soviet Bloc in the IMF and IBRD* (Boulder, Colo.: Westview Press, 1988).

39.   See Organization for Economic Cooperation and Development, International Monetary Fund and the World Bank, *The Economy of the USSR: Summary and Recommendations* (Washington, D.C.: World Bank, 1991), and International Monetary Fund, The World Bank, Organization for Economic Cooperation and Development, and European Bank for Reconstruction and Development, *A Study of the Soviet Economy*, 3 vols. (Paris: Organization for Economic Cooperation and Development, March 1991).

40.   See *Journal of Commerce* (December 13, 1991): 2A:1, and *Financial Times* (December 14, 1991): 2:3. But Yeltsin, while wanting IMF membership, has insisted

that he does not agree with all of the IMF provisions, and will not be dictated to. See *Financial Times* (April 29, 1992): 8:4.2.

41. In Summer 1992, Yeltsin appointed Deputy Prime Minister Aleksandr Shokhin as Russian representative to the IMF and IBRD.

42. The International Finance Corporation had a successful test pilot project in Nizhny Novgorod, and developed a privatization plan based on its experiences. The project and the plan are considered a model for privatization efforts throughout Russia. See Business Information Service for the Newly Independent States, "Commercial Overview of Russia" (Washington, D.C.: U.S. Department of Commerce, 1993).

43. For more background on the Soviet Union/Russia and GATT, see Jozef M. van Brabant, "Planned Economies in the GATT Framework: The Soviet Case," *Soviet Economy*, vol. 4, no. 1 (1988); Kevin C. Kennedy, "The Accession of the Soviet Union to GATT," *Journal of World Trade Law*, April 1987.

44. Office of the Press Secretary, White House Press Release, "Fact Sheet: Russia and the GATT," Washington, D.C., April 4, 1993. According to this fact sheet, a request from Russia to enter GATT would start discussion and negotiations among members to evaluate Russia's entry. President Clinton has offered to host informal bilateral discussions with Russian officials to encourage Russia's official entry into the organization.

45. "The U.S.-Russia Business Summit, June 17, 1992, Remarks by Boris Yeltsin," *Business America*, vol. 113, no. 13 (June 29, 1992): 8.

46. For more on early American trade policies toward the Soviet Union, see Philip J. Funigiello, *American-Soviet Trade in the Cold War* (Chapel Hill: University of North Carolina Press, 1988).

47. "The U.S.-Russia Business Summit, June 17, 1992, Remarks by President George Bush," *Business America*, vol. 113, no. 13 (June 29, 1992): 7.

48. Statement by Secretary of Commerce Barbara Hackman Franklin on signing the Terms of Reference for the Intergovernmental U.S.-Russia Business Development Committee, June 16, 1992, in speech entitled "Let a New Era of Russian-American Business Begin," *Business America*, vol. 113, no. 13 (June 29, 1992): 12.

49. Ibid.

50. Russia, as the largest republic of the FSU (encompassing one sixth of the earth's surface) has almost one-half of the world reserves of oil, natural gas and coal; has one-third of the world's timber resources; has 67 percent of FSU's gold reserves; is a large producer of platinum and diamonds; and has major untapped reserves of uranium and other strategic minerals including rhodium and palladium; and has other resources including copper, bauxite, molybdenum, iron ore, and precious stones to name only a few. Russia's coastal waters hold vast amounts of fish. Despite a sagging economy, Russia is still a major industrial nation, both in heavy and light industrial sectors.

Russia's population (1991 statistics) is 148.5 million. Moscow's population is 9 million; St. Petersburg's population is 5 million. Russia's geographical territory encompasses 6.6 million square miles and 11 time zones. Russia is twice the size of the United States. See "Commercial Overview of Russia," May 25, 1993.

51. Note that the agreement was first reached in June 1990 and approved by Congress in November 1991. It went into effect June 17, 1993.

52. See BISNIS Bulletin, September 1992, U.S. Department of Commerce.

53. See *Interflo*, vol. 11, no. 9 (July 1992): 4; *Business America*, vol. 113, no. 13 (June 29, 1992).

54. See Joint Statement on Creation of Intergovernmental U.S.-Russia Business Development Committee, June 16, 1992, in *Interflo*, vol. 11, no. 9 (July 1992): 3–4.

55. Ibid.

56. See BISNIS, February 28, 1993, U.S. Department of Commerce.

57. Office of the Press Secretary, White House Press Release, "Joint Statement of the Presidents of the United States and the Russian Federation: Vancouver Declaration," Washington, D.C., April 4, 1993, p. 1. Both leaders also reaffirmed the principles of the Camp David Declaration of February 1, 1992, and the Charter of the U.S.-Russian Partnership and Friendship of June 17, 1992.

58. Office of the Press Secretary, White House Press Release, "Press Conference by President Bill Clinton and President Boris Yeltsin, Canada Place, Vancouver, B.C." Vancouver, B.C., April 4, 1993, p. 1.

59. Ibid., p. 2.

60. Ibid., pp. 4 and 5.

61. Office of the Press Secretary, White House Press Release, "Fact Sheet: Generalized System of Preferences," Washington, D.C., April 4, 1993. This document notes that the U.S. GSP program expires July 1, 1993, and this would be a target date to begin including Russia.

62. "Commercial Overview of Russia," May 25, 1993.

63. The Export-Import Bank provides credit insurance, medium-term guarantees, and loans to support U.S. company exports to Russia. These transactions are entered into with Rosvneshtorg or Vneshekonombank guaranteeing the terms of the agreements.

64. Ronald H. Brown to OPIC Conference on investment opportunities in Tomsk and Chelyabinsk, Russia, quoted in featured article "Building Business Ties with Russia/NIS/Eastern Europe," *Business America*, vol. 114, no. 6 (March 22, 1993): 2.

65. BISNIS now has an automated "FLASHFAX" system whereby U.S. companies can make information requests via touchtone phone and receive the information back by fax in a short period of time.

66. The program expects an additional $7 million by October 1993 to create six more centers.

67. Numerous congressional delegations are visiting the NIS to gain a better perception of how best to frame U.S. trade policy toward the NIS. House Majority Leader Richard A. Gephardt, after returning from such a journey, concluded that the United States needed a substantially expanded exchange program; to continue repealing Cold War restrictions on trade and aid; and to refocus aid programs with an "in-the-field and out-of-Foggy Bottom" management approach. See Press Release, News from the House Majority Leader Congressman Richard A. Gephardt, Remarks to the Center for National Policy, "A New Partnership: U.S. Relations with Russia and the New Republics," April 22, 1993.

2

Foreign Investment, Economic Growth, and Market Transition

Eileen M. Crumm

The republics of the former Soviet Union (FSU) are enthusiastically pursuing connection with the world economy through joint ventures (JVs) and foreign direct investment (FDI). Foreign investors are expected to bring in scarce resources in capital and technology as well as marketing and management skills that FSU industries need to become internationally competitive. Since the post-planning economic free fall dramatically illustrates the drawbacks of autarkic policies of development, FSU states view integration into the world economy as the path to domestic prosperity, and foreign investment as the first step in that direction. But the opportunities and problems presented by foreign investment are extremely complex for these states. Not only do the post-Soviet republics hope to use foreign investment in the "traditional" sense to spur economic development but also many FSU leaders wish to employ foreign investment as a tool to break down some of the more intransigent barriers blocking the road to economic transition. This chapter examines the current and evolving patterns of foreign investment in the FSU republics and uses this information to assess its probable effects for these two goals. It demonstrates that these two aims are best served by very different patterns of investment and concludes that, therefore, FSU states face, at best, significant trade-offs between the growth and transition and, at worst, a situation characterized by irreconcilable aims.

Any evaluation of the probable effects of foreign investment needs to begin with a look at the shape and extent of foreign penetration into an economy. Therefore, this assessment begins with an overview of the patterns of investment in the FSU republics, focusing on data from the end of the Soviet era. The point made all too obvious by this data is that foreign investment is still a minor force in the economies of these states. For many republics, the immediate concern is not the need to regulate foreign investment and shape it to the goals of the states, but the more basic challenge of attracting foreign businesses to their economies. Therefore, this section also briefly reviews the factors deterring investors from the post-Soviet republics, and discusses what the republics are doing to entice foreign businesses to locate in their states.

After this, the focus shifts to a deeper examination of the two FSU goals for foreign investment, economic growth and market transition, and their relationship to patterns of foreign investment. These goals are analyzed to show the types of investments that are most likely to help the FSU republics successfully achieve them. Concentrating first on economic growth, I take an abbreviated look at scholarly work and developing country experience to show why, from this perspective, the most desirable investments are export-oriented JVs in resource extraction and in mature manufactures. The available evidence suggests that host states are best able to bargain with the owners of these investments to get concessions that contribute to economic growth. Turning to the second goal of market transition, I detail the anticipated roles that could be played by investment in post-Communist market transition, which revolve around its power as a force for demonopolization. These tasks are more suited to a dramatically different investment profile than the export-oriented resource joint ventures most beneficial for growth. In fact, what the post-Communist states need for transition is a kind of foreign investment most developing states have tried to avoid, that is, one consisting of wholly owned foreign subsidiaries selling manufactures to FSU consumers.

This analysis of patterns of investment establishes three characteristics of the external sector as most significant and predictive of the effects of foreign investment in the FSU: whether industries are export or domestic market oriented, whether they are new firms or joint ventures, and the economic sector in which they are located. The final part of the chapter considers existing and probable FSU patterns for each of these characteristics. After examining all of these points, I conclude that five FSU states most likely to use foreign investment to aid growth are Azerbaijan, Kazakhstan, Turkmenistan, Russia, and, to a lesser degree, Uzbekistan. These states possess characteristics that give them a stronger bargaining position vis-à-vis potential investors than do other FSU republics. The conclusions for the potential of investment to aid market reform are more pessimistic, as it is unlikely that foreign businesses will provide substantial assistance to market transition.

PATTERNS OF FOREIGN INVESTMENT IN THE
REPUBLICS OF THE FORMER SOVIET UNION

Historical Background: Foreign
Investment in the Republics of the USSR

Significant foreign investment in the FSU republics began during the Gorbachev period. Soviet leaders turned to foreign capital for two reasons. The most immediate was a traumatic shortfall in hard currency earnings in 1986.[1] Foreign exchange was essential to the viability of the program of perestroika, for Gorbachev planned to modernize Soviet industry through purchases of Western technology that required foreign exchange. Second, Soviet leaders believed that foreign investment would encourage greater domestic efficiency and innovation by providing competition to domestic producers, thus, providing a second avenue for reinvigorating the sluggish Soviet economy.[2] Thus, in mid-1986, Moscow requested Western firms to present proposals for JVs. In 1987, the Soviet economy officially opened to massive foreign investment, allowing JVs that required majority ownership to remain in Soviet hands.

Initially this announcement was met with enthusiasm by Western businessmen, and a tremendous number looked with interest to the Soviet market. Despite this early activity, only a little more than half of the ventures went into operation over the next few years. While over 2,900 JVs had been registered in the USSR by January 1991, at the time of the coup in August only 1,604 were operational.[3] These represented an insignificant 0.2 percent of the Soviet gross national product.[4] Business people lay most of the blame on Soviet officials and the Soviet economic environment. They argued that to do business in the USSR required a great deal of time, creativity, and money. Businesses were particularly dismayed by the fact that both initial negotiation and later operation took place in an environment preoccupied by bureaucratic procedure, which meant that government officials had considerable direct influence on the success of an enterprise. Many bureaucrats saw foreign ventures as a threat to their power and position and thus stifled or stalled such enterprises. One businessman revealed in an interview that he had to negotiate a major investment for over 9 years before he was able to begin construction, and the famous McDonald's restaurant was the result of 14 years of bargaining.

In addition to bureaucratic resistance, businesses faced a number of other obstacles to operating in the USSR. They had difficulty obtaining needed supplies and services like office space, employee housing, bank transfers, and telecommunications access. Businesses also had to figure out a way of dealing with ruble profits, because Soviet currency was not convertible and businesses were only allowed to take out of the country foreign currency that they directly earned (not obtained through currency exchanges). The JVs that did go into operation handled this difficulty in a number of different ways. Some companies opted to hold sizable amounts of rubles in the expectation that they would eventually be convertible. Others developed inventive means of repatriating profits. These included counter trade strategies, such as the Pepsi/Stolichnaya venture, where production of one good that was sold domestically was bartered for another to be sold externally. Some dealt with the problem by producing solely for export to the world market. Others created multiple marketing plans, where part of production was sold for hard currency to foreigners in the USSR and part for rubles, with the hard currency used to pay the Western partner. Still others set up dual factory arrangements where one factory was set up in the USSR, and one in the West, but both were staffed by Soviet workers paid by their government. The profits generated by the Western factory were used to compensate the foreign investor. Due to the many obstacles facing the external sector, many analysts held that only large multinational corporations (MNCs) could operate in this challenging environment, because they could build up supply networks outside of the control of interfering bureaucrats and design inventive means of repatriation. However, those same MNCs were likely to have equally attractive and less troublesome opportunities elsewhere, so many passed on the chance to invest in the Soviet Union.

Over time and with experience, the initial enthusiasm of business for Soviet investments declined, plummeting even further as the Soviet Union's political and economic troubles intensified. Likewise, the Soviet leadership found that foreign investments did not turn out to be all that had been expected. They had hoped for investments in manufacturing industries, which would create competition for domestic industries and increase their efficiency. But most JVs tended to concentrate in services. These services failed not only to create competition for Soviet industries but also to bring the advanced technology, managerial, and marketing know-how that Soviet leaders had expected. In addition, the system was reportedly extraordinarily corrupt. An *Izvestia* reporter argued that many JVs were unholy unions between Western firms looking for a quick buck and Soviet partners hungry for hard currency. He claimed that some were nothing more than schemes to export cheap Soviet raw materials at great profit and import electronics into the Soviet market to parlay the gains even further.[5] Mutual disillusionment characterized the relations between external investors and Soviet leaders in the early 1990s. Even so, Soviet leaders continued to offer incentives to investors, even allowing for complete foreign ownership in July 1992. This is explained by the fact that while leaders were not completely pleased by the performance of the external sector, they saw little alternative to it.

Nonetheless, at the end of the Soviet period, foreign investment in the FSU states stood at a relatively low level. The most comprehensive data available (see Table 2.1) shows that as of January 1991, the bulk of the investment focused on the Western republics with a total of $4.1 billion, followed by the Baltics with $243 million, Central Asia (and Kazakhstan) with $225 million, and the Caucuses with $105 million. Firms investing in the Western republics exported $235 million worth of products, $29 million from the Baltics, $18 million from the Caucuses (all from Georgia), and $12 million from Central Asia. Nor was the foreign sector a major employer. Only in Russia and Ukraine did hires reach more than 10,000: Latvia, Estonia, Georgia, Uzbekistan, and Belarus had between 3,000 and 8,000 nationals working in the external sector; Armenia, Kazakhstan, and Azerbaijan had less than 1,000.

Foreign Investment in the FSU Republics

Anecdotal evidence suggests that growth of the external sector has accelerated in some of the republics in the post-coup period. During 1991, the number of joint ventures operating in Russia doubled. At the end of 1992, Russian joint ventures were employing 137,000 people and had produced goods and services worth $18.4 billion. Four hundred JVs were operating in Ukraine as of September 1992 and 300 had been set up in Kazakhstan.[6] Kazakhstan and Belarus have been frequently cited as attractive by investors, but these republics are the exception rather than the rule. For the most part, dissolution of the Soviet state did not mean that disincentives to investment dissipated in the FSU republics. Most republics retained the characteristics that had dissuaded investment in the Soviet era, including inconvertible currency, high levels of corruption, opaque regulatory activities, and the lack of adequate physical, legal, and financial infrastructures. Investors continue to see the FSU states as economically and politically unstable and fear arbitrary state intervention once investments are in place.[7] Skeptics point to the problems encountered by the White Nights oil venture, which was the first to begin drilling new oil wells in Russia. This venture was forced to drastically cut production when oil taxes passed by the Russian parliament after the investment was in place made the operation unprofitable.

The fall of the Soviet government also intensified competing claims of ownership by a wide body of conflicting interests, particularly in Russia. Managers, workers, central (republican) governments, krais, and oblasts all asserted property rights to the enterprises and resources of a region. Foreign businesses faced uncertainty about which FSU organizations had the ability to make deals and follow through on commitments, and this increased uncertainty decreased the attractiveness of investment. In addition, companies in existing JVs found that, post-coup, lines of authority within ventures had blurred as the hierarchical relations of the Soviet system broke down. For example, the Brooke group reported that after the manager of a cigarette

TABLE 2.1
Foreign Direct Investment in the Former Soviet Union Republics
(in millions of dollars)

	Estonia	Latvia	Lithuania	Armenia	Azerbaijan	Georgia	Kazakhstan
Flow of FDI, 1989–90 (Ann. Av.)	57.7	25.8	38.3	27.7	19.7	65.0	9.0
FDI Stock, 1990	115.3	51.6	76.5	55.4	39.4	130.0	17.9
Employment in Foreign Affiliates	3,973.0	7,649.0	na	141.0	179.0	2,457.0	804.0
Sales of Foreign Affiliates, 1990	12.0	2.0	8.0	15.9	0.3	1.0	14.4
Number of Foreign Affiliates, 1990	168.0	69.0	28.0	22.0	18.0	90.0	22.0
Sales of Foreign Affiliates	12.0	2.0	8.0	0.0	0.0	1.0	0.0
Value Added of Foreign Affiliates	84.2	148.7	na	15.9	0.3	131.9	14.4
Employees in Foreign Affiliates	3,973.0	7,649.0	na	141.0	179.0	2,457.0	804.0
Exports of Foreign Affiliates	11.0	16.0	2.0	0.0	0.0	18.0	10.0
Imports of Foreign Affiliates	15.0	9.0	9.0	0.0	0.0	16.0	2.0

	Kyrgyzstan	Tajikistan	Turkmenistan	Uzbekistan	Belarus	Moldova	Russia	Ukraine
Flow of FDI, 1989–90 (Ann. Av.)	0.3	1.5	2.0	40.1	48.3	22.8	1,867	51.6
FDI Stock, 1990	0.5	2.9	4.0	80.1	96.5	45.6	3,735	206.5
Employment in Foreign Affiliates	na	na	na	4,016.0	3,444.0	1,511.0	65,633	13,854.0
Sales of Foreign Affiliates, 1990	0.0	0.0	0.0	171.7	14.0	3.0	581	32.0
Number of Foreign Affiliates, 1990	1.0	5.0	2.0	31.0	59.0	29.0	2,224	148.0
Sales of Foreign Affiliates	0.0	0.0	0.0	0.0	14.0	3.0	581	32.0
Value Added of Foreign Affiliates	na	na	na	171.7	186.7	26.3	3,180	374.0
Employees in Foreign Affiliates	0.0	0.0	0.0	4,016.0	3,444.0	1,511.0	65,633	13,854.0
Exports of Foreign Affiliates	0.0	0.0	0.0	2.0	2.0	1.0	189	33.0
Imports of Foreign Affiliates	0.0	0.0	0.0	62.0	10.0	3.0	729	88.0

Source: United Nations, *World Investment Directory 1992: Volume II Central and Eastern Europe* (New York: United Nations, 1992).

joint venture was fired by the city of Moscow, that manager continued to show up for work and even posted armed guards at his door to protect himself. The problem was that the manager disputed the right of the city to fire him, as it was not clear which government organization now owned part of the venture.

While the demise of Soviet communism allowed some states to successfully pursue investment capital, for most it only amplified the existing disincentives for investors. A German official interviewed about possible investment in Estonia captured the sentiment of many businessmen when he said that companies were interested, but that for the time being they are just analyzing the situation.[8]

The FSU states are undertaking all types of programs in an attempt to change the attitudes of like-minded investors. But unfortunately for these states, the early 1990s are characterized as a competitive environment for international investment, which meant that investors had their choice of states for investment. While foreign capital remains scarce, the investments in many post-Soviet republics seem less and less attractive. Many FSU economies have been marked by crisis and decline, while their political systems have been in upheaval. This combination of factors severely limited the bargaining leverage that the FSU had in dealing with foreign businessmen. In addition, the FSU republics are competing against each other, as well as against Eastern Europe and developing states, which means that businesses are able to play the states off each other to obtain the most favorable conditions. To induce greater competition, and hopefully get better deals, a few of the republics are actively courting competing firms, notably Kazakhstan, Belarus, and Uzbekistan.

However, most of the republics can do little to obtain concessions from foreign investors; rather, they find themselves offering incentives to obtain their capital and expertise. Over the last few years, the FSU republics have been passing legislation in an attempt to fashion friendly legal and economic environments. Many republics (Belarus, Estonia, Turkmenistan, and Uzbekistan) are guaranteeing that the investments will not be subsequently nationalized, and Uzbekistan has gone so far as to announce that both the state's share of a joint venture as well as the profits are to be backed by gold deposits in international banks. Kazakhstan, Russia, and Kyrgyzstan have legislation promoting free economic zones, which are specially allocated areas with relaxed legal arrangements. Belarus, Estonia, and Latvia are offering tax holidays to investors. Estonia, Belarus, and Uzbekistan are exempting imported capital goods for new ventures from export duties. The Turkmen government is giving special concessions to investors opening businesses in consumer goods and manufactures.

The problem for the FSU republics is that many of the characteristics that interest investors are either difficult to achieve or beyond the control of the government. These include factors such as advancement toward market reforms (the Baltic republics), political stability (Belarus, Kazakhstan, Turkmenistan, and Uzbekistan), and historical, religious, or ethnic ties between the potential investor and the host state (Arab investment in Central Asia, Armenian community investment in Armenia). One interesting note is that the reluctance of investors to enter unstable political situations has even become a ploy in political battles in some republics. Mihalosko reports that defenders of the status quo in Belarus are basing their objection to new elections, in part, on the need to stimulate foreign investment in the Belorussian economy.[9] With no great natural resources to offer multinational investment, one of the most inviting characteristics of investment in Belarus has been the stability of the state. Unlike in some other republics, businessmen are relatively confident that the Belorussian government will be able to deliver on a contract. As mentioned above, this has been a problem in other republics, as businessmen have found that they had to renegotiate the same deal with numerous layers of government administrators with overlapping and contradictory claims of sovereignty. Conservatives in the Belarus parliament point out that new elections could decrease the state's attractiveness at a time when it is competing for a limited investment pool.

The evidence indicates that the most important asset for attracting investment in the post-Communist states is the possession of scarce natural resources. The exception to the general rule of foreign investor disinterest is the case of ventures in extraction of natural resources, notably oil and natural gas. States with oil and natural gas are being pursued by investors, and are subsequently able to obtain greater concessions. For example, Kazakhstan is a stable state with rich natural resources and an active policy of recruiting investors. Kazakhstan has enough activity from investors that it has been able to demand business concessions. Large investments are required to provide special spending for social development, a demand that less well endowed republics are unable to make.

Russia, Azerbaijan, Turkmenistan, and Kazakhstan have the most substantial resource bases, followed by Uzbekistan. Recent media reports indicate that these states are getting the most play from investors. Other republics have not been as blessed by nature. Ukraine has substantial coal deposits, but estimates are that most of these will be needed to support domestic industry. Limited oil reserves are also present in Estonia, Lithuania, and Ukraine. The least endowed states are Tajikistan and Kyrgyzstan, which only have the potential for cheap hydro power to recommend them. A summary of the known FSU natural resources base is shown in Table 2.2.

TABLE 2.2
Known Resource Base for FSU Republics

Republic	Resource Base
Armenia	negligible: agricultural land
Azerbaijan	substantial: oil, natural gas, iron ore, agricultural land
Belarus	negligible: agricultural land, peat, potassium salts
Estonia	limited: timber, oil shale, limestone
Georgia	limited: agricultural land, tourism
Kazakhstan	substantial: oil, chrome, coal, lead, zinc, gold, iron, copper
Kyrgyzstan	limited: cheap hydropower, coal, gold, mercury, negligible amounts of oil and gas
Latvia	limited: peat, dolomite, limestone, gypsum, amber, gravel, sand
Lithuania	limited: agricultural land, lumber, small oil and natural gas deposits, peat, lime, sand, gravel
Moldova	negligible: agricultural land
Russia	substantial: coal, oil, natural gas, phosphorites, potassium salts, iron ores, gold, diamonds, rare metals, uranium, copper, lead, tin, bauxite, manganese, silver, graphite, nickel
Tajikistan	negligible: cheap hydropower
Turkmenistan	substantial: oil and gas, indications of gold and platinum
Ukraine	modest: coal, agricultural land, modest amounts of natural gas and petroleum, iron ore, manganese, uranium
Uzbekistan	modest: petroleum, natural gas, coal, hydropower

Sources: International Monetary Fund, *Economic Review* (from each of the aforementioned republics), Washington, D.C.: International Monetary Fund, 1992.

FOREIGN INVESTMENT AND LONG-TERM GROWTH: THE RECORD IN DEVELOPING STATES

While the FSU states are concentrating on getting the attention of international investors, scholars continue an ongoing debate about whether foreign investment provides a net benefit to the economies of developing states. While scholars have looked at developing states in Africa, Asia, and Latin America rather than the post-Soviet states, the literature that they have generated on the effects of external capital investment is enormous. In a chapter of this length it is impossible to do justice to its depth and complexity.[10] Sacrificing subtlety for simplicity, this chapter presents a somewhat uncomfortable marriage of a variety of perspectives to make some generalizations about the pattern of foreign investment most likely to encourage economic growth in the FSU.

The empirical record shows that developing states have sought a number of specific concessions from foreign investors that are believed to increase the value of the foreign investment by directing more of the profits toward the host state and society.[11] These include higher taxes, joint marketing, employment of nationals in managerial positions, shared ownership, production of more value-added products, expansion of linkages to the host economy, and increased export of products.[12] Developing states have pressed particularly hard for joint ownership of ventures, as host states believe that joint ownership will cut down on outflow of resources from a country and increase the local economy's control over the operation of the foreign owned facility.

Analysts point out that even if the host state is not able to get these concessions initially from foreign investors, it is better placed to renegotiate the terms of the venture over time, either explicitly or tacitly.[13] Once an enterprise is profitable and vested in an area, the state is able to get greater benefits because the multinational's bargaining leverage has diminished relative to the point of entry. Now the MNC has sunk capital costs, the initial risk of the venture has been reduced, and world wide technological diffusion has reduced the MNC's preeminence as a provider of advanced manufacturing processes. While the foreign investor's position has weakened, the state's position has become stronger. The state has had time and experience to acquire bargaining, regulatory, and managerial skills and, thus, is better able to shape the terms of investment to its advantage. The most persuasive analyses of this have focused on investments in natural resource or extractive industries,[14] but some research indicates that states can also achieve gains on the terms of manufacturing investments in industries where technological diffusion has taken place but not in those that employ rapidly changing technology over which the company maintains exclusive control.[15] Host states can try to improve the balance of strength by developing their own research and development programs, and many scholars indicate that this is the best policy when dealing with manufactures that use evolving technologies. The general finding is, however, that investments in sectors with rapidly changing technological bases, such as in the pharmaceutical industry, are the least likely to be willing to cede additional benefits to the host over time.[16]

Another factor beyond sectoral location has been identified as significant to a state's ability to shape foreign investment to growth, and that is the host state's regulatory capacity. Scholars have pointed out that investors are sometimes able to get around a state's rules and requirements for investments. Multinationals have employed a variety of strategies, both legal and illegal, to circumvent the host state's demands.[17] Scholars have pointed out that states like the FSU, which have a high level of corruption, might not have the capacity to effectively control the external sector.

In summary, the prior record of foreign investment argues that for FSU states to obtain the best bargain from investment, they should try to negotiate with potential investors for concessions that will maximize the domestic impact of that investment. In particular, FSU states should encourage investment into joint ownership rather than direct foreign investment so that profits are more likely to be returned to the host economy and enterprises oriented to export that will bring hard currency into these economies. Given their weak position, the FSU states should actively seek multiple partners to take advantage of international competition within industries to compensate for the "buyers market" for investors.[18]

However, given the fact that potential investors have lots of choices and FSU states comparatively few, FSU states might not be able to successfully bargain for such favorable arrangements. In these likely circumstances, FSU states might have to shift the focus to the longer term and plan on altering the terms of the investment later on, either through explicit negotiation or by pressuring investors. In this, as in all questions of regulation, the FSU states face a major barrier in the pervasiveness of corruption in these societies.[19] However, if this problem can be overcome, the FSU republics are more likely to have a favorable outcome if the industries they are working with are either in resource extraction or mature manufactures. As noted, only 5 of the 15 republics (Russia, Azerbaijan, Turkmenistan, Kazakhstan, and Uzbekistan) have the wherewithal to get investments in extractive or mining industries. This suggests that the others should solicit investment in mature manufactures (such as automobile production as the Daewoo JV in Uzbekistan). In summary, the developing state experience suggests that states with greater regulatory capacity, technological research facilities, and natural resource endowments appear to be best situated to harness foreign investment to the goal of economic growth.

FOREIGN INVESTMENT AND MARKET TRANSITION

The FSU republics are looking toward foreign investment for more than help in improving prospects for long-term growth. As shown above, hoped for effects from foreign investment in the FSU resemble those desired by developing states. Like leaders of developing economies, leaders of the FSU republics expect foreign investment to bring an infusion of capital, management skill, technology, and market access to firms. They hope that this will enhance exports to hard currency markets and that it will improve the state's balance of payments. In addition, FSU leaders are hopeful that foreign investment will help solve growing unemployment problems through the creation of new jobs. This is particularly significant in the FSU, as large numbers of individuals have been and will be displaced in the transition to market as inefficient industries go bankrupt.

In other ways, FSU ambitions for foreign investment are more comprehensive than those of other developing states. Unlike most states before them, the republics of the FSU are attempting to transform their economies from central planning to the market. Mandlebaum (1993) argues that there are three major tasks to market transition: stabilization, economic institution building, and liberaliza-tion.[20] It is believed that foreign investment can play an important role in stabilization by improving balance of payments and in liberalization by assisting in demonopolization. These contentions have been carried over from the Gorbachev period, which expressed this idea in its draft law on transition. This document argued that foreign investment would ease transformation to a market economy.[21] Faith in the benefits of for-eign investment was so pervasive to the Soviet elite that during pere-stroika the idea even found support among ultraconservative groups like Soyuz. In fact, some observers note that Soviet elites viewed for-eign investment as the magic cure for the major ills of the Soviet-style planned economy.[22]

Like the Soviet Union before them, the FSU republics are looking at foreign investment as an aid to transition, for foreign investment can (but not always) help solve one of the most thorny problems of liberal-ization, demonopolization of the economy. Under certain circumstances, MNC investment fosters a more competitive environment by introduc-ing new and efficient firms into the market. This aspect of investment is important to FSU states because one of the more detrimental legacies of communism was the high level of monopolization of the industrial base, which was dominated by large Soviet-built enterprises. Some comparative statistics illustrate differences between Soviet cir-cumstances and those in less concentrated markets.

While 25 percent of enterprises in the Soviet Union employed more than 500 employees, only about 1 percent of firms in the United States and Japan did so.[23] In addition, only 15 percent of Soviet firms employed less than 15 workers, while this describes 90 percent of the firms in the United States and Japan. Moreover, in the Western states, unlike in the Soviet Union, monopoly power is frequently reduced by the foreign competition.[24]

Soviet firms were mostly inefficient and produced less output rela-tive to input than the international best practice level.[25] This ineffi-ciency was largely a result of the planning process, where prices were used primarily as a means of accounting rather than as a mechanism for allocation of scarce resources. During the Soviet era, enterprises used more inputs than best practice level because those inputs were essentially costless. In the planned economy, where inputs and outputs had to be balanced against each other, balancing was simplified when enterprises were small in number, which necessitated that they be large in size. In addition, Soviet planners equated size with efficiency and thus further favored large scale industry.[26] This created the system of large, inefficient, concentrated industries inherited by the FSU republics. The problems created by this industrial bloc for the FSU are many, both economically and politically.

To start with the economic problems, the high concentration of Soviet industry meant that even after price reforms were put in place, these firms were not forced to become more efficient. Since they were monopolies they could just charge higher prices rather than cut their costs. This inefficiency led to a reduction of both state and consumer welfare. The state was less well off since these resources could be put to better use in other investments. In addition, since many enterprises operated at a net loss, they had to be subsidized from state budgets in order to remain in business. Consumer welfare was also reduced because the goods produced were less tailored to consumer desires and more expensive than they would be in a competitive environment.

In competitive markets, such inefficient enterprises would go bankrupt. However, this was not possible with concentrated industries, for they were a major influence on the economic welfare of a region. When a firm is a big fish (or the sole fish) in a small pond, it gives the enterprise considerable clout with local authorities because these firms are the major source of employment and revenue. This situation is aggravated in post-Soviet economies. In addition to the advantages that accrue to any monopoly, in the post-Soviet republics industrial political clout in the FSU has been enhanced by the inability of government organizations to provide social and welfare services.[27] Enterprises are now the major source of these politically significant services. The power that industrialists exercise over post-Soviet markets as a source of employment, social services, and welfare is often translated into political influence. In short, a highly monopolized market is both economically inefficient and politically powerful.

Part of the process of liberalization is changing the environment within which enterprises operate, notably the degree of market concentration. But to date, the republics have made only minimal moves toward reduction of market concentration. Most FSU republics have antimonopoly policies that propose reducing market concentration by dismantling some conglomerates into their component factories. There has been little official progress on this, although nomenklatura privatization has seen enterprise managers transforming the better parts of a conglomerate into private businesses for themselves. Most FSU republics do not have programs for promoting competition other than privatization, which will take years and may not reduce industrial concentration very much.[28] In post-planned economies, foreign business could increase the competitiveness of the domestic market as well as augment productive resources by bringing in capital and technology.[29] This in turn can reduce state expenditures and improve the quality of life for the population.

But before expanding on the benefits of increasing competition through foreign investment, I want to address why foreign firms are more capable of achieving this goal than domestic entrepreneurs. Pitting domestic entrepreneurs against these monopolies and oligopolies creates a David and Goliath situation. It is not impossible that the small business will prevail against a larger established monopoly or near monopoly (witness the Apple success against IBM in the United States), but the odds are heavily against it. While the relative advantages will differ by sector, preexisting firms usually have substantially more economic and political resources than the small entrepreneur.

Analysts have found that in post-Communist societies, these concentrated industries are well placed to capture regulators and politicians and lobby for protection. These industries use their influence to craft a legal and economic environment that maintains their profits and prevents others from entering the market and diluting their influence. One way that industry has tried to exercise its power in the post-planned environment is by controlling the availability of capital in creating largely or wholly owned commercial banks. These enterprise managers can prevent these controlled banks from extending credit or capital to possible domestic competitors. The environment in which new businesses operate is quite hostile in the post-Soviet republics, and most exist in a parasitic, or at best symbiotic, relationship to state enterprises.[30] Large enterprises have the opportunity and the capability to destroy nascent domestic competitors by erecting political and economic barriers to market entry.

Foreign firms have the resources to better match those of domestic monopolies. MNCs are best able to get around legal and economic barriers to market entry; that is why they became multinational firms in the first place.[31] For example, if entry in a particular industry necessitates a large capital outlay, the domestic entrepreneur would not be able to obtain the capital from the captured local bank and the credit ratings of the FSU republics make it unlikely that it could be raised from international commercial sources. The MNC is able to raise the capital from other sources, either from commercial lenders or from its own resources. Likewise, if a local monopolist pressures suppliers not to provide competitors with inputs, the domestic entrepreneurial enterprise can be strangled because it is unlikely to have the hard currency to import such supplies from abroad. The MNC can import inputs from other markets or set up its own suppliers, vertically integrating, as McDonald's did by setting up its own bakery and farm to ensure quality sources of supply.

It is vital to remember that foreign investment does not necessarily reduce industrial concentration in a host state.[32] If a foreign firm creates a new firm (green field entry), then another seller is added to the market. However, if investment is made through existing firms in a JV, it may increase competitiveness by reviving a defunct firm, but it does not necessarily do so. From the perspective of increasing competition, the creation of new firms producing for the domestic market is preferable to JVs. This conclusion directly opposes the one reached above on economic growth, where shared ownership is the preferable vehicle as it is believed to lead to more capital remaining within the host state.

Foreign firms are desirable from the perspective of liberalization because they are better placed to compete with existing firms and, therefore, contribute to the dilution of the political and economic influence of such firms. Decreased market concentration should lessen the ability of industry to exert pressure on government for protection and subsidies and ease the pressure on FSU budgets. Since enterprise managers are often characterized as a conservative political force opposed to reform, decreased market concentration may also weaken resistance to the process of transition from industrial leaders.

Increased competition in domestic markets should also lead to cheaper prices for consumers. If the foreign firms are producing consumer goods for sale to the population, this would improve the quality of life for the average citizen. When analyzing Soviet reform, the International Monetary Fund (IMF) speculated that increased availability of these goods could help build public support for reform.[33] The same logic should be applicable to the FSU republics, which would mean that the FSU should seek firms interested in producing consumer goods for consumption within the FSU host state, as Turkmenistan has by offering special benefits to such investors. Such production would reduce the scarcity of goods and help to stem hyperinflation in states like Russia.

Thus, this analysis concludes that for transition, the most beneficial foreign investment would be in monopolized sectors and in manufacturing industries producing consumer goods for domestic consumption. Like the argument above for "green field" entry, this contradicts other conclusions developed above that indicated that other developing states believed that investments oriented toward export sales were more beneficial for growth than those aimed toward the domestic market.

ASSESSMENT OF FORMER SOVIET UNION FOREIGN INVESTMENT PATTERNS

The analysis has indicated that certain patterns of investment (export oriented, mature manufactures, natural resources, joint ventures) are believed to be most beneficial for the long-term growth prospects of developing states, but that a quite different pattern (domestic market oriented, consumer manufactures, green field entry of new firms) has the greatest potential in aiding the process of transformation. This section reviews the available data on foreign investment and FSU policies toward investment and anecdotal evidence of foreign incursion, and assesses the probable pattern and effect of foreign investment in the republics. To do this, I look at these three issues individually: the sectoral patterns of investment, joint venture versus green field entry, and export versus import oriented production.

Sector of Investment

An analysis of the development literature suggested that states will have opportunities to renegotiate the terms of investment, and that the sector of investment is likely to be a good indicator of success in these renegotiations. Prior studies suggest that states are most successful with extractive industries and mature manufactures not dependent on rapidly changing technology because of such factors as state learning, technological diffusion, and sunk costs. States are likely to do less well in areas where technological evolution is vital and located out of country, as well as in areas where sunk costs are minimal, such as in service industries. Given the limited information on sectoral distribution of investment in the republics, it is helpful to look at investment figures from the Soviet period before speculating on the pattern in the post-Soviet era.

At the end of the Soviet period the largest number of JVs was in the service sector. PlanEcon analysts argued that investment was concentrated in services because of the lower degree of risk associated with their operation.[34] Starting with service industries organized by number, JVs in early 1990 were registered in personal computer production and programming (208); business consulting (149); research and development and engineering consulting (129); construction and construction materials manufacturing (117); tourism, hotel operation, and passenger transport (87); retail trade and public dining (71); health and medical care (56); and film, video production, and concerts (56). In manufacturing, consumer goods (123), chemicals and wood products (97), machine building (91), and agriculture and food processing (91) had the highest number of registrations. These numbers can be a bit misleading, since they report only the number of registrations and not characteristics such as size, amount of capital investment, or success in implementing the venture that would be better indicators of the economic significance of these enterprises.

However, if the PlanEcon analysts were correct in their surmise that investment is constrained by high uncertainty about the political and economic conditions in the republics, it is reasonable to assume that investors will continue to invest in the service sector as they did in the Soviet period.[35] Recent data from Lithuania, which has released information on sectoral distribution through 1993, shows that this pattern is repeated. Foreign investment is concentrated in financial services, tourism, and trade.[36] If this pattern holds in other republics the way it has in Lithuania, then it is highly unlikely that the FSU republics will be able to use these investments for either of their goals of transition or economic growth. Services represent little sunk costs and tend to be transitory or mobile. If FSU host states attempt to extract concessions from such ventures, it is relatively easy for the investor to choose to move to a new location (exit), rather than give the host state a greater percentage of its profits or accommodate other state demands.

Several analysts have speculated on the types of investments that will gravitate to the various republics, given their individual mix of resources, such as the investment in extractive industries discussed above. Such forecasting is based on factors such as geographic position, existing resource base, and existing industrial base. For example, both the IMF and PlanEcon[37] argue that Georgia is well suited to tourism and agriculture. Presently Georgia is getting little play from investors because of the Abkhazian conflict, but this suggests that eventually Georgia's foreign investment will focus on these areas. PlanEcon also proposes that Latvia and Belarus are admirably positioned to serve as gateways to the post-Soviet market from the West. This suggests that foreign investment in these states might develop in transportation and trade. For manufactures, the European republics offer a highly educated work force at a bargain price. States that were highly industrialized by Soviet planners (Russia, Ukraine, Belarus, the Baltics) also have existing factories that can be modernized and converted and a more highly developed physical infrastructure than republics in areas like Central Asia. Plants from the defense sector offer particular promise; these were located in Belarus, Ukraine, Russia, and Kazakhstan. Thus, for manufactures, the European portions of the FSU seem to have the greatest potential for attracting foreign investors because they have an existing, even if poor in quality, infrastructure and a large, educated work force.

Joint Ventures and Direct Foreign Investment

The next question of interest is what form the investment will take, JVs or FDI. Joint ownership is seen as a means of keeping control and profits in the host country, and is, therefore, desirable from a developmental standpoint. Complete ownership is more likely to induce greater competition and is preferable from a transition perspective. The data on this JV versus foreign investment is completely anecdotal, but it does come down strongly for JVs rather than for complete foreign ownership of the business. This is because from the investor's perspective, there are numerous advantages to a JV over complete ownership in any host state.[38] Business people note that JVs provide greater control over production, management, and quality; give the business an opportunity to obtain otherwise unavailable technology or natural resources; are able to employ less expensive and more qualified labor; have greater access to potential markets; and tend to be more firmly established in their relationships with local authorities and enterprises.

In addition, there are benefits to JVs that are specific to the post-Soviet republics. The Soviet system was one based largely on personal connections between individuals. As businesses attempting to enter the

Japanese market have found, operating in such a system without an indigenous partner is difficult and frustrating. And, in addition to being outside the network, completely foreign owned firms face restrictions that those with indigenous partners do not have, despite the fact that most of the foreign investment laws promise equal opportunities. There are numerous examples of these disadvantages. In Russia and Estonia, external firms have not been able to acquire land but are only able to get long-term leases. In Kyrgyzstan, foreign participation in privatization auctions (or other competitive bidding) requires special government permission. Belarus has put a few sectors of the economy off limits to foreign capital. Given that there are still some restrictions on the activity of foreign firms and given the general benefits of having a local partner in the short run, the probable pattern of investment will be in JVs rather than new or green field entry. The consequence of this pattern for the FSU is that while foreign investment may bring capital, technology, and management skills to the economy, such firms will probably not provide a major means of demonopolizing the economy and thus may be of minimal assistance to the task of transition through demonopolization of markets.

Export versus Import Oriented Production

The final issue to be addressed is whether the FSU republics will attract investment focused on production for the domestic market or that which is export oriented. Domestic production would prove useful for transition in building public support and helping to stem hyperinflation; industries that export would aid balance of payments and growth. On this point, the post-Soviet republics represent a rather unusual case, because the empirical findings of economists suggest that most foreign investment in developing states is done to penetrate the domestic market of those states, not as a base of operations for export. However, in the Soviet Union before it and in the FSU republics, the lack of a freely convertible currency has meant that enterprises would have to have an export component, engage in cross-trade, or barter to be able to get profits in hard currency. But without convertible currency or goods that are fairly fungible for cross-trade, the FSU republics will probably only see investment that is oriented toward export. Ventures geared toward the domestic market will probably cater to the small portion of society that has hard currency, and thus not have the stabilization effect that would prove an aid to transition.

To develop this point in a bit more detail, it is necessary to look at why MNCs invest in developing states in the first place. The notion that an MNC would invest in a certain state to export is based on the assumption that MNCs are accounting for comparative advantage in their decision to invest in a specific region. Economists agree that states become important hosts because they are low cost locations to do what MNCs do. However, there is no compelling empirical evidence that backs up this assertion.[39] Rather, research suggests that the decision on whether to invest in a state and whether to export to that state are jointly determined questions. The decision is between exporting to that state or setting up production facilities there to sell in that market, not between different places for putting a particular factory. Foreign investment, in this view, is chosen over export when it minimizes transaction costs and uncertainty and eases company access to that market. This means that it is anticipated that a foreign firm will be oriented toward production in the host state for consumption in that state. Companies choose investment rather than export to overcome tariff protection of a market.

Now, the market potential of the republics, particularly the large ones like Russia and Ukraine, is enormous and relatively untapped. Some claim that the magnitude of opportunity is unmatched in the world.[40] The population is familiar with Western products and brand names, which were a symbol of status during the Soviet period. It is a market with a preexisting demand for Western style goods that is very attractive to potential investors. However, what is lacking is the ability to easily get out the profits of a venture. This is a powerful explanation for the low level of foreign investment; the MNCs are unable to successfully achieve the primary goal of foreign investment — profitable sales to the host market. This indicates that currency convertibility is a necessary first step in encouraging investors to produce for domestic consumption in the FSU republics. I say currency convertibility rather than encouraging a policy of barter or cross-trade, even though such policies are presently being used. This is because the policies of cross-trade and barter offer opportunities to corrupt officials, and may lead to less-than-market-price sales of FSU goods and a less efficient use of resources — problems associated with JVs during the Gorbachev era. This means that without currency reform, the investment levels will remain low and most ventures will remain at least partially export oriented.

CONCLUDING REMARKS

The FSU republics have great hopes for foreign investment. It is seen as the means of modernizing industry, spurring competition, increasing productivity, quelling social discontent, improving the balance of payments, and decreasing unemployment. Multinational capital can be a vehicle for future growth as well as aid economic transformation from central planning. But as the analysis above indicates, these two tasks call for quite different sectoral patterns of investment. The experience of developing states indicates that export oriented JVs in extractive industries or mature manufactures are most likely to gain FSU states the kinds of concessions from business that are believed to aid economic growth. Given their rich resources, Russia, Azerbaijan, Turkmenistan, Kazakhstan, and perhaps Uzbekistan may be able to use foreign investment as such an engine of growth. It will be much more difficult for the remaining republics to achieve this goal.

The analysis of the role of foreign investment in transition suggested that domestically targeted "green field" manufacturing (especially of consumer goods) in highly concentrated sectors would be the greatest aid to the process of transition. There are two important barriers to foreign investment fulfilling this role. First, the FSU republics lack a convertible currency. Therefore, MNCs are only able to sell their product domestically if they make arrangements to export at least part of the product or if they develop counter trade arrangements. While companies such as Pepsico have achieved such arrangements, anecdotal evidence from businessmen suggest that it is an arduous and time consuming process. Second, anecdotal evidence suggests that doing business in the post-Soviet republics without a local partner is quite difficult. Thus, businessmen are attracted to JVs rather than the green field entry that would decrease market concentration. While these two barriers, the lack of convertible currency and the need for local partners, exist, the process of foreign investment is likely to be less effective to aid the process of transition from central planning.

NOTES

1. Anders Aslund, *Gorbachev's Struggle for Economic Reform: The Soviet Reform Process, 1985–1988* (Ithaca, N.Y.: Cornell University Press, 1988), p. 141.

2. See H. Steven Gardner, "The Implications of Greater East-West Economic Cooperation for the Soviet Economy," in *Perestroika and East-West Economic Relations*, eds. Michael Kraus and Ronald D. Lebowitz (New York: New York University Press, 1990).

3. Michael Bradshaw, *The Effects of Soviet Dissolution* (London: Royal Institute of International Affairs, 1993), p. 35.

4. Carey Goldberg, "Joint Ventures Failing to Lift Soviet Economy." *Los Angeles Times*, May 26, 1991, p. D1.

5. Ibid., p. D16.

6. These figures are taken from Bradshaw, *The Effects of Soviet Dissolution*, pp. 35–37.

7. Cassandra Cavanaugh, "Uzbekistan's Long Road to the Market," *RFE/RL Research Report*, vol. 1, no. 29 (July 17, 1992).

8. "Investment Hopes to Survive Current Difficulties," *The Baltic Independent*, July 31–August 6, 1992.

9. Kathleen Mihalosko, "Political Crisis in Postcommunist Belarus," *RFE/RL Research Report*, vol. 1, no. 22 (June 12, 1992).

10. For reviews of this literature, see Thomas J. Biersteker, *Distortion or Development? Contending Perspectives on the Multinational Corporation* (Cambridge: The MIT Press, 1981); Theodore H. Moran, *Multinational Corporations: The Political Economy of Foreign Direct Investment* (Lexington, Mass.: Lexington Books, 1985); and John M. Rothgeb, Jr., *Myths and Realities of Foreign Investment in Poor Countries: The Modern Leviathan in the Third World* (New York: Praeger, 1985).

11. Raymond Vernon, *Storm Over the Multinationals: The Real Issues* (Cambridge, Mass.: Harvard University Press, 1977), pp. 166–73.

12. See Moran, *Multinational Corporations*, pp. 6–9.

13. See the obsolescing bargain argument in Raymond Vernon, *Sovereignty at Bay: The Multinational Spread of U.S. Enterprises* (New York: Basic Books, 1971).

14. See Moran, *Multinational Corporations and the Politics of Dependence: Copper in Chile* (Princeton, N.J.: Princeton University Press, 1974).

15. See Gary Gereffi, *The Pharmaceutical Industry and Dependency in the Third World* (Princeton, N.J.: Princeton University Press, 1983).

16. Ibid.

17. Thomas J. Biersteker, "The Illusion of State Power: Transnational Corporations and the Neutralization of Host-Country Legislation," *Journal of Peace Research*, vol. 17 (1980).

18. See Joseph M. Greico, *Between Dependency and Autonomy: India's Experience with the International Computer Industry* (Berkeley: University of California Press, 1984).

19. Daniel Treisman argues that in Russia at least, there is still genuine confusion over concepts of fair and unfair influence. See Daniel Treisman, "Korruptsia," *The New Republic*, May 11, 1992, p. 16.

20. Michael Mandlebaum, "Introduction," in *Making Markets: Economic Transformation in Eastern Europe and the Post-Soviet States*, ed. Safiquil Islam and Michael Mandlebaum (New York: Council on Foreign Relations Press, 1993), pp. 3–4.

21. See *Perekhod k Rynku: Kontsentsia i programa [Transition to Market: Conception and Progress]* (Moscow: Arkhangel'skoe, 1990).

22. Perra Sutela, "The Role of the External Sector during Transition," in *The Post-Soviet Economy: Soviet and Western Perspectives*, ed. Anders Aslund (London: Pinter Publishers, 1992), p. 86.

23. Herbert S. Levine, "The Future of the Soviet Economy," in *Rubles and Dollars: Strategies for Doing Business in the Soviet Union*, ed. John L. Hecht (New York: HarperCollins, 1991), p. 213.

24. Heidi Kroll, "Monopoly and Transition to the Market," *Soviet Economy*, vol. 7, no. 2 (1991).

25. Abraham Bergson, "Communist Economic Efficiency Revisited," *AEA Papers and Proceedings*, May 1992, p. 28.

26. For a detailed argument about the Soviet monopolistic practices, see Kroll, "Monopoly and Transition to the Market," pp. 144–49.

27. Richard E. Ericson, "Economics," in *After the Soviet Union: From Empire to Nations*, ed. Timothy J. Colton and Robert Legvold (New York: W. W. Norton, 1992).

28. James H. Noren, "The Russian Economic Reform: Progress and Prospects," *Soviet Economy*, vol. 8, no. 1 (January–March 1992), p. 20.

29. Elias Dinopoulis and Timothy D. Lane, "Market Liberalization Policies in a Reforming Socialist Economy," *IMF Staff Papers*, vol. 39, no. 3 (September 1992), p. 485.

30. Ericson, "Economics," pp. 59–60.

31. Richard E. Caves, *Multinational Enterprises and Economic Analysis* (Cambridge: Cambridge University Press, 1982), p. 100.

32. Ibid., p. 102.

33. International Monetary Fund, *A Study of the Soviet Economy* (Washington, D.C.: International Monetary Fund, 1991), p. 361.

34. "Soviet Joint Ventures: Developments through the First Quarter of 1990," *PlanEcon*, April 27, 1990.

35. Bradshaw presents a counterargument to this, arguing that manufacturing ventures take longer to come on-line, and that the numbers of operating

manufacturing firms will soon begin to balance this skewed picture.

36.   See Economist Intelligence Unit, *Country Report: The Baltics*, no. 1 (1993).

37.   *PlanEcon Report*, March 27, 1992, and the 15 IMF Economic Reviews on the republics.

38.   R. Pipko, "Joint Ventures: A Practitioner's View," in *Rubles and Dollars: Strategies for Doing Business in the Soviet Union*, ed. John L. Hecht (New York: HarperCollins, 1991).

39.   Caves, *Multinational Enterprises and Economic Analysis*, p. 67.

40.   John L. Hecht, "Why Do Business in the Soviet Union," in *Rubles and Dollars: Strategies for Doing Business in the Soviet Union*, ed. John L. Hecht (New York: HarperCollins, 1991).

3

Russian Banking and Finance: A Crisis of Credibility

Eric A. Stubbs

The pre-perestroika banking and financial system of the Soviet Union was one component of a larger central planning system. In many ways it operated as a financial and accounting shadow of the state's more prominent material planning mechanism. Its three primary responsibilities in that role would be unfamiliar to Western central banks: audit and verification of enterprise transactions; maintenance of financial equilibrium between aggregate supply and demand; and reinforcement of a macroeconomic strategy of isolation of the consumer, enterprise, and foreign trade sectors. There was no role for private commercial or investment banking in these functions.

One of the challenges of Russia's attempts today to develop a coherent model of economic reform is to solve the complicated task of devising a modern and pluralistic banking industry out of the remaining pieces of that legacy.

The job of banking and financial reform involves the government's mechanisms for central banking and finance, the profusion of private commercial banking institutions that have opened their doors, and the state enterprises, private citizens, and entrepreneurs who are the clients of the new system.

The transition is complicated by the heated political contests surrounding economic reform as a whole. Not surprisingly, these have been reflected in debates over the roles of central and private banking and a variety of political institutions and bureaucracies in Russia's transition. In many instances the financial institutions have been held hostage by

---

The views expressed in this chapter are those of the author and do not necessarily represent the views of Price Waterhouse.

the warring political factions. In other cases, they have been parties themselves to the disputes.

The difficulties of transitioning to a new central and commercial banking and financial system, and even of identifying appropriate goals and strategies for the system over the last two years, have led to a succession of confused and contradictory policies and vacillation culminating in a Gordian knot of financial crises. The symptoms of the crisis include spiralling inflation rates, unconstrained expansion of the money supply and enterprise credits, an exploding government deficit, declining industrial investment and production, free-falling ruble-dollar rates in internal auctions, and a demonetization of the domestic economy.

In part, the financial crisis reflects two years of political confusion over reform strategies. The mix of elements from both a macroeconomic reformist financial agenda and a microeconomic institutional "preservationist" strategy has resulted in contradictory and incoherent financial strategies marked by episodes of shifting objectives and reversing initiatives, and, in many cases, the imposition of increasingly onerous burdens on the citizen population.

The domestic and international credibility of Russian efforts to contain and control the financial crisis has suffered as a result. This crisis in credibility has impeded the rehabilitation of the Russian financial and banking system. Symmetrically, the restoration of domestic and international confidence in Russian macroeconomic financial management is an essential first step to stabilizing the ruble and ensuring the effectiveness of the economic reform program of the Russian government.

Although the conflicts over reform agendas are relatively new, the origins of this crisis of credibility reach back several decades into Soviet-era financial management practices and institutional organization. The political skirmishes over strategy and direction that have surrounded the Central Bank of Russia's management of the financial and monetary system in a strongly pluralistic and contentious government bureaucracy have added to the crisis. Layered on top of these issues is the competition among conflicting programs for industrial production support and for sharing the burdens of reforms across sectors of the economy and society.

This chapter outlines the nature and extent of the current crisis in Russian banking. It traces the Soviet historical legacy and institutional background that have set the stage for the erosion of the domestic credibility of the ruble. The organization of the Soviet financial system — both from a macroeconomic perspective and in the microeconomics of the traditional government-enterprise relationship — is a second facet of the historical foundations of Russia's financial crisis. These are outlined in the third section of the chapter.

The sections that follow describe the issues that confront the Russian government in its efforts to make the transition to a new banking and financial system that is supportive of the overall goals of economic reform in its immediate applications and for the longer term requirements of the Russian banking and finance sector. These issues are grouped into three categories: those that center around the problematic relationship between the Russian government and enterprises, those that arise as a result of the politicization of the role of the Central Bank of Russia, and those concerning the valuation of the ruble and Russian progress toward convertibility.

Whatever reform strategy Russia ultimately adopts, its success in restoring economic growth, curtailing inflation, assembling a political constituency that supports a coherent plan of reform, and progressing toward international viability for the ruble, depends on monetary stability and the credibility of Russian central banking policies. The concluding section of this chapter outlines some of the difficult choices and strategies that are available to the Russian government in its efforts to reestablish the stability and credibility that it requires.

THE CURRENT RUSSIAN BANKING
AND FINANCIAL CRISIS

Russia's economic derailment is clear from its accelerating inflation, mushrooming money and near-money supplies, growing government debt, and precipitous declines in real production, the auction value of the ruble, and investment. Table 3.1 traces the history of selected indicators from 1988 through 1993. Figures prior to 1991(6) refer to the USSR as a whole. Table values in parentheses denote estimates.

The figures in Table 3.1 illustrate the extent of the deterioration in the Russian economy over the last two years. Visible retail price inflation had maintained a stable rate between 2 percent and 5 percent per year throughout the mid- and late-1980s. Increases in the money supply and government debt levels in the last years of the Gorbachev era led to mounting inflationary pressure and a doubling of inflation rates.

With the dissolution of the Soviet Union in the middle of 1991, a number of changes with profound implications for Russian economic management occurred simultaneously. As republics declared political independence they became increasingly resistant to Russian economic direction. As a consequence, anticipated tax revenues were neither collected nor remitted to Moscow. Domestic enterprises and those across republic borders discovered too that the new government was unable in most cases to compel payment for receipt of goods. Payments slowed or ceased altogether. Reductions in interrepublic deliveries of intermediate goods compounded the problem by crippling production of final goods and collections of payments for deliveries. Cascading shortages

TABLE 3.1
Deterioration of Russian Economic Performance

	1988 (6)	1989 (6)	1990 (6)	1991 (1)	1991 (6)	1992 (1)	1992 (6)	1993 (1)	1993 (6)
Price Index	100	105	(110)	114	N/A	221	2,210	5,770	16,312
Cash Rubles (R bil.)	80	(95)	118	132	(165)	234	(560)	1,741	(3,100)
R/$ Auction Rate	N/A	N/A	N/A	28	42	230	144	489	1,030
Government Debt (R bil.)	312	398	N/A	566	875	996	N/A	2,571	N/A
Ent. Credits (R bil.)	22	22	234	365	557	775	2,200	3,000	6,000

Notes:

(1) values in January of the year addressed

(6) mid-year values

Sources: Based on a speech by A. A. Khandruyev, "Let Us Define Our Priorities," *Rossiyskiye Vesti* (2 March 1993), p. 5 in FBIS-USR-93-026 (26 March 1993), pp. 32–34; Paulo Vieira da Cunha et al., *Russian Economic Reform: Crossing the Threshold of Structural Change* (Washington, D.C.: The World Bank, 1992); Marie Lavigne, *Financing the Transition in the USSR: The Shatalin Plan and the Soviet Economy* (New York: Institute for East-West Security Studies, June 1989); Eric Stubbs, *Soviet Domestic Economic Reforms and the International Business Environment* (Providence, R.I.: Center for Foreign Policy Development, 1980); "Soviet Banking in 1990," *Interfax* (1800 GMT, 31 May 1991) in FBIS-SOV-91-107 (4 June 1991), pp. 24–25; "The USSR Economy over the Period January–September 1991," *Ekonomika i Zhizn*, no. 43 (October 1991), pp. 7–10 in FBIS-SOV-91-216 (7 November 1991), pp. 20–36.

along production chains resulted. These were manifested both in declining production and in declining enterprise revenues.

The national government found itself facing unexpected operating deficits as its own revenues declined and requirements to provide working capital to enterprises grew. In the last year of Soviet government, for example, profit tax collections equaled only 36 percent of expected levels; sales taxes, 31 percent; and government foreign trade income, 26 percent of anticipated levels. Some economizing did occur, with expenditures limited to 77 percent of planned levels. Nonetheless, the government deficit ballooned to at least four and a half times budgeted levels.[1] As government borrowing increased the money supply, government debt, and enterprise credits rapidly rose.

The sources of Soviet, and later Russian, collection difficulties included declines in officially recorded trade volumes (hence reduced turnover and sales tax revenues), declining export capabilities, reduced remittances of taxes by enterprises, reduced payments to the central government by republic governments, and reductions in interrepublic trade remittances.[2]

Under the traditional Soviet model for financial management, increasing money and near-money (credit) supplies would not necessarily result in higher price levels for consumers. With pervasive price controls, money supply increases might appear as *hidden inflation* (spurious creation of new classes of goods to justify inflated prices) or as *repressed inflation* (typically manifested through rising savings rates, goods shortages, and longer lines). However, loosening government authority over enterprise production and management and preference among reformers within the government to allow greater pricing freedom to enterprises combined to ensure that the money supply increased prices instead. Over the course of 1991 retail prices grew by 94 percent.

The inflationary cycle was accelerated at the beginning of 1992 by a government decision to abruptly decontrol prices on roughly half of the nation's consumer goods. The inflation rate for the month of January 1992 skyrocketed to 345 percent. Prices rose by an additional 756 percent over the next 11 months after the initial shock of price liberalization. For 1992 as a whole, inflation amounted to 2,609 percent, or an average of 31 percent per month, compounded monthly.

The January 1992 price liberalization was motivated by a belief that the profits generated by the price increases would encourage existing producers to increase production. With time, large profits would also encourage new producers to enter markets, raising output and creating jobs. The anticipated spurt of inflation itself was expected to absorb excess liquidity in the money supply, restoring a stable (albeit higher) price level to the economy. Eventually, price competition would ensure that the alignment between prices and household incomes was restored. The actual situation evolved much differently.

The price liberalization effort did not account adequately for either Russian industrial organization or politics. Expanding production and realignment of prices depend on adequate competition among producers to create an incentive to expand production and to capture a greater market and to ensure that inputs are readily available at a reasonable price.

Neither condition held in Russia. As Russian economists quickly recognized, a rational monopolist faced with opportunities to increase prices and difficulties to obtain inputs will restrict output supply and increase prices as much as possible.[3] But, what is rational for an individual monopolist is disaster for an entire economy. When copied by all the monopolies (70 percent of Russian industry), that behavior triggers cascading shortages and economy-wide production declines. Ironically, as input shortages stymie production, producers face increasingly desperate working capital shortages and an inability to cover costs.

As pressure mounted on the Russian government to alleviate the liquidity shortage and quell the industrial panic it had created,[4] the government confronted a Hobson's choice: extending credits to industry would fuel inflation and reverse government efforts to compel enterprises to act as independent producers. The alternative, however, risked massive unemployment and industrial decline as production continued to tumble in a continuing liquidity crisis.[5] The government appeared reluctant to embrace the first strategy of liberalized credit, thereby avoiding a more severe production crisis in the short term but perpetuating the underlying problems.

Russian inflation slowed slightly during the first half of 1993 to an average of 19 percent per month (282 percent over the first six months of the year). Similar rates continued to the end of the year, leading to an, overall Russian inflation rate of about 800 percent during 1993.[6]

While inflation is both a direct visible sign and a symptom of the disintegration of the Russian economy, its indirect effects have been equally corrosive for the macrofinancial economy. Two aspects of high inflation often have debilitating impacts on government and business efforts at recovery by inhibiting long-term investment — uncertainty and inflation tilt.

Inflation rates at the levels experienced by Russia make it nearly impossible to collect reliable statistics on production, market trends, incomes, or even inflation itself. That uncertainty translates into difficulties in setting interest rates consistent with positive real returns for banks and other lenders. The unstable and dynamic nature of the economy increases lending risks as well. As a consequence, commercial rates that would compensate lenders for informational uncertainty and commercial risk are far higher than most borrowers could contemplate. Long-term loan financing becomes virtually impossible to find.

Russian commercial banks extended 7,970 billion rubles in commercial credit as of the middle of 1993. Of that amount, only 351 billion rubles, or 4.4 percent is in loans with maturities longer than a year.[7] Most of the long-term loans are old loans that are likely to mature shortly. In February 1993, only 0.4 percent of new loan issues by commercial banks were for maturities exceeding a year. In March that ratio fell to 0.2 percent.[8]

Nominal interest rates on these loans have averaged only a little above 100 percent per year. The implied real interest rates are consequently strongly negative. However, banks paid an average of 75 percent per year on deposits in early 1993, resulting in a profitable spread for their lending operations. Moreover, the banks enjoyed preferential centralized credit disbursement from the Russian government of Viktor Chernomyrdin, which effectively subsidized their lending operations.[9]

The second problem associated with banking in a high inflation environment is inflation tilt. Inflation tilt refers to the phenomenon with installment loans that with higher nominal interest rates, the borrower is compelled to pay a larger fraction of the present value of the loan sooner than with a lower nominal rate loan, even when real interest rates are identical. Higher nominal rate loans place a greater burden on the borrower's immediate cash flow, making the loan prohibitively expensive to pay back in the short term. Inflation tilt makes it more difficult for borrowers to match their cash flows to the requirements for debt service in the short term.

The combination of political factors relating to relaxed government control over enterprise performance and payments, inflation, and the political and economic confusion that have surrounded Russian reforms have taken a toll on Russian production. According to official Russian measures, gross domestic product growth rates fell from +5.5 percent in 1988, to +3.6 percent in 1989, −2 percent in 1990, −8 percent in 1991, and −19 percent in 1992. The expected decline through the end of 1993 is another 10 percent.[10] Unofficial recalculations of Russian gross domestic product suggest that the decline actually began in 1986 and that national income fell by 5 percent each year from 1988 to 1990 and by 24 percent in 1991.[11] These statistics imply a decline in production of between 34 percent and 47 percent since 1989.

The decline in domestic production was coupled with an alarming drop in new investment. Real investment decreased by 45 percent in 1992, with 38 percent of the funds used for investment coming from the Russian government.[12] The declines in real investment continued throughout 1993.

Russian industry appears to remain plagued by inefficiency in the use of available investment resources, as it was when the enterprises were controlled by the previous Communist government of the Soviet Union. Only 1 percent of investment projects scheduled for completion in 1991–92 were actually finished.[13] Work in progress ties up investment capital without producing increasing output or improving performance.

Some of the effects on Russia's population of these recent economic events are easy to predict. Others are more difficult to decipher. Inflation has devalued the savings of the Russian population over the previous decades to the point where an average worker's monthly income today (about 30,000 rubles) is five times greater than the entire savings of an average family at the end of 1991.[14] With savings bank interest rates generally running below 100 percent per year even now, the real value of deposits and accrued interest halves every four months.

The decline in national output has also reduced living standards for Russians. It is impossible, however, to reliably ascertain the extent of the decline. Wage rates increased 28-fold between the beginning of 1992 and the middle of 1993, while retail prices increased at more than twice that rate. That would suggest a 50 percent fall in real wages. The statistics are questionable, however, as increasing proportions of both earnings and commercial transactions occur in ways that defy reliable collection. These include off-the-book transactions, private sector exchanges, barter arrangements, and, increasingly, gray and black market trading. Official statistics are likely to underestimate earnings and may overestimate effective inflation as a result.

However, the aggregate average statistics also mask important disparities in the incidence of Russia's economic decline. The greatest burdens have fallen on the urban middle-aged workers and the older population who often have neither the skills nor access to participate in the private economy, and on those with fixed incomes.

ORGANIZATION OF THE RUSSIAN MONETARY ECONOMY

The Russian monetary system has evolved into a pluralistic organization where institutional jurisdictions and responsibilities are still in flux. At times, the major institutions, including the Ministry of Finance, Ministry of Economics, the Supreme Soviet, and the Central Bank of the Russian Federation (CBRF), appear to pursue convergent policies in relative harmony. Since 1991, however, it appears to have been the case more frequently that policy has been the product of a political competition between two blocs — the executive government and the Supreme Soviet. That competition appears to be based on fundamentally different perceptions of the problems currently facing Russia and of fudamentally different prescriptions for solutions.

It is useful to review briefly the historical backgrounds of the institutions involved in Russian monetary and financial policy as a preface to an exploration of their recent actions.

Government Financial Institutions in the Soviet Economy

In the early 1980s, prior to perestroika, the Soviet financial system was regulated and directed by the Ministry of Finance, and under its supervision, by Gosbank (State Bank), Stroybank (Capital Investments Bank), Vneshtorgbank (Bank for Foreign Trade), and the Savings Bank of the USSR.

Perestroika brought a number of major bank reforms that contributed to the decentralization of central banking activities. Decentralization was accomplished primarily by spinning off of specific functions from Gosbank to five newly created or reorganized specialized sector banks. Sector banks received their initial funding from the State Bank and have been paying interest on the money to the State Bank. The newly formed sector banks raised additional funds from Soviet enterprises, cooperatives, and Soviet citizens.

The six formally co-equal banking institutions included Gosbank — the original state central bank — and five banks specialized by the sectors they served: *Promstroibank* — industrial and construction banking; *Agroprombank* — agriculture and agro-industrial banking; *Sberegatelnyibank* — retail savings and credit banking; *Zhilsoszbank* — housing, municipal services, and social development banking; and *Vnesheconombank* — foreign economic activity.[15]

Bank policy for the six official banks was developed by the USSR Banks Council, which was subordinated to the Ministry of Finance. Gosbank's chairman served as the permanent chair of the council, while the chairmen of the newly formed sector banks were council members. While part of the Banks Council's activities diminished Gosbank's authority in a technical sense, Gosbank remained the central bank of the USSR and could use its preeminent position on the Banks Council to exercise its influence over Soviet banking as a whole. The banks were not authorized to undertake independent policy formulation, nor could they independently develop or execute credit or loan policies.[16]

Gosbank's power was guaranteed in part under Soviet law through provisions dictating that all of the newly formed commercial banks and cooperatives in the USSR had to maintain reserve deposits with Gosbank. Gosbank effectively served as a regulator of commercial banks. The commercial banking sector itself was, however, only in its very initial formative stages. In January 1989, there were 41 private banks in the USSR, including 24 cooperatives. A year later the numbers had swelled to 225 and 78 respectively, and grew to 1,307 and 133 by January 1991. With a few notable exceptions, such as the *Energomash Bank*, which served the needs of the giant Energomash enterprise, and the *Technokhim Bank* of Leningrad, most of these banks were small and precariously undercapitalized.

Commercial banking rules, then as now, existed through a patchwork of legislation. The legislative basis for commercial banking was far from complete. For example, it was only in late 1989 that a reserve requirement (of 12.5 percent) was imposed on commercial bank lending activities. Until that time, no explicitly stated reserve requirement was in force, although this was understood to mean that the implicit requirement was 100 percent.

Although many new Soviet commercial banks were extremely undercapitalized, a few, like those mentioned above with the security of a major enterprise conglomerate behind them, were reasonably secure. Apart from the potentially precarious nature of their banking activities, commercial banking activity represented another avenue for the weakening of the government's control over the money supply. Commercial banks also represented the growth of a new and competitive alternative to state banking for Soviet enterprises and consumers. They pay a higher interest rate on deposits, can issue industrial bridge loans, and finance private housing and construction projects. They have also been known to launder illicit gains from criminal activities (as defined by the Soviet government).

The Ministry of Finance had a number of critical roles in the Soviet economic structure. Technically, the Ministry supervised Gosbank. Government deficits were, therefore, readily converted into short-term credits and disbursements of circulating currency. Currency was transferred to individuals through subsidies, government and enterprise wage payments, and contractual payments to enterprises and social programs. These, in turn, increased circulating money stocks to the extent that price increases and inducements for individuals to increase their savings deposits did not withdraw currency. In contrast to most other economies where the retail purchase of government instruments tends to reduce the inflationary pressure of deficits, government retail bonds were not significant in Soviet finance in the 1980s.

The Ministry of Finance was also responsible for developing the state budget. That task had required direct communications and negotiations with the Ministries of Finance of the 15 republics and used additional information from state enterprises and the various ministries. Once the budget was developed it required approval from the State Council and the Supreme Soviet prior to implementation. Once the budget passed, the Ministry of Finance was responsible for ensuring adherence to the budget.

One of the Ministry of Finance's most important functions was that of controlling the nation's hard currency reserves. The Ministry of Finance provided the very important service of converting rubles into hard currency for different republics and ministries for their imports. Additionally, the Ministry of Finance was responsible for auditing the expenditures of the republics and all of the other state ministries.

Five departments of the Ministry of Finance were key to its administration of the Soviet financial system:

Budget Division was responsible for preparing the state budget. Following approval, it was charged with budget oversight.

State Revenue Division collected revenues from state, cooperative, and public enterprises.

Department of Industry and Agriculture Financing was made up of a number of specific divisions that oversaw the revenues and cash flows of heavy industry, the agro-industrial complex, transportation and communications, light industry, and state trade.

Division of Credit, Money, and Wages participated in designing the state budget. It controlled interactions between the state budget and credit system and performed analytical tasks related to the setting of wage rates and money supply.

Main Currency-Economic Division participated in the design of the portion of the state budget that dealt with import and export strategy and currency distribution.

Other departments under the Ministry of Finance included the Division of Finance for Culture and Public Health, Division of Finance for Social Security, Central Staff Division, and the Price Division. The State Committee of Social Insurance of the USSR and the State Committee for Production and Quality Control Certification were also under the jurisdiction of the Ministry of Finance.

The Soviet model for administration of the financial system central-ized in the Ministry of Finance most of the functions that we identify today with macroeconomic management. Between its direct responsi-bilities and oversight authority over Gosbank, the ministry controlled government outlays and revenues, money supply, government and enterprise credit, import and export trade and revenues, industrial cash flows and investment, government and commercial banking, and industrial regulatory compliance.

Interaction among Soviet Financial Sectors

The routes by which inflation emerged in the Soviet economy were very different from those that we normally associate with inflation in a Western market-oriented system. Although the political tenor of the system has changed under the Russian, non-Communist government, many aspects of the organization, institutions, and relationships remain. An understanding of those holdovers is useful to perform an analysis of the implications of continued inflation for Russian banking and finance.

Traditional banking, financial, and monetary management under the Soviet Communist system had four primary purposes:

- to isolate the four separate monetary sectors of the Soviet economy,
- to maintain the intersectoral monetary balance and to avoid undue accu-mulations of cash in the consumer sector,
- to monitor material production transactions for audit and control purpos-es, and
- to maintain units of account and trade within the economy.

A useful way to understand the organization of the Soviet monetary system is to regard it as four separate but interconnected subsystems, each using its own form of currency for transactions and accounts: the consumer sector, using cash rubles; the domestic enterprise sector, using bank drafts; and the foreign trade sector, using convertible rubles. More recently, a fourth sector has become more prominent: the domestic hard currency sector and the gray market, using barter, for-eign currency, and sometimes rubles.

One of the explicit goals of the Soviet monetary authorities was to maintain stability by enforcing a quarantining of these sectors and minimizing spillovers among sectors. The goal of balance within each sector has generally been a higher priority for the Soviet Ministry of Finance than the goal of economy-wide balance of supply and demand.

The official industrial sector executed most of its transactions through bank drafts that were cleared and administered through the central banking authority. This, incidentally, provided the central bank with an additional role as de facto government auditor for the industrial sector. Payments for interenterprise contracts were generally made through these drafts, issued by the bank only upon evidence of the completion of a contract or requirement of interim payments. Industrial utilization of ruble currency was limited to authorized withdrawals to meet payroll and deposits of ruble revenues from retail operations.

The central bank had the additional responsibility of greasing the wheels of commerce by providing bridge loans and long-term loans to cover industrial revenue shortfalls.[17] When capital depreciation is taken into account, about one-half of Soviet enterprises lost money each year.[18] Tax rates were set to provide revenues to the government and to withdraw excess credits from this sector. Typically, an enterprise paid 32–35 percent of its profits in taxes, although at various times the definition of profits changed to include or exclude wage payments and capital consumption reserves.[19]

Monetary balance in the enterprise sector entailed careful control of enterprise finances and expenditures. It was complemented by the explicit distinction in the Soviet economy between the possession of funds for a transaction and authorization to undertake the transaction. For example, enterprise investment in structures and equipment generally used rubles drawn from the enterprise's budget resources (about 35 percent) and from state disbursements (about 65 percent). However, even with an adequate budget in place, investment resources could not be procured legally without authorization from the supply agencies and investment agencies for actual material supplies.

In contrast, commerce in the consumer sector occurred almost entirely in cash rubles from receipt of wage packets to payment for food and goods. The exceptions were taxation and sometimes rent, which were usually deducted at the source. Although checking accounts were technically available in the consumer sector their use remains minimal because of unfamiliarity on the part of the people and hostility in stores. The technical means of check verification remains nearly absent in the USSR and is one aspect of a broader problem of absence of accurate, timely, and broadly disseminated financial information.

By 1990, total savings by Soviet consumers totaled about 700 billion rubles (funding for more than one year's consumption) split evenly between banks and hoarding at home. Individuals save primarily because of the shortages of goods in stores. In a market system, where money implies a command over resources, loanable savings fuel investment. Under the Soviet model, in contrast, administrative authorization was required before investment could occur so there was no natural connection between individual choices to save and enterprise or government access to fund and resources for investment.

Among its consequences, this disconnection of saving and investment generated a short-term equilibrium problem in that aggregate supply and demand of consumption and investment goods and services did not necessarily balance out — shortages and surpluses plagued the economy and were not resolved by price adjustments. It also resulted in a long-term problem: the collective desires of citizens for more or less of particular goods and services in the near term and trade-offs between consumption today and consumption tomorrow were largely ignored by a system that did not translate long-term private consumption and investment goals into societal economic action.

Traditionally, the Soviet foreign trade economy was entirely isolated from the industrial economy, with Foreign Trade Organizations (FTOs) of the central government requisitioning exportable goods from enterprises, paying for them in rubles, then selling the goods abroad for hard currency and remitting revenues to central government accounts. The central government then exercised its authority in determining import decisions on behalf of the entire nation.

Tight central control was relaxed progressively after 1986, with enterprises exercising more control over a fraction of their hard currency earnings. Nonetheless, the lion's share continued to go to the central government. Enterprises were compensated for export sales in accounting rubles on Soviet books. The value of a $100 export in accounting rubles depended on the type of good and region of the country where the goods were produced. A Siberian oil producer might be credited with 500 accounting rubles, while an Odessa textiles plant might only receive credit for 200 accounting rubles for generating $100 in foreign sales. Whatever the specific accounting rate, it bore little relation to either prevailing world and Soviet prices for the particular export good or equilibrium exchange rates.

Import authority as granted along with rights to *valuta*, or convertible rubles. On Soviet enterprise accounting books, these rubles signified a right granted by the central government for an enterprise to use hard currency for imports. As with exports, the conversion rate between accounting convertible rubles and dollars depended on the industry, region, and other factors.

A new monetary sector emerged in the USSR in the 1980s: the domestic hard currency sector. In 1990 an estimated $3 billion was in circulation in the USSR, fueling a thriving black market and lubricating gray-market transactions. The Soviet nonagricultural black market probably constituted 15–20 percent of GNP then (and 25–30 percent today). That this sector has expanded at an impressive rate is a testament to the breakdown of conventional commerce in the USSR. Dollars are preferred to rubles not only because they are considered a stable token of purchasing power as the ruble continues to erode but also because all the administrative authorities that must accompany a ruble transaction may be bypassed by the customer who holds dollars.

From the government's point of view, the rise of the domestic dollar economy has made the task of macroeconomic monetary management nearly impossible, given the impotence of government control over this sector.

Soviet government efforts to isolate these sectors were necessary to mitigate some of the difficulties caused by the Soviet economic management approach. Much of Soviet-era economic policy can be interpreted as an attempt to override collective private consumer preferences for consumption and saving and to impose a set of collective social preferences on production and consumption instead.

Many of the complex and layered decisions adopted by Soviet governments affecting the economy over time may be distilled down to a political objective to devote resources to their interpretation of social needs — ranging from military hardware, to inexpensive food and medical care, to ambitious agricultural and industrialization projects — while maintaining price stability.

Soviet emphasis on social goals that were discordant with the private preferences of the people meant that typical and automatic private market criteria for the allocation of resources, such as profitability, surpluses, and shortages, were discarded in favor of a variety of political criteria. To the extent that the government deemed it a priority to make a particular good universally available — for example, bread — its retail price was reduced by fiat for consumers. As a consequence, profitability of bread factories could not be used to guide the appropriate levels or locations of investment in bread production.

In this environment, too, subsidization of some Soviet industries became inevitable. Consider once again the bread bakery. To the extent that the bakery sold below production costs, greater production would be associated with greater economic losses to the bakery. Moreover, it would be difficult through an examination of the bakery's finances to distinguish a bakery that lost money because it satisfied the government's political and social objectives from one that was merely inefficient.

The Soviet government's reluctance to rely on the relatively simple economic criteria of private productive efficiency and demand, such as profitability, created a number of problems for the production and finance sectors of the Soviet economy. Monitoring of enterprise performance became difficult and led to the promulgation of increasingly elaborate and convoluted production measures. A single factory production line might find itself encumbered with 300 different production objectives relating to use of inputs, quantity of outputs, wage payments, prices, and deliveries. Often the criteria were contradictory or related to aspects of the production process that were not under factory control.

The convoluted performance measures raised an even deeper problem for Soviet efforts to allocate investment resources across economic sectors. Typical Western private financial systems would not operate effectively where profitability could not be used as a measure of factory performance. Moreover, Western banking systems that allocate funding on the basis of firms' relative abilities to pay back debts could not function where all enterprises are owned by the government, and the government effectively guarantees that all debts will be paid through subsidies. In the extreme, if they remained unconstrained, those guarantees would lead enterprises to develop an insatiable appetite for (free) inputs and investment resources. As a consequence, the Soviet government was compelled to ration and allocate investment resources according to its political criteria without necessarily referring to the economic performance of the enterprise or its liquidity.

This system of government-guided investment required that Soviet investment and savings decisions should be disconnected. Because savings and investment were disconnected, as were pricing and consumer demand, the financial system could function only if the major sectors — production, retail consumption and foreign trade — were isolated. Because the costs of investment and access to production supplies were underwritten by the government, there was a risk that enterprises would become magnets for all of the resources in the economy. The development of essentially separate currencies and stringent political control over enterprise resource allocation evolved to avoid that outcome.

The fundamental problem with the Soviet system of financial control and sectoral isolation was that total isolation was impossible and engineering the balance in each sector was a complex undertaking. Mismatches frequently and inevitably occurred between salary and wage payments to workers and the subsidized prices charged for consumer products. In essence, workers were paid more than their share of the value of the goods produced by the enterprises. Through wage payments, a large fraction of the subsidies to enterprises became subsidies to workers. These subsidies were not associated with actual production.

In the context of these efforts at isolation and balance, one interpretation of Soviet/Russian inflation is that the means for controlling credit disbursements and for withdrawing excess cash currency disintegrated. Credit grew because the government leverage over enterprises that had maintained production for decades deteriorated. Production slowed but bankruptcy remained impossible. Implicit and explicit subsidies to the production sector resulted. Leakage into the consumer sector followed as wages increased, but no mechanism remained by which the government could withdraw excess currency under the new system without compulsion. A vicious circle of inflation was the consequence.

During his short tenure as prime minister, Valetin Pavlov launched a misguided effort to correct the escalating monetary imbalance through more traditional Soviet means of coercion and fiat. The Soviet government declared on short notice that as of January 15, 1991, all 50- and 100-ruble banknotes would be removed from circulation. Those holding these banknotes were given three days to exchange quantities equal to up to one month's salary (or 300 rubles for pensioners) at their enterprises. Those with more than 300 rubles worth of large notes would have to seek permission and account for the source of their money before additional exchanges would be permitted. Officially, this measure was justified as a move to deprive the mafia of ill-gotten gains — presumably salted away in large notes — and to counter an alleged foreign plot to destroy the Soviet economy by (according to Pavlov) reintroducing into the USSR the 10–15 billion rubles in large notes that U.S. and other bankers have been quietly accumulating on the cheap.

In reality, the reform was an attempt to withdraw currency from circulation to avoid the building inflationary pressures that the Soviet government had created by issuing more than 25 billion rubles in new currency during the previous year. Pavlov hoped that this measure would remove 10–15 billion rubles from circulation.

The resistance of the Supreme Soviet and Soviet media and the outrage of the republic governments who refused to back the effort doomed the reform attempt. The deadline for redemption of large notes was extended and enterprises were exchanging up to 10,000 rubles for their employees without verifying sources. Since rumors of the impending reform began circulating before the previous November, many people, including organized crime, had disposed of their large bills by January in any event.

Reportedly, the reform led to a withdrawal of 7 billion rubles from circulation, although even Soviet officials express doubts about this figure. The most significant result of this episode was that money panics ignited by the rumors led to an emptying of goods from the stores as individuals tried to dispose of their currency and an exhaustion of government wholesale reserves of goods, intensifying the shortages and discrediting well-intentioned reform efforts as well. The government policy was regarded by the long-suffering population as merely another attempt to saddle the workers with the costs of reform while rendering the government and enterprise structure harmless. In addition, the rebelliousness of republic governments and enterprises sounded the death knell on the central government's ability to impose its will through unilateral decrees.

A BRIEF HISTORY OF SOVIET AND
RUSSIAN FINANCIAL INSTRUMENTS

The first Soviet government bonds, called "natural bonds," were issued in 1922. They were issued by the government to farmers as a form of payment by promissory note for the requisition of agricultural produce. Farmers were forced to exchange corn, bread, or sugar for a bond that entitled them to a ruble payment within 10 years.

With the reestablishment of a financial system in the mid-1920s, the government could return to using bonds denominated in rubles. Prior to World War II, bonds in the Soviet Union served two specific purposes: to help redistribute funds within the state-owned sector (take profits out of enterprises that were in the black to subsidize those that were losing money) and as a means of controlling inflation by withdrawing excess cash.

Under Stalin's leadership in the 1930s, people were simply forced to buy quantities of 20-year bonds, yielding no interest, at a fixed percentage of their income This measure was introduced as a way of fighting inflation because of a severe shortage of goods. During World War II, Stalin introduced another mandatory bond. Twenty-year war bonds were issued as a way to pay for the war. When the bonds were due for repayment 20 years later, Khrushchev delayed the payment of these bonds for an additional 20 years. Finally, 20 years later, President Brezhnev paid back all of the bondholders. However, without any interest payments and 40 years of inflation, the relative value of the bond repayment was minimal.

The next form of bonds introduced in the Soviet Union were 3 percent lottery bonds that were distributed by the Sberegatelny (Savings) Bank of the USSR through its national network of 100,000 local savings branches. These bonds, which sold poorly, gave the investor two alternatives: a chance to enter a lottery and win up to 10,000 rubles or a 3 percent interest payment to be repaid after ten years. Notwithstanding, interest income that was considered unearned income was inconsistent with socialist principles and Soviet citizens were expected to use their savings in a noncapitalistic fashion.

In the mid-1980s, the Soviet Union introduced a new type of bond. The "purpose bonds" entitled a Soviet bondholder to the right to purchase a specified commodity like a car, television, or refrigerator at a set price on a specific future date. These bonds did not sell well because of a lack of confidence in the Soviet system to deliver the promised goods. In fact, very few of the promised commodities were ever made available to the bondholders.

In 1989, with the Soviet budget deficit exceeding 10 percent of the countries' GNP, the Soviet government decided to sell more than 75 billion rubles worth of long-term treasury bonds on the domestic market to institutional and individual investors (of these, 49 billion rubles worth were to be issued by the central government to institutional investors, 15 billion were earmarked for the consumer market, and, for the first time in Soviet history, republics were authorized to issue up to 11 billion rubles worth of bonds. The new bonds paid a 5 percent return, had coupons attached, a call feature, and a maturity of 16 years. These bonds were backed by the central government and by the state bank of the USSR and were distributed by the savings bank branches, which sell bonds on behalf of the state bank and the USSR Ministry of Finance. To the surprise of few, these treasury bonds sold miserably because the low interest rate was only 2 percentage points higher than those paid on savings accounts, while inflation was running at 10 percent and more. As a result, the government had to raise the interest certificates on the bonds for individuals to 10 percent for the bonds to sell. A small secondary market in these bonds and subsequent issues, trading up to 500 million rubles worth per month, has since developed.[20]

The government again issued "compulsory bonds" in 1992, following the bankruptcy to the Vneshekonombank. Vneshekonombank's liabilities to state enterprises, cooperatives, foreign trade organizations, and joint ventures have been reported variously as $5 billion, $8 billion, and $9.11 billion with that last figure considered the most reliable estimate. In lieu of redemptions of these deposits, the Finance Ministry issued hard currency bonds carrying interest rates of up to 3 percent per year, with maturities of up to 15 years.[21]

The Russian government recently attempted to issue a short-term bond of its own. In February 1993, the Supreme Soviet passed a decree to permit the government to float a loan in the amount of 650 billion rubles through short-term zero-coupon bonds. Eighteen Russian banks indicated their willingness to purchase the bonds at discounts that guarantee returns greater than 80 percent per year.[22]

The purpose of the bond issues is reported to be for noninflationary financing of the state budget deficit, to modify the money supply through open secondary markets operations, and to create a sound banking asset to act as collateral for credit extended by the CBRF to commercial banks.[23]

POLITICIZATION OF THE CENTRAL BANK OF THE RUSSIAN FEDERATION

The ambiguous political position of the CBRF and its involvement in a number of hotly contested policy debates reflects the volatility of the political and economic environment of Russia. That volatility has been an impediment to financial reform in Russia. While most Western governments have concluded that the merits of central bank independence outweigh the costs, that is an issue that is far from resolved in the high inflation, newly pluralistic political scene of Russia.

The issue is further complicated in Russia by the absence of any explicit enumeration of the responsibilities of the bank. The bank's jurisdiction has come to include:

- clearing operations and reciprocal settlements for the enterprise and commercial banking sectors,
- lending to the government and to state enterprises (via a network of commercial banks and directly),
- currency administration,
- foreign exchange auction activities,
- commercial bank regulation and examination, and
- treasury operations related to monitoring of state budget utilization.

For a time, the bank was also the focus of efforts to maintain a unified ruble monetary union across the former republics of the USSR.[24] Because the jurisdiction of the bank was nowhere well defined, it has been the subject of continual contention since the CBRF's creation.

Historically, Gosbank operated under the supervision of the Ministry of Finance. That status was consistent with both the political strategy of the government, which emphasized the monolithic nature of its control, and with the functional requirements of the government, given the responsibilities delegated to Gosbank.

The fragmentation of Russian political power among the executive, the legislative, and the operational branches and erosion of the central government's financial functions with the centrifugal force of regional autonomy, growing enterprise independence, and an emerging commercial banking sector led to a reconsideration of the role and organization of the CBRF. It led also to a struggle for control of the bank and the responsibilities that it had inherited.

Leadership Transition at the Central Bank of the Russian Federation

The first political skirmish pitting Yeltsin's government against the more conservative legislative branch was precipitated by the resignation of the first chairman of the CBRF, Georgiy Matyukhin, and his deputy, Vladimir Rasskazov, in June 1992.[25]

The circumstances surrounding Matyukhin's departure from the bank are difficult to unravel but appear to have been the culmination of several smaller frictions. Matyukhin, whose appointment was originally supported by R. Khasbulatov and the Russian parliamentary conservative wing, antagonized both the Yeltsin government and parliament during his tenure. The immediate cause of his departure was his refusal to acquiesce to parliamentary demands that the CBRF reduce its interest rates on enterprise credit from 80 percent to 50 percent per annum, while inflation was over 700 percent.[26] Market commercial bank interest rates ranged from 130 percent to 200 percent at the time.

Before his resignation, Matyukhin had also earned the enmity of the Yeltsin government by implementing a system of postal clearing of enterprise and commercial bank accounts to replace the wire system. The new policy, which delayed clearing by up to a month, was apparently instituted as a deliberate effort to reduce the velocity of transactions to fight inflation. The Yeltsin government regarded it, however, as a critical impediment to the workings of the market economy.

Matyukhin also sided with the parliament against the executive branch by opposing efforts to print more rubles to alleviate the liquidity crisis confronting enterprises and consumers. Furthermore, Matyukhin pressured Russian enterprises to withhold deliveries to Ukraine and other non-Russian newly independent states (NIS) who had not paid previously incurred debts. The government expressed grave reservations over the impact that this policy might have on Russian production and on escalating trade tensions with other nations.[27] Matyukhin's resignation also apparently interrupted plans to issue up to 1 trillion rubles in credit to enterprises to cancel mutual interenterprise- and enterprise-bank debts.[28]

Ironically, Matyukhin's successor was Viktor Gerashchenko, who had a reputation as a capable but conservative international banker. Gerashchenko apparently owed his appointment to the intervention of the Russian parliamentary leadership.[29] He had served previously as chairman of Gosbank under Gorbachev, and retained his post after the August 1991 coup attempt only because of his credibility with the international financial community.[30]

Issuance of Credit to Enterprises

Gerashchenko's first policy statements appeared to align the CBRF with Yeltsin government policy.[31] Addressing the question of provision of credits to enterprises, Gerashchenko indicated immediately after his appointment that the CBRF had no intention of writing off enterprise debts, as had been the practice in the past.[32] He appeared to reverse that position a mere ten days later, however, with a telegram (July 28, 1992) to enterprises and commercial banks indicating that credit would be forthcoming to cancel mutual debts.[33] Pressure from the Yeltsin government compelled Gerashchenko to reverse his position once again in a revision to the original telegram.[34] However, shortly thereafter, the deputy chairman of the bank, Vyacheslav Solovov, announced bank plans to lower the interest rate charged to commercial banks who lend to enterprises from 80 percent to 50 percent or 60 percent per year.

Among the criticisms of the policy was the charge that it would violate understandings between the Russian government and the International Monetary Fund (IMF) that were underpinnings to credit agreements critical to Russia's recovery.[35] Another criticism of the debt forgiveness program was that it benefited state enterprises but did not provide similar relief for private businesses also caught in the working capital crisis.[36] Some government officials contended that the financial pressure on private businesses could lead many to bankruptcy. Of course, there were also serious concerns that the credit policy would ignite a new round of hyperinflation.

Gerashchenko's CBRF justified the liberal credit policy as critical when nearly half of all products produced by state enterprises traded without any payments. In the view of the bank, relief of the working capital crunch was necessary to avoid precipitous declines in output.[37] Government involvement was required, the bank contended, because, unlike developed Western economies, Russia lacked a capital market.

One continuing source of contention between the government and the bank has been the relative rights of the two entities to grant credits to enterprises. The government has argued that state enterprise credit policy is a budgetary issue and, therefore, falls under the jurisdiction of the Ministry of Finance and the Ministry of Economics.[38] Moreover, according to the government, the bank issued credits to particular enterprises on the basis of enterprise requests, rather than by following any specific guidelines or procedures. The government cited a 190 billion ruble credit to Roskomsever as an example of the bank's arbitrary policy.[39] The bank, however, has defended its position by asserting that its jurisdiction over enterprise clearing operations extends to credit issuance.

At certain times during 1992 and 1993, the bank, the government, and the parliament were each independently issuing credits to enterprises using different sets of criteria for their disbursements. As the total volume of credit increased to 3.5 trillion rubles by the end of 1992, the inflationary impact of the credits became clear. Each of the three power centers blamed the others for the uncontrolled disbursement of credit. The government argued that bank preferential credit allocation policies amounted to an industrial policy that was beyond its jurisdiction. The bank in turn argued that it was responsible for direct allocation of only 6 percent of the credit, with the rest allocated by the government and parliament with 45 percent going to agriculture, 18 percent to the Far North, and 28 percent going to industry.[40] The CBRF argued also that it was disingenuous for the government to argue against the issuance of enterprise credits when the Ministry of Finance itself had received over 1.2 trillion rubles of credit from the bank at a 10 percent interest rate.[41]

By January 1993, however, the government had reversed its opposition to CBRF targeting of credit, giving it explicit written support for efforts to target defense enterprises undergoing conversion, among others.[42] A compromise of sorts appeared to be in the works later in 1993 as the government and bank agreed that the credits and subsidies would be granted only through the state budget, using credit auctions and involving commercial banks.[43] Commercial banks, however, have charged that the central bank used this leverage to allocate credit selectively among the commercial banks, and that obtaining access to CBRF credits often entailed making payments of 10–15 percent to intermediaries.

Jurisdiction over the Central Bank of the Russian Federation

The disputes over bank policy during the transition from Matyukhin's leadership to Gerashchenko's led to increasing calls from the executive branch for parliament to cede jurisdiction over the bank to the government.[44] That pressure only increased as Gerashchenko became more explicit about his alignment with the parliamentary economic program.

As the government-parliament-bank frictions intensified, the government attempted a variety of strategies to exert more control over the CBRF or to attenuate its powers by creating alternative banking structures. Vladimir Shumeyko, first vice premier of the Russian government, for example, asserted that the bank should either be transformed into an independent state reserve bank to supervise commercial bank activities or it should be transferred to direct government control.[45] Vice Premier Anatoli Chubais adopted a different strategy by suggesting that a presidential decree to include the bank chairman in the government's cabinet was necessary so that President Yeltsin could exert sufficient control over the bank to ensure success in the fight against inflation.[46]

Another strategy of the Yeltsin government was embodied in presidential directive number 872, which created the Russian Bank for Reconstruction and Development on December 30, 1992. The new bank was created to function as a counterweight to the CBRF in government efforts to promote development and private investment by directing the utilization of foreign aid and credit resources. Creation of the Russian Bank for Reconstruction and Development was immediately opposed by parliament.[47]

Commercial Banking Regulation

CBRF policies with respect to the regulations of the commercial banking sector have been another source of continuing controversy within the Russian governmental and financial communities. The bank has contended that in light of its limited resources for examination and regulation of the 1,700 or more commercial banks that were operating by the middle of 1993, the best strategy for limiting improper commercial bank activities is to restrict the number of operating banks.

In mid-1992, about half the banks in Russia were capitalized under 20 million rubles. The CBRF proposed to impose a minimum capitalization requirement of 100 million rubles to effect a consolidation of the sector, up from 5 million rubles for privately owned banks, and 25 million rubles for joint-stock institutions.[48] The bank argued that smaller institutions were unable to guarantee the safety of deposits or to extend standard financial services to enterprises. Also, as part of its consolidation efforts, the bank advocated the renationalization of the Sberbank — the retail savings bank — as a subsidiary of the CBRF.[49] The bank was not successful in that effort.

At various times, too, the CBRF attempted to restrict commercial bank lending activities through a variety of measures that included increases in reserve requirements (to 20 percent with efforts to raise it to 30 percent and 50 percent). The reserve requirements were intended to control potentially inflationary credit expansion.[50] The commercial banks argued for a 5–7 percent reserve requirement.

In 1993, the bank went further by attempting to restrict the operations of foreign banks in Russia. Among other moves, the bank intended to restrict the abilities of foreign banks to repatriate earnings, arguing that money earned in Russia should be invested there.[51]

Bank-Enterprise Relations

The bank's involvement in apparently selective issuance of credits to favored enterprise — a de facto industrial policy — is one aspect of the bank's overall influence on the state enterprise sector. Apart from its superficial purpose of providing working capital to enterprises, the credit policy had a second important component. It prevented bankruptcies. Because credits were issued to efficient and poorly performing enterprises without regard for ability to service the debts, it was clear that bank policy included support for enterprises as state institutions quite apart from their economic viability. While the policy served an important social purpose by forestalling mass unemployment, many in the government argued that it violated the fundamental spirit of market reform.

In addition to its participation in credit operations and the settlements process more generally, the bank was involved in enterprise operations in other ways. In particular, the bank attempted to exert control over the allocations of credit by requiring enterprises to sequester credit receipts in separate accounts in an unsuccessful attempt to prevent leakages through rising wages into the consumer sector.

In addition, the bank and the Yeltsin government imposed restrictions on enterprise disposition of hard currency earnings, requiring enterprises to sell first 50 percent, then 100 percent of earnings to the bank to prevent enterprises from depositing hard currency receipts in foreign banks.[52] The terms of sales also varied across a series of decrees. Early versions specified fixed exchange rates while later versions indicated that enterprises would be compensated at the auction market exchange rate prevailing at the time of sale. Many in the government argued, however, that the fundamental problem was one of credibility of bank and parliamentary policy toward business: "The main problem, however, lies in the fact that enterprises do not believe the authorities. Through the chaos in our economy, we are increasingly forcing out of the country new capital."[53]

CONCLUDING REMARKS

The skirmishes between the CBRF and the government can be interpreted as the natural outcome of a system in profound transition, where roles and jurisdictions have yet to be established. Another interpretation, however, would identify the policy disagreements as symptoms of a deeper confrontation between two visions of economic and financial reform. On the one hand is the Western model of rapid and uncompromising reform favored by Gaidar and most leaders of the government; on the other hand, the bank and parliamentary alternative is a gradualist model that focused on preserving the power and productive capacity of the enterprise sector and traditional centers of power in the economy and political structure.

Both visions, however, suffered from a common problem: The vacillation and maneuvering created uncertainties with very tangible costs to the agents and institutions of the economy. Moreover, the inability of either side to deal effectively with inflation imposed a tremendous burden on the consumers in the society, while disproportionately benefiting the government, the established enterprise, and free market participants. Inflation rates of 700 percent and more per year have rapidly destroyed the value of a lifetime of savings for the Russian people. In the process, the government, the bank, and parliament destroyed any shred of credibility that they enjoyed with the Russian population.

Russia's credibility problem not only affects its domestic financial policy but also extends to its international relationships as well. A perennial issue in Russian financial policy is the timing of a transition to a more freely convertible ruble — the Holy Grail of Russian market reform. That move has been postponed on numerous occasions over the last six years for a variety of reasons that boil down to the government's conviction that some set of technical conditions on price structure have not been achieved. These conditions generally involve alignment between Russian domestic prices and world prices for major commodity groups.

What is missing from Russian strategies for convertibility, however, is serious consideration of the importance of the credibility of government financial policy, and as a result, the credibility of the ruble as a stable unit of value. The Russian approach to ruble convertibility is based on the idea that convertibility is a goal that can be achieved through the right configuration of currency exchange policies, supported by a stabilization fund. At its foundation, however, convertibility is not driven so much by the supply of rubles as it is by the demand. That demand is dependent on foreign perceptions of the stability of the ruble as a store of value and as a unit that commands access to resources.

The willingness of foreign businesses or banks to deal in rubles is based on domestic and international confidence. That confidence is lacking today for two reasons:

- Administrative rules and government actions limit the usefulness of the ruble as a right to resources on demand.
- Absence of credibility and commitment of government policy to overall domestic monetary stability render the ruble a precarious store of future value.

As a consequence, ruble convertibility is actually best regarded as an indirect confirmation of international confidence in Russian domestic monetary and fiscal policies and acknowledgment of the credibility of Russian commitment to monetary stability rather than as a goal that might be realizable external to the context of domestic banking and finance.

As described by one Russian economist, the issue of credibility can be distilled down to a simple concept: "When they believe you, they will lend you money, and not with land or natural resources as collateral, to which we will never agree, but rather on the honest promise of the government, bolstered just in case, by printed promissory notes."[54]

NOTES

1. "Business Today," *Moscow Interfax*, 1500 GMT (27 May 1991) in FBIS-SOV-91-102 (28 May 1991), p. 46. The trend has continued under the Russian government with revenues at least 40 percent below expected levels in 1992: I. Ivanov and G. Talalayev, ITAR-TASS, 1327 GMT (17 September 1992) in FBIS-SOV-92-18 (17 September 1992), pp. 21–22.

2. Moscow *TASS International Service*, (1555 GMT, 27 May 1991).

3. In the words of one Russian economist, "Another significant factor determining the crisis in the development of industry is the deep-seated monopolism which grips all spheres of production and which excludes the emergence of a competitive environment. . . . Thus most industrial enterprises will, as in the past, continue to lack the incentives for increasing product output, because under conditions of

general shortage, a systematic increase in prices coupled with a reduction in volumes of production will allow them to retain their financial well-being." A. Frenkel and V. Galitskiy, "Russia's Economy in 1993," *Delovoy Mir* (11 March 1993, pp. 10–14 in FBIS-USR-94-044 (9 April 1993), pp. 14–38.

4.   A. Borodenkov, "Andrey Nechayev: How to Maintain the Balance," *Moskovskiye Novosti*, no. 11 (14 March 1993), p. A13 in FBIS-USR-93-041 (1 April 1993), pp. 21–23.

5.   The deputy chairman of the CBRF, A. A. Khandruyev, expressed the dilemma as: "Is it necessary to fight inflation at the expense of growth of unemployment and decline of production or, on the contrary — to fight against the decline in production at the expense of intensification of the inflationary processes?" From Khandruyev, "Let Us Define Our Priorities," p. 32.

6.   Reference PlanEcon numbers from Washington *Post*, Monday, September 6, 1993.

7.   Speech by V. Gerashchenko, "Current Goals of the Monetary and Credit Policy and Trends in the Development of the Banking System in the Russian Federation," *Biznes i Banking*, no. 23 (June 1993, pp. 4–8 in FBIS-USR-93-083 (6 July 1993), pp. 18–26.

8.   Nikita Kirichenko, Vladimir Bessonov, Tatyana Gurova, Valeriy Fadeyev, and Yelena Vishnevskaya, "New Policy to Hold Back Inflation," *Kommersant*, no. 12 (29 March 1993), pp. 15–18 in FBIS-USR-93-053 (28 April 1993), pp. 13–25. Vice-Premier Boris Fyodorov observed in this context that no commercial credit can exist under current Russian inflation rates: N. Garkushka, "A Time for New Alternatives," *New Times International* (May 1993), pp. 18–20 in FBIS-USR-93-076 (21 June 1993), pp. 16–22.

9.   N. Garkushka, p. 22.

10.   Reported in "The Corridor of Agreement; Anti-Crisis Measures: What Do They Consist Of?" *Ekonimika i Zhizn*, no. 16 (April 1992), pp. 4–5 in FBIS-USR-93-060 (14 May 1993), p. 36. Conclusions based on these and the statistics below assume that Russian production changes were similar to those of the USSR as a whole prior to 1991.

11.   "Dynamics of Russian Economy: Official Indices and Alternate Assessment," *Commonwealth Business News*, no. 1 (January 1993), p. 1 in FBIS-USR-93-064 (22 May 1993), p. 6.

12.   The Russian government's proportion of investment funding is nearly the same as the ratio contributed by the previous Communist regimes of the Soviet Union in the 1980s. See Frankel and Galitskiy, "Russia's Economy in 1993."

13.   Only 3 of 329 investment projects that were to begin production in 1991 were actually completed that year. In general, the Soviet and successor Russian government has continued previous practices of spreading investment resources too thinly to permit timely completion of projects. Despite a 50 percent decline in available investment resources, the number of projects underway increased by 10 percent in 1992–93: "The USSR Economy over the Period January–September 1991."

14.   Because Russians typically hold their savings in a variety of forms, including cash hoarding at home, it is difficult to estimate average savings reliably. A comparison of cash in circulation and savings account balances with cash issuance by the government suggested that, in 1990, average total family savings were about 5,000–6,000 rubles. Survey data from the end of 1991 indicated that the median savings account balance was 500 rubles, suggesting a drop in savings, as one would expect with rampant inflation: *Interfax*, (0733 GMT, 9 December 1991) in FBIS-SOV-91-239, p. 24.

15.   The split into six banking institutions reversed the Soviet banking reforms of 1956 to 1963 when the State Bank took over the Agricultural Bank, Central

Communal Bank, Industrial Bank, and Trade Bank as discussed in J. Wilczynski, *Comparative Monetary Economics* (London: Macmillan, 1978), p. 25.

16. Roundtable on Soviet Inflation, *Moscow News* (English ed.), no. 3 (15 January 1989), p. 10.

17. Long-term interest rates were on the order of 0.8 percent per annum with a 50-year payback period while inflation was running 10–14 percent per year. In many instances, the loans were explicitly identified as "soft loans" — loans that were provided to make up for losses or to ensure an accounting balance for the enterprise that the government did not anticipate calling at any point in the future.

18. Pravda Economic Policy Department, "Profitable Enterprises: A Review of the Cornerstone of the Economically Accountable Economy," *Pravda*, 19 January 1988, p. 1.

19. For a detailed exposition of Soviet enterprise financial accounting standards, see Erika Nobel, ed., *Soviet Cost-Accounting in the Machine Building and Metal-Working Sector* (Falls Church, Va.: Delphic Associates Inc., 1988).

20. "Bonds Selling Well," *Rossiyskaya Gazeta* (8 September 1992), p. 3 in FBIS-SOV-92-179, p. 25.

21. *Interfax* (1346 GMT, 18 May 1992) in FBIS-SOV-92-097, p. 22; *Interfax* (1150 GMT, 26 July 1992) in FBIS-SOV-92-144 (27 July 1992), p. 27.

22. "The First Civilized Experiment," *Rossiyskaya Gazeta* (12 February 1993), p. 3 in FBIS-USR-93-023 (3 March 1993), p. 25.

23. Gerashchenko, "Current Goals of the Monetary and Credit Policy and Trends in the Development of the Banking System in the Russian Federation.Ú

24. A. Diordiyenko, "Boris Yeltsin Has Signed an Edict 'On the Federal Treasury' to Stabilize Finances," *Rossiyskiye Vesti* (17 December 1992), p. 1 in FBIS-SOV-92-247 (23 December 1992), p. 39.

25. M. Leontyev, "Epidemic of Change on the Russian Olympus: President, Parliament, Government, Central Bank Mingle in Fight for Control of Economic Policy," *Nezavisimaya Gazeta* (3 June 1992), p. 1 in FBIS-SOV-92-110 (8 June 1992), p. 32.

26. A. Tabachnikov, *ITAR-TASS* (1457 GMT, 1 June 1992) in FBIS-SOV-92-106 (2 June 1992), p. 18.

27. V. Sluzhakov, "Harsh Sanctions by Central Bank of Russia Cost Freedom," *Rossiyskaya Gazeta* (26 June 1992), p. 2 in FBIS-SOV-92-127 (1 July 1992), pp. 36–37.

28. *Interfax* (1913 GMT, 8 June 1992) in FBIS-SOV-92-111 (9 June 1992), p. 53.

29. G. Vinitskaya, *ITAR-TASS* (1519 GMT, 16 July 1992) in FBIS-SOV-92-138 (17 July 1992), p. 37.

30. V. Mikheyev, "West Won't Stake All While Central Bank Is Without a Head," *Izvestiya* (3 June 1992), p. 1 in FBIS-SOV-92-110 (8 June 1992), p. 31.

31. I. Zasurskiy, "The People Who Like Order Are Back," *Nezavisimaya Gazeta* (24 July 1992), pp. 1–2 in FBIS-SOV-92-1444 (27 July 1992), pp. 29–30.

32. T. Karyakina, "Everyone Is In Our Debt," *Rossiyskaya Gazeta* (18 July 1992), p. 2 in FBIS-SOV-92-141 (22 July 1992), pp. 35–37.

33. *Moscow Radio Rossii Network* (1000 GMT, 10 August 1992) in FBIS-SOV-92-157 (13 August 1992), pp. 27–28 refers to the July 28 telegram.

34. *Interfax* (1344 GMT, 4 August 1992) in FBIS-SOV-92-151 (5 August 1992), pp. 38–39 reports that minister of the economy Andrey Nechayev had indicated that telegram number 166-92 on credit issuance would be largely retracted through an agreement between chairman Gerashchenko and acting premier Yegor Gaidar.

35. P. Filippov, "Central Bank Head's Directive Threatens Catastrophe," *Izvestiya* (4 August 1922), pp. 1, 2 in FBIS-SOV-92-151 (5 August 1992), pp. 39–40.

36. S. Parkhomenko, "'I Did Not Come to Torpedo Gaidar's Financial Reform' Says Georgiy Khizha, Deputy Prime Minister of Russian Government," *Nezavisimaya*

Gazeta (23 July 1992), pp. 1–2 in FBIS-SOV-92-143 (24 July 1992), pp. 34–36.

37.   P. Ryabov, *ITAR-TASS* (1605 GMT, 4 August 1992) in FBIS-SOV-92-152 (6 August 1992), p. 33.

38.   *Interfax* (1614 GMT, 31 July 1992) in FBIS-SOV-92-149 (3 August 1992), p. 26.

39.   Borodenkov, "Andrey Nechayev: How to Maintain a Balance."

40.   Din Inamov, *ITAR-TASS* (1618 GMT, 25 September 1992) in FBIS-SOV-92-189 (29 September 1992), p. 20; A. Chernyak, "Will Ruble Be CIS Currency?" *Pravda* (16 October 1992), pp. 1–2 in FBIS-SOV-92-202 (19 October 1992), pp. 33–35.

41.   *Interfax* (1816 GMT, 22 September 1992) in FBIS-SOV-92-185 (23 September 1992), p. 27.

42.   "Stabilization Strategy," *Rossiyskiye Vesti* (26 January 1993), p. 3 in FBIS-SOV-93-016 (27 January 1993), p. 33.

43.   V. Ozerov, "The Government and the Central Bank of Russia Got Married," *Delovoy Mir* (27 May 1993), p. 1 in FBIS-SOV-93-079 (25 June 1993), pp. 19–20.

44.   *Moscow Teleradiokompaniya Ostankino* (Television First Program Network) (1700 GMT, 3 June 1992) in FBIS-SOV-92-108 (4 June 1992), pp. 41–42.

45.   S. Parkhomenko, "Control of the Central Bank: Desire to Wrest It Away from Parliament Intensifying in Government Circles," *Nezavisimaya Gazeta* (18 September 1992), p. 2 in FBIS-SOV-92-183 (21 September 1992), pp. 29–30.

46.   *Interfax* (1359 GMT, 23 November 1992) in FBIS-SOV-92-227 (24 November 1992), p. 31.

47.   A. Shinkin, "The President's Pocket Bank," *Pravda* (16 January 1993), p. 2 in FBIS-SOV-93-012 (21 January 1993), pp. 38–39.

48.   *Interfax* (1234 GMT, 5 September 1992) in FBIS-SOV-92-174 (8 September 1992), p. 23; A Melnikov, "Government Continues to Squabble with Central Bank," *Kommersant-Daily* (2 March 1993), p. 3 in FBIS-SOV-93-041 (4 March 1993), p. 33.

49.   N. Zhelnorova, "There Will Be No Monetary Reform," *Argumenty i Fakty* (February 1993), pp. 1, 4 in FBIS-SOV-93-025 (5 March 1993), pp. 16–19.

50.   *Interfax Business Report* (1443 GMT, 17 May 1992) in FBIS-SOV-92-100 (22 May 1992), pp. 30–31.

51.   I. Petrov, "Foreign Banks — Evil or Boon?" *Rossiyskiye Vesti* (25 March 1993), p. 7 in FBIS-SOV-93-043 (7 April 1993), pp. 19–21.

52.   A. Bogomolov, "Commentary," *Rossiyskaya Gazeta* (9 October 1992), p. 7 in FBIS-SOV-92-200 (15 October 1992), pp. 30–31.

53.   A. Bekker, "The Government's Reforms Prove to Be Only in Words," *Megapolis-Express* (5 May 1993), p. 14 in FBIS-SOV-93-072 (11 June 1993), pp. 50–52.

54.   A. Livshits, "The Economy of Russia in . . . 1995," *Izvestiya* (8 April 1993), p. 4 in FBIS-USR-93-050 (23 April 1993), pp. 10–11.

4

The Yeltsin Revolution and Russian Export Protectionism

William E. Schmickle

The essence of the process of transition to a market economy has changed fundamentally. Now it is necessary to bring about a transition to the market not from a centralized planning system, under which at least we were able to live, but from a situation of the anarchical disintegration of the entire economy.

— Aleksandr Rutskoi, February 1992

The figures were startling. Having steadily fallen from a high in 1986, Soviet foreign trade was now plummeting in 1991. Exports were down 23 percent from the previous year; imports had sunk 48 percent. And it was just October.

The Gorbachev era of foreign trade reforms was about to close at statistical levels not seen since the Brezhnev stagnation. But even stagnation would have been better than the "descent into Hell" feared by one Moscow insider.

GORBACHEV'S ATTACK ON SOVIET SYSTEMIC PROTECTIONISM

This was not the fate Mikhail Gorbachev planned.[1] He had inherited a flagging industrial base hobbled by autarky, and he started pushing managers toward competing in pace-setting international markets.

Other Soviet leaders had tried to stimulate the economy with imports, but Gorbachev was the first to attack the socialist system itself for creating a black hole of endemic scarcity into which imports sank without any outward rippling, stimulating effect. What concerned him even more was that this same gravitational pull had also protected industry from pressures of having to export to competitive markets.

Gorbachev's key export oriented development strategy, then, took more than a mere shift in policy. It required perestroika, a deep restructuring of the domestic economic mechanism and the state trading monopoly to enhance incentives and the ability of industry to move with greater agility in foreign markets. Yet, by the third quarter of 1991, the national economy was stumbling headlong behind a closing trade door, until Boris Yeltsin began shouldering it open in the process of dismantling the Soviet economic system in the waning months of that revolutionary year.

PERESTROIKA'S TRANSITIONAL EXPORT PROTECTIONISM

Yeltsin paid scant attention to foreign economic policy. His bent was toward politics; his grasp of economics was suspect, and more than one economic adviser had resigned over it. But he evidently cared little for the repressive, supposedly temporary system of administrative trade — mainly export — controls that the Gorbachev government had slapped on newly independent traders in 1989 to stanch the hemorrhaging of resources abroad. He blamed Gorbachev's half measures — market oriented reforms that had loosened the command economy without yet putting the USSR on a sound market basis.

Disoriented by these partial reforms, production had fallen. Deepening scarcities and surging inflation drove many producers to foreign trade simply to get hard currency. Disciplined by neither socialist plan nor capitalist marketplace, and frequently inexperienced in foreign commerce, they often sold at any price what was badly needed at home to buy at any price what the domestic economy could not provide.

The government of Prime Minister Nikolai Ryzhkov was forced to impose registration of traders and export-import licenses, quotas, and bans to protect the economy in its transition to market relations and to defend the perestroika process itself against mounting social discontent. But protectionism is costly, and the price was perestroika's soul: the worsening economic situation had made a virtue of reluctance to implement the export strategy. Five years to the day after perestroika had been ushered in by the first foreign economic reform decrees of August 19, 1986, critics on the right launched their abortive coup d'etat.

YELTSIN'S ATTACK ON TRANSITIONAL PROTECTIONISM

Yeltsin, too, made foreign trade liberalization one of his first moves toward radical economic reforms. On November 15 he rescinded Soviet protectionist regulations within Russian Soviet Federated Socialist Republic (RSFSR) jurisdiction, dismantling administrative management levers (registration, quotas, licenses) and initiating economic ones (tariffs, taxes). In the process the Russian economy became more open than at any time since 1918. The decree ended restraints on barter and intermediary trading, suspended mandatory deductions for state purposes from hard currency (*valuta*) transactions, and provided for a market-based domestic ruble exchange rate. Only a narrow, but unspecified, list of goods would be subject to quotas, and licenses were to be distributed on a competitive basis.[2]

Groundwork for this unilateral Russian initiative had been laid on August 20 with Yeltsin's decree on Russian republican economic sovereignty. On August 31 he put the USSR Foreign Economic Bank (Vneshekonombank) under Russian control. The State Licensing Committee was created in September to control export and import operations. In late October, Yeltsin formed the RSFSR Customs Committee to protect republican interests, having swept aside the authority of USSR customs services in August.

The assault on the former Soviet state foreign trade apparatus was completed when on November 15, following the cessation of the USSR Ministry of Foreign Economic Relations (MFER), an administratively inexperienced economist, Petr Aven, was appointed to chair, without ministerial rank, the new Russian Committee on Foreign Economic Relations within the RSFSR Ministry of Foreign Affairs. The Committee on Foreign Economic Relations was designed as a "compact" control structure, Aven said, to oversee implementation of the new, less interventionist, trade policy.

Mourners at the passing of the MFER were few and, among outsiders, limited to those who lost privileged access to a bureaucracy that had never shaken its aura of venality. Yeltsin's action was doubtlessly motivated partly by a reformist determination to clean house.

But the radical easing of closure policies that accompanied the decision was, on its face, a reckless move since the problem of scarcity that had generated the transitional system of export controls in 1989 had worsened. In some ways it was simply a case of law catching up to practices that had evolved extralegally in the post-coup revolutionary environment. Yet another understanding of its rationale emerges from considering renewed openness in terms of Yeltsin's domestic economic revolution in Russia.

REDUCING THE ROLE OF THE STATE IN FOREIGN TRADE

By early 1991, Soviet economists had largely agreed that, in order to ease export restraints, freedom for traders would have to be fitted to a comprehensive program for taking the domestic economy into a

liberating and disciplining free marketplace capable of guiding investment, production, and import-export decisions. But along the way,
Gorbachev insisted, the Soviet state had to be preserved to avoid economic catastrophe and popular revolt.

Critics on his left, including Yeltsin, countered that the state could
not solve problems of disorder; it could only get out of the way of a market solution. Radical economists argued that transitional trade protectionism was more likely to be self-perpetuating because it depended on
bureaucracies with vested interests in central control.

Thus, when he began Russia's forced march to a liberating, disciplining market, Yeltsin told *Der Spiegel* that the "first thing that had to
be done was to make sure that this system collapsed."[3] That meant
pulling the struts from under the institutions of Soviet political and
economic power, including central control of foreign trade.

Petr Aven joined Yegor Gaidar, a close personal friend and Yeltsin's
recently chosen deputy prime minister for economics and finance
reform. Grigory Yavlinsky has reflected on the circumstances of
Gaidar's appointment, which later led to service as acting prime minister until December 1992. It had been Yavlinsky who had, as Yeltsin's
adviser in 1990, germinated the 500 Days market transition plan identified with Stanislav Shatalin. After the coup he became deputy chairman of the USSR Operational Management Committee under Ivan
Silayev and a working colleague of Arkady Volsky, president of the
USSR Scientific and Industrial Union and Gorbachev's main link to the
committee. Considered by many to be Russia's most capable liberal
political economist, Yavlinsky was a leading contender for the job of
heading up the next round of reforms. But by his own admission he took
himself out of the picture by telling Yeltsin that Russian political independence, which meant the loss by Russia of key parts of the geographically integrated Soviet economy, was incompatible with a sound
reform strategy. Gaidar, however, as the leading exponent of the economic shock therapy strategy backed by the International Monetary
Fund (IMF), had no such compunction standing in the way of Yeltsin's
overriding political goals — "first and foremost," according to Yavlinsky,
"the instantaneous . . . disintegration, not only political but also economic, of the Union and the elimination of every conceivable coordinat-
ing economic body."[4]

Such virtual clear cutting of agencies, Yavlinsky said, was prologue
to a reform process seen as both "swift" and "attractive." As much as
Yeltsin may have counted on IMF support and believed Russia's future
lay with the world economy, it is unlikely that he fully shared Gaidar's
confident optimism and its theoretical underpinnings. If Gaidar was
right, the quickly emerging market system could, among other economic advantages, impose economic rationality on freer trade operations, compensating for the loss of administrative regulation. But the
market strategy itself also had a compelling political rationale for

Yeltsin's efforts to consolidate power in Russia — a rationale that had appealed to Gorbachev, too, in the months before the failed coup d'etat.

THE POLITICS OF GORBACHEV'S REFORM STRATEGY

Back in the fall of 1990 Gorbachev had advocated a "full-blooded market" as "common sense." But the spreading "war of laws" among republics, which he later said "brought about paralysis of power and economic collapse," put politics uppermost in his mind. He withdrew his support from the Shatalin plan that presumed a foundation of republican sovereignty in a not yet agreed new state system.

Gorbachev then struck a deal in April with Yeltsin and leaders of eight other republics. He got them to agree to seek a more decentralized union in exchange for more, and more painful, market reforms, both to meet republican demands for economic self-determination and to solidify unity. "For the market makes it possible," he had said, "to unite the peoples [of the USSR] not by dangerous force of arms but by reliable economic interest."[5]

Conservatives were not convinced. They launched their fateful putsch the day before the new Union Treaty was to have been signed on April 20. Gorbachev treated it as an interruption. Republican leaders saw it as evidence of the center's implacable hostility to change. They bolted, and the USSR came undone.

THE RUSSIAN REVOLUTION OF 1991

For a time Yeltsin backed a looser political arrangement among the 12 Soviet republics remaining after the exit of Estonia, Latvia, and Lithuania. Opposing Yavlinsky's stronger draft Treaty on Economic Union prepared in mid-September, he preferred concentrating power in republican governments under Moscow's primacy. But the Ukrainian independence vote on December 1 must have given him pause.

Nationalism was the maul on the wedge that split the union. But the large pro-independence vote among the 12 million Russians living in Ukraine showed the wedge itself was antagonism to Moscow, important both as the seat of Soviet power and as the capital of the Russian Federation. Now others were threatening. In the Caucasus, along the Volga, in the Urals, and across Siberia people resented Moscow's past expropriations of their resources and more general abuse. Many, like the Tatars and Chechens, harbored deeper ethnic tensions sporadically erupting in violence. Once begun, Yeltsin had to wonder where the splitting would end.

Vice President Aleksandr Rutskoi warned that those who had cheered Yeltsin in partitioning the USSR would not stop with Russian independence: "Lately everybody has been yelling: 'The center means dictatorship!'" he told the popular *Argumenty i facty* in January. "But was it worth it to destroy a great power in order to destroy the dictatorship of the center? And why not destroy Russia now," he asked sarcastically, "in order to avoid the dictatorship of the Russian center?"[6]

Yeltsin himself was committed to maintaining a unitary Russian economy. Within hours of the passing of the USSR, he decreed invalid all local or regional enactments restricting movement of goods and services within Russia. Yet his hope lay not with stitching up the fraying legal order but with the emerging marketplace, where mutual economic interests could dissolve secessionist ambitions. As reforms got underway in January 1991, his trusted adviser, Gennady Burbulis, spoke of the separatist Tatar Autonomous Republic and said, "I am convinced that the more rapidly the reforms proceed, the more quickly we will see the disappearance of the following way of looking at things: 'Give me independence at all costs, and come what may I will have a better life than you will, amid all this chaos.'"[7]

Gorbachev knew the strategy well, though he could do little more than watch as perestroika passed away in a new Russian revolution. In the process, the broader problems of the newly formed Commonwealth of Independent States were all but left to languish at the periphery.

THE YELTSIN-GAIDAR ECONOMIC REVOLUTION

The Yeltsin-Gaidar fast-track market transition effort resembled perestroika in its opaqueness and seeming lack of coherent concept. But where Gorbachev had used perestroika against an ossified system to prize open opportunities for a calculated rolling reform process, Gaidar and his lieutenants often spoke not about a program but about crisis management.

Incipient systemic collapse had been hastened in the autumn of 1991 by the spreading domino effect of raw material shortages as industries and entire regions held back resources to barter for scarce commodities. People brought "to the brink of indigence and despair," in one writer's words, were slipping away into incivility and nationalistic reveries.

Gorbachev had started from the "position of an omnipotent ruler," his adviser, Oleg Bogomolov, said, while Yeltsin had taken power "at a time when events [had] already developed their own dynamism, when many things [were] no longer under control." In such a situation, he suggested, "the easiest thing" for the government to do was "to lift restrictions, to announce freedom, and to see what will happen."[8]

This is, in fact what Yeltsin and Gaidar did. In order "to get back our economic freedom," Yeltsin said on October 28 in his first nationally televised address on the proposed reforms, "we must remove all obstacles to freedom for enterprises and entrepreneurship." And what of the consequences? Gaidar's economic shock therapy strategy — featured by liberalization of prices together with sharp cuts in state spending — foresaw a quick dip in living standards in the near term, followed by an upswing with filling markets and falling prices in as soon as six months, with noticeable changes for the better in three to four weeks after releasing most state price controls on January 2. But the key political question was whether the people of Russia would respond to this Polish-style "big bang" with their own social explosion. Yeltsin declared, "I am banking on the trust and understanding of the citizens of Russia."[9]

Gaidar's reform team, however, were political novices for the most part, young economists whose own primary trust lay in the central tenet of classical free market theory: that lying beneath extant economic deformities was an immanent natural order, a self-regulating mechanism governed by objective economic laws that were at once simple, harmonious, and beneficial. They frequently spoke of the "normal market," and with Burbulis of tasking themselves to "replacing the social system and freeing the oppressed natural forms of life."[10]

They could vector Russia's reforms by Poland's experience because, as Aven argued, "economics is a science with its own laws," making "all countries similar . . . as far as economists are concerned." When dissenting economists pressed issues of difference, as Yavlinsky did ("In a crumbling state one cannot carry out economic reform. That is the most important difference between our situation today in Russia and shock therapy in Poland."[11]), Aven dismissed the importance of factoring the political situation into the government's strategic line: "It is like the weather getting bad. . . . There is nothing we can do about it."[12]

Former Gorbachev adviser Nikolai Petrakov criticized the younger generation's "elementary mistake" of proceeding from classical market theories rather than from the more complex and politically textured realities of the Russian economy.[13] Ruslan Khasbulatov, speaker of the Russian Supreme Soviet, or parliament, charged the government with naivete for its "hope that in removing control over the state sector . . . everything [would] tick all by itself."[14]

But in an inadvertent way, this is, in fact, what happened according to Central Bank acting chairman Viktor Gerashchenko. In the presence of endemic shortages, he pointed out, dominant state industries not yet brought to heel by privatization and antimonopoly legislation "quite naturally" and with the "logic of the market" had cut back on production while prices and profits soared.[15] As the government began to recalibrate the reforms, Burbulis had to tell parliament that inflation was "plundering the people beyond belief" — and without relief, since Gaidar's tight monetary policy undercut social protection.[16]

THREE FOREIGN TRADE SCENARIOS

What prospects for foreign commerce might be expected from these beginnings? Predictions in Russia divided over three basic scenarios, none mutually exclusive of the others, and each offering a perspective on the actual course of events over the first two years after the August coup.

Foreign Trade under Presumed Success

The first scenario saw Yeltsin succeeding soon, in one to two years, through a combination of price reform, fiscal restraint, and privatization and demonopolization of state property. But where Gorbachev's export strategy had been framed for a strong state industrial sector up to — but too long sheltered from — the rigors of foreign competition, under Yeltsin many of those industries were made vulnerable by restructuring. In terminating Gosplan (the State Planning Committee), Gossnab (the State Committee for Technical and Material Supply), and sectoral industrial ministries and departments after the coup, Yeltsin had sundered the vertical links of Soviet centralized resource allocation on which 90 percent of domestic producers still relied despite perestroika's decentralizing innovations. Almost overnight, state enterprises became "super-independent," as Vladimir Shumeiko put it in the absence of horizontal wholesale and distribution replacement links to take up the slack. Starved of production resources, the 26 giant machine-building and electronics factories in Ryazan, for example, had closed down or cut the work week in half by July 1992.

With unemployment climbing and the rate of declining production in double digits, tighter import and export policies were indicated for Russia to have any hope of conserving, much less furthering, the industrial advances of the Soviet period. Newly formed private sector industries, as well as privatized divisions of demonopolized state industries, would also have to be protected from foreign competition.

This time, however, a market economy emerging with the beginning of an early industrial recovery could be expected to bring forth a modernized tariff and nontariff system committed to long-term openness. As Gaidar put it, "otherwise, by remaining behind . . . protectionist barriers, we will create a crippled, materials intensive and backward . . . industry which will not work to benefit people."[17]

Foreign Trade under Prolonged Difficulties

The second prospect considered a protracted, rocky transition, with public trust disintegrating amid unchecked inflation, unemployment, profiteering, speculation, chaotic privatization, spreading mafia networks, and corruption in state industry and trade and in the private commercial sector. With minimal conditions for a disciplining market nowhere in sight, predatory traders would continue to loot domestic resources for private gain, corroding the industrial age and turning Russia into a raw materials appendage of the West. As before, the state would have to step in, this time with strong regulatory agencies to manage both private and state sector foreign trade operations.

Warnings of another antigovernment putsch to restore centralized power and state planning hovered at the edges of debate. But in parliament the more credible challenge to the Yeltsin-Gaidar reforms was inspired by less democratic, but market influenced, Asian Pacific Rim development models: a strong regime (perhaps "an empire of lesser evil," in A. A. Deryabin's phrase), capable of maintaining order, could in a regulated market, using wage and price controls and state subsidies to industry and social supports, manage an industrial restructuring aimed at export markets while protecting the home market with a combination of economic and administrative instruments.

This alternative course was most closely identified with Volsky, who became head of the Russian Union of Industrialists and Entrepreneurs (RUIE) after January 1992. RUIE's political wing, the Renewal Union (chaired by Aleksandr Vladislavlev), later joined with Nikolai Travkin's Democratic Party of Russia and Rutskoi's People's Party of Free Russia to form the centrist coalition called Civic Union. Volsky was the recognized leader of the opposition faction representing business and the still powerful industrial complex.

Foreign Trade under State Disintegration

The last script was less hopeful, but not entirely gloomy. It calculated that Russia might no longer have executive authority to maintain the unitary economic space predicated by the other two options. With no one obeying Moscow and with the Russian federal government unable to cushion the shock of change, local authorities in autonomous republics, oblasts, and krais could shut themselves off from one another, setting their own internal, interregional, and foreign economic policies. Opportunism and interethnic discord could turn discontent with the Yeltsin-Gaidar program to separatist political advantage, finally tearing the state apart.

But some critics, like Yavlinsky and democratic activist Yury Afanasyev, suggested that rule from the center should be relaxed to enlist loyal regional leaders as allies in change in a softer federal or a new confederal arrangement, a clustering of administrations each managing reforms and external trade policies suitable to its own conditions. Those regions with easily marketable resources, like Sakhalin or Yakutia, or with advanced foreign trade infrastructures, as in Vladivostok and Nakhodka in the Maritime *krai*, would likely press ahead with vigorous trade and foreign investment policies. Optimists predicted that in a cooled political atmosphere geographical and economic realities would encourage a gradual process of reintegration.

THE STRATEGIC RAW MATERIALS EXPORT PROBLEM

Moscow's relations with outlying localities were not helped by Yeltsin's heavy handed appointment of regional and city executives and presidential representatives to assure conformity with his government's new course after the August coup. Yet the apparent incidence of official insubordination (with 200,000 complaints filed against local enactments by the federal procuracy in 1992) shows how tattered the fabric of rule of law was in Russia. As Peter Reddaway pointed out, this made a safe haven for covert syndicates of provincial officials, locally powerful enterprise managers, and mafia to sell state property abroad, bribing customs, and failing to report transactions and earnings to Moscow.[18]

In this environment strategic raw materials (SRMs) — called "strategic" because of their economic value, not military significance — disappeared from the country in unprecedented volume, with fuels, petroleum products, mineral fertilizers, nonferrous metals, and timber products leading the list. Uncontrolled SRM exports became the most serious foreign trade problem of 1992, forcing deep revisions in the government's external economic policy.

These exports were not forced out of the domestic marketplace by insufficient consumer demand, despite rising prices. Nor were they driven abroad by import competition. With empty shelves and demand for cheap goods everywhere, factories were suspending production. What was happening was a supply-side depression — perhaps the world's first, according to Marshall Goldman — caused by the break-up of the Soviet Union and the collapse of its centrally organized distribution system.[19] By September, Gaidar was reporting a 16.6 percent drop in industrial output over the first eight months of 1992, caused by "disrupted or incomplete deliveries of raw materials and components."[20]

With as little as 3 percent of all *valuta* circulated through the new domestic currency exchanges, demand for foreign currency drove quoted ruble rates downward and the value of hard currency sales sharply up.[21] Even at giveaway prices, yawning price disparities between domestic and international markets made SRM export sales hugely profitable. As the ruble continued its descent, SRM profiteers were suspected of hiding billions of dollars in earnings abroad, though estimates varied widely.

Evasion of export duties (exacted after January 1) on SRMs and other products was also costly to the state, which had expected payments to form 40–45 percent of the federal budget in 1992.[22] As wholesale prices climbed after deregulation, the extra expense for private traders of export quota certificates and licenses (also required after the new year and averaging a fifth of prices on the new commodity exchange) drove down profitability and encouraged evasion. Some regions openly exceeded their powers in creating their own export licensing authorities. Even so, Mark Kolesnikov, director for nontariff regulations at MFER, claimed in early 1993 that "an overwhelming majority of strategic goods leaves Russia without any accompanying documents at all."[23]

Part of the problem was the continuing attack on the already demoralized foreign trade bureaucracy and its replacement with inadequate structures. Slowness in defining customs borders with ex-Soviet republics provided nearly unregulated side-door transit routes for Russian raw materials to third countries. Then, too, within Russia the MFER and the Ministry of Trade and Resources had separate quota systems. The latter delegated issuance to regional and local administrations as it chose, and neither ministry made much effort to cooperate with the Russian State Customs Committee.

Another contributing factor was Yeltsin's penchant for governance by ad hoc, sometimes poorly framed, and often uncoordinated and contradictory decrees. From the very start, critics charged that the foreign economic reforms lacked a coherent conception.[24] The overall result was an unsettled commercial climate and a lack of confidence in the unevenly developed body of customs and currency law.

Export tariff, quota, and licensing regulations were subjected to repeated amendments and delays. They were frequently administered arbitrarily or without reference to available supplies. Regulations also meant approvals and an unholy dilemma: the procedures themselves were fertile ground for recrudescent corruption, real or suspected, in the distribution of lucrative quotas. The stature of the new regulations was further undermined after February by the government's public assurances to the IMF of its intention to remove most export quotas and licenses by July 1.

Despite early hopes for the appearance of free market mechanisms to regulate export-import activity, Moscow analyst Yevgeny Khartukov summed up the actual situation in September 1992: "There is no market environment although there are market aspirations. The vacuum is filled by malpractice, corruption and disillusionment . . . compounded by sheer ignorance among managers of how to behave any differently."[25]

TOWARD A NEW CENTRALIZED
REGULATORY SYSTEM FOR EXPORTS

From June 12 to June 14 Yeltsin issued a series of decrees signaling a retreat from liberalization and toward recentralized state control of foreign trade operations.[26] Politically, too, this policy was heralded by a shift toward the center.

In early April, centrist parliamentary forces maneuvered Yeltsin into replacing Gaidar (who became acting prime minister) at the Ministry of Finance with Vasily Barchuk, who had been deputy Soviet finance minister in Valentin Pavlov's precoup government. Then, at the unexpectedly aggressive Sixth Congress of People's Deputies (CPD — Russia's highest legislative body), the entire cabinet was brought to the brink of resignation before a compromise was reached. The CPD, which had given Yeltsin extraordinary powers at its fifth session in December, finally agreed to extend the government's term until December in exchange for further executive appointments suggesting a slower and less austere reform pace. Viktor Chernomyrdin, formerly USSR minister of the gas industry, became deputy prime minister for energy. Georgy Khizha and Vladimir Shumeiko joined an expanded cabinet as "pragmatic practitioners" (in contrast to "brilliant theoreticians") with personal backgrounds in industry and, like Chernomyrdin, close ties to Civic Union.[27]

According to Aven, who wondered publicly about why he had been left in place, the same lobby that had reshaped the cabinet had also pressured the MFER to protect the position of monopolist producers against upstart trading competitors and the usurpation of industrial resources.[28] Its interests and those of the state intersected at the issue of controlling exports of SRMs.

Russian analysts called the June decrees "the legal basis for a fundamentally new system" of foreign economic regulation.[29] Russia's deepening foreign debt and the Central Bank's nearly empty foreign currency coffers, which prevented it from managing exchange rates, put pressures on the freedom of private transactions and valuta holdings. Three of the four edicts that went into effect on July 1 covered payments and settlements, export tariffs and mandatory sales of valuta receipts, and a provisional import customs tariff. Some results were predictable: evasion and hard currency flight intensified in the presence of paper enforcement mechanisms, and many enterprises dependent on imports of raw materials and components suffered. The fourth decree outlined procedures for the sale of SRMs that resuscitated a key aspect of the former Soviet state foreign trade monopoly in its last years.

"VELVET" RE-MONOPOLIZATION
OF STRATEGIC EXPORTS

Gorbachev had ended the highly centralized state trading monopoly inherited from Stalin in order to put industry directly into world markets. In 1989, registration of new traders had become the means for certifying and controlling recipients of direct trading rights. Yet six months after abolishing the practice and promising unrestricted trading rights to all, Yeltsin was forced to reinstate selective registration.

The intention, according to Aven, was to hand pick a "narrow circle" of special exporters selected for experience and the transparency of their financial dealings.[30] Anyone could still bid for export quotas at exchanges (which would be surpluses from producers' quotas or let by the MFER's control board), but only registered traders could actually conclude and execute contracts at fixed commission rates.

Registration requirements, procedures, and financial incentives were biased in favor of traders registered before the coup, and they virtually guaranteed that trading would be monopolized by a restricted club as in the former Soviet Union. It came as no surprise that most of the first 50 approvals in August went to the successors of foreign trade organizations formerly within the orbit of the USSR Ministry of Foreign Economic Relations. And in a troubling development harkening back to the conflict-of-interest riddled regulatory mechanism before August 1991, in more than half the commodity groupings the MFER registered its own Main Department for Cooperation as a foreign trade broker.

Low fixed commission rates (from 0.5 percent to 2.0 percent by commodity) and a rule against refusing service to any legitimate quota-bearing exporter did provide a check against the fee gouging and insolence of officially sanctioned intermediaries in the last Soviet period. But they also meant that trading was profitable only for very large volume brokers. "Meanwhile," Tatyana Korotkova observed, "the small producers and intermediaries again find themselves out in the cold and isolated from direct participation in foreign trade activity."[31] By the end of December the estimated 35,000 entities that had been trading in SRMs were reduced to some 500 only, which was still deemed too permissive.

The turn toward monopoly operations was limited to a commodity structure encompassing some 80 percent of Russia's exports in 1991, leaving the full range of manufactures free of quotas, licensing, export duties, and registration. Even as the government embraced this combination of administrative and market approaches, it anticipated (as had the earlier Ryzhkov administration) that the special exporters corps and other nonmarket restrictions would be transitory. In comparison with past Soviet practices, it was indeed a policy, in one commentator's summation, of "velvet" control.

TIGHTENING OF QUOTAS AND LICENSES

According to later reports, these efforts did not begin to solve the problems of regulation. In a frank address on reform difficulties in October, Yeltsin distanced himself from his cabinet, emphasizing deep dissatisfaction with the MFER and charging it with "lack of professionalism, drive, firmness and consistency in upholding Russia's interests."[32] He blamed Aven but kept him on when Gaidar intervened. The result was an expansion of staff exceeding the former Soviet MFER by some 40 percent, including an expansion of upper level posts. With this strengthening came a tightening of customs borders with the

Commonwealth of Independent States and a new round of strict quota and licensing regulations marking a further retreat into administrative export controls.

Under the ordinance signed by Gaidar on November 6, not all goods were subject to licensing; in fact, previous lists were shortened. And not all those needing licenses were tied to quotas. But all categories of SRMs were covered, though extent varied depending on specific product nomenclature, and violators were faced (at least on paper) with tough criminal and administrative penalties.[33]

The edict recognized four types of export quotas, effective January 1, 1993: quotas tied to state needs in meeting international obligations; general enterprise quotas allocated to producers for their own output; general regional quotas distributed from the center to republics, oblasts, and major cities for allocation to producers; and auctioned quotas put up as revenue earners by the MFER and by regional, local, or enterprise quota holders.

Unlike quotas, export licenses were nontransferable, and issued only upon presentation of an initialled contract and, if required, a quota certificate. SRM licenses were issued only to registered special exporters. There were two types of licenses: general licenses for several categories of goods in one commodity type, valid for a year for export operations meeting state needs; and one-off licenses for single transactions involving one category of goods only.

As in the last years of perestroika, protectionism was uniquely focused on exports. Imports were largely quota and license free, though soon laden with value-added taxes and excise taxes. There was only a provisional tariff in 1992 as work proceeded on a permanent tariff scheduled for 1993. Exports of finished industrial products were mostly left unregulated and free of export duties in order to lure trading houses away from primary commodities.

"VALUE" SUBTRACTION AND THE PROBLEM OF INDUSTRIAL EXPORTS

Gaidar told parliament in October 1992 that Russian strategy should first use the processing industry as a "bridgehead" for breaking into world markets, for turning the face of industry toward "real competition" in preparation for the day when rising extraction costs in the inefficient natural resources sector would price fuel and raw materials out of the marketplace. Long-term replacements, he said, potentially lay within metallurgy, engineering, and other equipment markets. Meanwhile, both export and import tariffs would be required for two to three more years in order to protect domestic industries from foreign competition.[34]

Simple in its formulation, this scenario embodied a deeper problem. Export duties not only raised state revenues. Set at 20–35 percent of world prices, they were also an important lever for keeping domestic prices for raw materials from rising to world levels faster than industry could adjust. Yet far more potentially explosive was the basic dilemma of value subtraction. Processing should *add* value to raw materials. As a result of the old command economy's administrative pricing system, however, the final subsidized price of product was frequently *less* than the value of its raw materials in world trade.

Even with export duties and other costs of conducting trade, prices for raw materials had been rising faster than those for finished goods holding back manufactured exports despite preferential export customs treatment and a falling ruble. Sooner or later as the country geared into the world economy the long awaited appearance of a domestic market mechanism would produce investment indicators favoring extractive over manufacturing enterprise. Degrees of foreign trade openness, therefore, directly influenced the extent of Russian deindustrialization. Without heavy state subsidies, many factories would go bankrupt and cause massive unemployment in a fully opened economy.

Already in 1991 regional economists in Khabarovsk had reported production costs so high that free trade with Asian neighbors, they said, "may force the Soviet Far East's manufacturing industries into bankruptcy, leaving their labor forces unemployed."[35] By the end of 1992, fully 24 percent of factory managers responding to a survey thought bankruptcy was a realistic threat to their enterprises over the next two years.[36]

ENTERPRISE INSOLVENCY AND CONFRONTATION WITH CIVIC UNION

Yeltsin's June 1992 state enterprise bankruptcy decree catalyzed the political contest between the government and its parliamentary opponents. Civic Union, the bloc of centrist deputies founded the next week with RUIE leadership, excoriated the edict for its hair-trigger insolvency mechanism, set at three months' delinquency or when debts doubled assets; its restructuring provisions, handing over state enterprises to private Russian or foreign management as the only chance to avoid liquidation; and its administrative arrangements, based in a government department instead of the courts.

Civic Union's counterproposals later formed a central part of its own anticrisis proposals in the fall. The basic argument was that Gaidar's reforms had failed; the Russian economy remained state-centralized, but in transition to market relations — a goal Civic Union shared. In that case, then, the state should maintain essential industries, moving many toward privatization while making certain that leading concerns in basic sectors stayed in experienced hands. "Nomenklatura privatization" was seen as the surest way to make reforms work while conserving past gains. Foreign economic policy in the present crisis, Civic

Union contended, should protect low domestic fuel and raw material prices and defend processing and manufacturing industries against foreign imports, and bankruptcy procedures should be the province of courts, not bureaucrats.

Conceptually, Civic Union argued that government policies attempted "to reach the market in one jump" — a "utopia," Volsky said.[37] But more persuasive was the argument from practice, which Jerry Hough has stressed: that what the government said about economic logic and what it did were frequently two different things.[38] Time and again, the government had intervened in an ad hoc manner to prevent crises or to satisfy separate requests from enterprises or regions. By reifying what Rutskoi called "mythical models" of market interactions — whether based in textbook theory or abstracted from Polish experience — radical reformers excused themselves, so critics charged, from elaborating a comprehensive plan for the state's role in the switch to market relations.

Volsky admired the practical model of China's state-facilitated search for the marketplace. Whereas Poland's post-Communist government had moved to demolish the state economy to clear the ground for a market system, the Chinese had taken an evolutionary, two-sector approach. Leaving the state industrial complex intact and supported, though rather neglected in terms of new investment, China had built a private-sector economy around it capable of drawing state resources into a market mechanism while maintaining impressive economic growth. Volsky argued that a similar, fiscally responsible approach in Russia would restore the supply-side of the economy, undergird social supports, ease protectionist pressures and, in the long run, provide for Russia's integration into the global economy with a stronger industrial export profile.

Gaidar faced his critics squarely in October. The democratic choice in Russia, he said, had closed off, "firmly and politically, the possibility of transforming our society and our economy along the Chinese path" that presumed a "powerful structure of authoritarian control."[39] Fiscally, the Chinese model would entail hyperinflationary social and industrial spending, hastening economic collapse and social upheavals, he warned. Yet by year's end, Yeltsin was in Beijing saying: "The Chinese tactic of reform is not to hurry, not to force, without revolutions, without cataclysms, . . . and I think that for us it has a certain significance. Russia doesn't need revolutions or cataclysms either."[40]

But that was after the Seventh Congress of People's Deputies had cornered a compromising Yeltsin into trading Gaidar for a packaged agreement that included a national referendum, set for April 11, on Russia's constitutional future. Viktor Chernomyrdin was installed as prime minister and the reform portfolio was handed over to Boris Fyodorov, Yeltsin's former dissident finance minister who had resigned from the pre-coup Russian government in 1990. Although most ministers kept their positions for the time being, the politically vulnerable Aven was replaced by his 32-year-old first deputy, Sergei Glazyev, and not by Vladislavlev, who as head of the Renewal bloc was said to be Civic Union's first choice.

EXPORT POLICY AND CHERNOMYRDIN'S ANTICRISIS PROGRAM

Chernomyrdin pledged to stay on a less ideologically plotted and more industry oriented reform course. Year end statistics for 1992 painted a grim portrait of Russian industrial production collapsing at an unarrested rate in the neighborhood of 20 percent per annum, against a rising national external debt of some $75 billion that was jeopardizing radical economic reforms. The steepest decline was in finished manufactures, according to the State Committee for Industrial Policy. With widespread bankruptcies and flooding imports predicted for 1993, Glazyev announced that the MFER would implement a "series of protectionist measures to support Russia's businesses."[41]

Through April 1993 the ministry worked on a complex of initiatives for the new government's slowly emerging anticrisis program.[42] Critical aspects involved developing a concerted strategy for stimulating manufactured exports while introducing a two-tier system for SRM export controls.

RENEWAL OF THE INDUSTRIAL EXPORT STRATEGY

In the first quarter of 1993 trade with the West was down 42 percent from early 1992 as traders waited for the distribution of quotas and licenses and the first auction of export certificates for SRMs.[43] Then, too, price adjustments for domestic fuels introduced in October were driving production costs of energy intensive SRMs (aluminum, copper, ferro-alloys) toward export unprofitability, as Gaidar had predicted. Crude oil output was down 13.5 percent and refined petroleum products were off 21 percent. With most of Russia's leading exports in jeopardy, the MFER turned its attention to plotting a new industrial export strategy.

These initial efforts focused on supporting the export of finished goods, whose trade share in 1992 had been "near zero," as Glazyev told the cabinet. The approach was to continue centralized purchases of industrial exports with ruble funds from both federal and local budgets, while stimulating development of export lines in focus sectors with tax breaks and low interest credits (up to 20 percent in hard currency) to export oriented enterprises.[44] New institutions, including a Russian export-import bank, would facilitate operations. Projected gains were a modest 5–10 percent rise in machinery deliveries. But the more active role of the center would, according to commentators, undoubtedly strengthen the MFER's control over foreign trade.[45]

ENHANCING STATE CONTROL OF STRATEGIC RAW MATERIALS EXPORTS

Parliament voted in January to establish monopoly control of precious metals to the consternation of gold producing regions. Glazyev denied that the resurrection of state monopoly exporters was on the agenda. But Oleg Davydov, his first deputy minister, publicly expressed regret that Russia had 33 registered oil traders while other countries had state owned monopolies. As dependence on valuta revenues from oil rapidly increased (up 62 percent over the early months of 1992) the MFER cleared the way for a cartel of super-special exporters, according to one report, monopolizing all government oil exports.[46] By the end of January, Kolesnikov reported sharp cutbacks, up to one-half or more, in the number of exporters listed for several strategic commodity groups.[47] Everything except public statements pointed toward a de facto monopoly of SRM exports by state sector traders.

Perhaps to deflect charges of stepped-up suppression of free trading rights, Glazyev told a news conference that in the course of 1993 a new federal system of tenders would become the sole method of allocating export quotas for meeting state needs, estimated by some analysts to cover some 40 percent of all Russian exports. The Tender Committee, however, invited only special SRM exporters to the first closed tender round scheduled for May, and it was anticipated that the bidding process would winnow the ranks of special exporters even more.

REGIONAL AND SPECIAL INTEREST ATTACKS ON CENTRAL CONTROL

The center's control over trade and hard currency resources was called into doubt as the politics of privilege and local authority heated up in the first months of 1993. On February 27, Yeltsin acceded to Bashkortostan's demand for higher oil export quotas, at twice the regional average. The Bashkirs, analysts said, had at last breached the federal system of export regulation that other regions had been assaulting, thereby setting a precedent undermining Moscow's management of regional foreign economic ties.

In March the oil and gas industry in Russia successfully negotiated exemptions from customs duties and obligatory sale of hard currency on the domestic market for state owned or controlled entities trading on behalf of state interests. The concessions may have been politically motivated to strengthen the opposition of the executive branch in its battle for primacy with parliament. The effect, however, was to cal down an avalanche of similar demands from Russia's outlying regions.

Yeltsin sought to make strength out of weakness by turning future duty exemptions into credits for investment, but many enterprises were still able to win outright privileges.

Concessions to regions — where additional trade rights meant political power — were more spectacular than to individual enterprises, and Yeltsin's deferment tactic was soon forgotten. For instance, all exports from Karelia were exempted from export duties, as were certain industrial sectors in the Murmansk oblast, Chuvashia, and Yakutia (now the Sakha Republic). Commentator Vadim Bardin predicted that given the "chronic crisis of central authority . . . the strengthening of the regions is becoming a guarantee that in the future the 'institution' of foreign economic privileges will survive as a major component of economic policy."[48]

TRADE AND THE POLITICS OF REFORM IN 1993

Crime, corruption, and political cronyism in the foreign economic sector were prominent in the campaign of allegations that Rutskoi waged against Yeltsin in the run-up to April's nationwide referendum. As chairman of the government's interdepartmental anticorruption commission, he told parliament he had eleven suitcases of evidence implicating officials at the highest levels, including Shumeiko, Burbulis, and Anatoly Chubais, who directed the State Property Committee's radical privatization agenda. "The people of Russia were robbed twice in the past year, through shock therapy and price liberalization on the one hand," he said, "and through the unchecked leaking to foreign countries of money and raw materials."[49]

As the political effect of raw material shortages escalated, their economic impact seemed to be moderating according to surveys of some 100 directors of mid-sized plants conducted from April to January. Where in April 63 percent of respondents had placed the lack of material inputs at the head of the list of factors identified with production holdups, the figure was down to 40 percent at the end of the period. Scarcity of resources had been overtaken by their high cost (up from 52 percent to 59 percent), shortage of working capital (up sharply from 29 percent to 56 percent), and by declining demand (up from 36 percent to 48 percent).[50]

The figures lent credibility to Minister of the Economy Andrei Nechayev's claim, "If an enterprise has money, it has no problems in acquiring material and technical resources."[51] The situation reflected in the statistics, however, was far from stable and featured price inflation, high interest rates, and expanding indebtedness. Whatever the cause of shortages — whether physical supply or finances — the State Statistics Committee was still reporting in April a "raw materials famine" in light industry and declining production continuing in most other industrial sectors. Yet the survey did suggest progress in industry's adjustment to postsocialist relations as factories began to settle debts and restore ties with suppliers, and it pointed to a rise in domestic competition, as reported by 39 percent of respondents.

Heartened by Chernomyridin's practical experience and pragmatic bent, many of Russia's top managers endorsed the government while doubting its grasp of strategy and criticizing various aspects of its industrial policy. But even as debate reshaped around the choice between quickening the pace of change or slowing to consolidate gains, the political ground shifted decisively to a contest between the president and parliament for control of Russia's constitutional development. Both, however, were shadowed by events in the regions beyond Moscow, where developmental forces from below were defining realities that would shape Russia's economic and political future.

In the closing months of 1992, the corps of more reform resistant state enterprise directors had been drifting to the political right finding more in common with hardcore statists — communists and "national patriots" united in the National Salvation Front against Yeltsin — than with the leaders of Civic Union who had worked hard to hold together the pivotal political center at the December CPD. Civic Union's scrupulous adherence to the formula of support for the president plus "constructive" criticism of the government was severely tested in the new year by Rutskoi's defection to the unbridled impeachment campaign waged against Yeltsin by Khasbulatov and a variety of factions in parliament. Volsky's own efforts to stay above the "political games of the upper echelons," as he called them, effectively put him out of political play. "The struggle for power has always simply offended me," he later said, while also debunking, perhaps disingenuously, his reputation as Russia's Deng Xiaoping, China's behind-the-scenes power broker.[52] Civic Union, too, found its considered positions marginalized by the politics of passion and personality unleashed at two sessions of the CPD convened in March 1993 by Yeltsin's opponents.

Centrist delegates held the line against impeachment at the Eighth Congress, but they were unable to prevent a dismantling of the December accord with the president. As Khasbulatov reached to assert parliamentary supremacy, Yeltsin impetuously threatened to impose special presidential rule. The Ninth Congress was hastily called, and Yeltsin, amid proceedings reported as both terrible and farcical, narrowly escaped impeachment with his prerogatives of office badly battered. Civic Union put a patch on its own internal rifts, and the national plebiscite was rescheduled for April 25. But it was evident that the centrifuge of events had cleaved the political forces in the capital into two broad factions stalemated over the issue of a parliamentary versus a presidential republic.

For Vasily Lipitsky, chairman of Civic Union's executive committee, the most alarming development at the congress was the comment of one regional leader that seemed to speak for many: "However this ends, federal power does not interest me any more." With the central authorities having only "enough forces to block one another," Lipitsky observed, "their decisions have less and less significance in the enormous territories of Russia, where the power of regional elites is strengthening before our very eyes."[53] This and other like-minded assessments registered concern for keeping the "war of powers" in the constitutional contest from precipitating an outright struggle against the state as such mounted by regions losing patience with Moscow.

In April's referendum campaign Yeltsin warned that any effort to reinvent the center would result in Russia's disintegration into warring fiefdoms. The heightened rhetoric inside Russia chilled the confidence of the international business community, while leading to predictions of dire consequences should the West fail to support Yeltsin against the "hard-line" opposition. The smart line in the West identified Yeltsin with democracy, free markets and rising trade. Thus Richard Nixon wrote in the *International Herald Tribune* in March:

Consider these facts: Russian GNP last year was seven times as great as China's. China's trade with the United States was eight times as great as Russia's. Why? Because China's private enterprise produces more than one-half of its GNP. Russia's private enterprise produces only one-fifth of its GNP. As Russia's private sector grows, this will mean thousands of jobs and billions in trade for the United States.[54]

The article's title was "The West Can't Afford To Let Yeltsin's Russia Fail." But even as the Russian president was moving toward a limited victory in the April vote, Nixon gave reason to consider the merits of the center's more subtle strategies for preserving an economically open Russia, with or without Yeltsin.

PROSPECTS FOR RUSSIA'S INTEGRATION INTO THE WORLD ECONOMY

Western assistance carried a price. The quid pro quos of the latest IMF-mediated financial aid package in May were a little more relaxed than in the period of Gaidar's stewardship. Yet few Russian observers thought that the government could deliver on all its pledges of monetary and credit asceticism, privatization, and liberalization of foreign trade policy. "On the whole, the agreements with the Fund imply one logic for the reforms," Aleksandr Bekker wrote in May, "while the political and economic alignment in Russia implies another."[55]

Not only were powerful parliamentary factions certain to oppose Fyodorov's quest to slash spending by 40 percent and Chubais' rapid privatization goals but also inside the government personnel changes in the top echelon had sharpened differences of opinion in the long-running debate on the draft economic program.

Post-referendum Industrial Policy and Economic Openness

Yeltsin confounded speculation that he would use his success at the polls in April to bring Gaidar back to reenergize radical reform. True, he had quickly isolated Rutskoi for "his apostasy" as *Izvestia* called it, and dismissed Khizha and Security Council Secretary Yury Skokin, both of whom had run afoul of reformers. But the appointments of two pragmatic economic managers, Oleg Lobov and Oleg Soskovets, who joined Shumeiko as first deputy prime ministers, marked a shift in the cabinet's balance of power toward state influence in the economy.

Lobov lost no time in fashioning a hotly contested plan for turning the Ministry of Economics, which he took over, into the leading central body of federal executive power[56] — a new Gosplan, less generous critics said. The Ministry of Foreign Economic Relations had reason to fear his ambitions, for he proposed demoting it once again to committee status, this time under his own ministry. But the proposal failed, and whatever animus it may have generated was leavened by Lobov's backing of the kind of aggressive state capital investment program needed by Glazyev's efforts to stimulate exports of advanced manufactured goods.

Once a Gaidar protege, Glazyev had split with shock therapy even before Chernomyrdin first joined the government. He remained a staunch advocate of foreign economic openness, in word and by deeds as he dismantled a number of trade barriers in the autumn of 1992. Yet his concept of the open door, like Gorbachev's, hinged on an export-oriented development strategy as the top priority task of national industrial policy.[57] His reformulation of the strategy to fit post-Soviet realities made him an ally of the industrial and defense lobbies and their representatives in the government's inner circle.

Thus his proposal to use 30–40 large financial-industrial groups to take state-of-the-art high-tech products into world markets pulling up the rest of Russia's economy with them, conflicted with Chubais' IMF-backed privatization plans. He was quick to defend science-intensive enterprise associations and their structural subdivisions against hasty privatization, arguing that their vertically integrated research-development-production links would be pulled apart and individually made vulnerable under existing unstable conditions. Instead, he suggested management by large holding companies, described as "diversified and mixed-type corporations with both state and private capital" capable of operating successfully in the emerging domestic marketplace as well as in foreign markets. These "embryos of export-oriented economic growth" would be nurtured by umbilical ties to research organizations, specialized foreign trade firms, and investment banks, as well as by major infusions of state assistance.[58]

New threats to industrial stability notwithstanding, Glazyev had to contend with one central fact: the enormous investments needed to bring product design and quality up to world standards were already scarcer, by far, in 1993 than before the revolution. Gorbachev's problems had been of a different order, and linked to the colossal wasting of state resources by over-protected domestic producers. But for Glazyev, the uncoupling of financial and material resources from industry that had occurred through 1992 was the principal barrier to the success of his export strategy.

Direct state subsidies for machinery and equipment exports were reportedly only 5 percent of what they had been four years earlier. Private commercial banks, on the other hand, shied before the prospect of becoming hitched to old state enterprise associations, seeing Glazyev's plan as a scheme for preserving former political and economic structures despite his reformist credentials.[59]

Glazyev's recentralization of trade operations and the strengthening of SRM controls also ran counter to the government's IMF commitment to work toward eliminating export quotas. In his strategy, however, protectionist quotas, licenses, and tenders were key levers for concentrating foreign currency in state hands and making additional state credits and technology imports available to targeted industries.

His drive to increase industrial competitiveness also needed protection from new privatization schemes for raw material producers. He pointed out that many independent extractive and processing firms had already rushed into higher priced export markets. Resulting price increases for domestic users were undercutting the competitiveness of technically sophisticated Russian products, advancing the "tendency toward the country's deindustrialization." Without a powerful state-managed industrial policy, he said, Russia's industrial complex would soon enter an "irreversible process" of disintegration, and the country's prospects would be diminished to shipping raw materials to competitors.[60]

In that event, he warned, foreign transnational corporations would take advantage of Russia's economic openness to acquire the more lucrative and promising enterprises, research centers and raw material resources. Lidia Malash had earlier reported that many of the federation's regions, "aspiring to complete independence," were offering their natural resources as collateral to foreign creditors. She correctly suggested that Glazyev's concept of geographically broad industrial-financial consortiums with subsidiaries in a number of regions was partly aimed at ensuring the country's economic, and by extension political, unity.[61]

According to an analysis of the April vote prepared at the Russian Academy of Sciences' Institute of Geography, support for Yeltsin had "unambiguously grown" since 1991 in 21 seaport and adjacent raw materials producing areas, which were almost "all export trade areas oriented toward the outside world."[62] Many, the report said, like St. Petersburg and the Arkhangelsk and Murmansk oblasts, had "predictable political sympathies and a rather stable orientation toward

Moscow." But in other less supportive regions, such as Tatarstan and Bashkortostan, as an earlier study had noted, political defensiveness against interference by Moscow was complicated by challenges from internal "radical-national" separatist movements. In those areas, many local authorities were "endeavoring, by hook or by crook, to take control of the power-wielding structures," while also setting up regional administrations to take over raw materials exports.[63] It was in light of such counter-trends that Malash concluded that Glazyev's efforts on behalf of national unity and a centralized trade policy were "perhaps . . . being made too late."[64]

The Glazyev Affair and Heightened Political Uncertainty

Such troubling portents could hardly comfort critics of the still running tide of corruption in the foreign trade sector. Some, however, were less intent on prosecuting wrongdoers than in hauling the government before the court of public opinion.

Caught in the middle, Yeltsin first used the momentum of the April referendum to strip Rutskoi of his chairmanship of the special inter-departmental anticorruption commission, accusing the vice president of using his position for personal political advancement. Yeltsin formally took over the commission's reins and promptly broadened its investigations.

Rutskoi did not go peacefully. Resisting pressures to resign the vice-presidency, he led Civic Union — whose prior ambitions were described by one commentator as not extending "beyond Yeltsin's waiting room"[65] — into a broader center-left coalition as a springboard for his own quest for the Russian presidency. The move was known to have disaffected Travkin's Democratic Party of Russia, one of Civic Union's main supporting factions. Yavlinsky, too, confirmed his own interest in the executive office during an appearance in Kazan. Meanwhile, other political blocs, for and against Yeltsin, were laying plans for parliamentary and presidential campaigns in anticipation of possible early elections. All, to one degree or another, made economic openness an issue.

Then in June, Glazyev wrote an article for *Rossiyskaya gazeta* bluntly charging unnamed forces in the government itself with complicitous foot-dragging in implementing control decrees aimed against "stable criminal groupings."[66] In mid-August the MFER announced cuts in the number of special SRM traders, which had burgeoned to some 700 licensed participants. Within a matter of days, Glazyev was called in to hear new corruption charges against his ministry and, it was rumored, against himself personally.

He resigned on August 21, forced out he said by mafia bands and a cabal of high-level government officials, including Shumeiko, whose involvement in questionable foreign trade deals was under investigation by order of parliament. Although Glazyev was criticized by Foreign Minister Andrei Kozyrev for not owning up to "political and professional mistakes," the cabinet refused to accept his resignation, at least for the time being. The whole affair was "symptomatic," Leyla Boulton wrote in the *Financial Times*, "of the chaos at the top of reformist Russia."[67]

But there was more to come. The anticorruption commission had, meanwhile, referred purported evidence of criminal currency and foreign trade transactions by Rutskoi to the Moscow procurator, unwilling to entrust it to the office of Russian Procurator General Valentin Stepankov, a known ally of the vice president. In fact, commission member Andrei Makarov accused Stepankov, who was handling the Shumeiko case, of conspiring with an informer to get rid of, presumably murder, Makarov himself.[68] On September 1, Yeltsin suspended both Shumeiko and Rutskoi, pending further action. Khasbulatov called Rutskoi's removal unconstitutional, and promised its recision by parliament.

True or not, these and many similar accusations against a growing list of top figures deepened public cynicism, further diminishing the government's — and the opposition's — moral and political authority outside Moscow. One thing was clear as the country braced for more unsettling revelations: foreign trade had once again, as at the beginning of perestroika, become a pivotal factor in strategies for change, however now for more starkly political than economic reasons.

When Glazyev got the summons on August 20 to respond to charges, he was en route on business abroad, and his plane turned back to Moscow. The story left an especially fitting image. For it was then seven years and a day since Gorbachev's first trade reform decree, and still the country was without a confident course into the world economy.

NOTES

1. The present chapter continues analysis introduced in William E. Schmickle, "Soviet Foreign Trade Reforms under Gorbachev," in *The U.S.S.R. and the World Economy: Challenges for the Global Integration of Soviet Markets under Perestroika*, ed. Deborah Anne Palmieri (Westport, Conn.: Praeger Publishers, 1992), pp. 27–53. The author wishes to thank editor Doug Barry at the Alaska Center for International Business for publishing an early version of part of the present study in *Russian Far East News*, vol. 2, no. 1 (March 1992): 14–16.

2. "On Liberalization of Foreign Economic Activity in the RSFSR," *Interflo: A Soviet Trade News Monitor*, December 1991, p. 4.

3. *Der Spiegel*, November 18, 1991.

4. "Borderline Situation," *Literaturnaya gazeta*, no. 44 (October 28, 1992), p. 11 in Foreign Broadcast Information Service, *Daily Report. Central Eurasia: Baltic and Eurasian States* (hereafter FBIS-USR with year and issue) 1992, No. 146, pp. 28–29.

5. Moscow Domestic Service, October 19, 1990, in FBIS-SOV-90-204, p. 33.

6. N. Zhelnorova, "I Am Like the Emperor without Clothes . . . ," *Argumenty i facty*, no. 2 (January 1992), p. 3 in FBIS-SOV-92-015, pp. 31–32.

7. "Gennady Burbulis: We Have No Time to Hope for a Miracle," *Komsomolskaya pravda* (January 21,1992), pp. 1–2 in FBIS-SOV-92-014, p. 39.

8. Joerg R. Mettke, "The People Will Defend Themselves," *Der Spiegel* (January 6, 1992), pp. 113–17 in FBIS-SOV-92-005, pp. 45–46.

9. Quoted in *Interflo*, November 1991, p. 31.

10. "Gennady Burbulis: Political Role — 'Killer'," *Nezavisimaya gazeta* (January 29, 1992), pp. 1–2 in FBIS-SOV-92-020, p. 35.

11. "It Cannot Work," *Wochenpresse* (January 30, 1992), p. 31 in FBIS-SOV-92-021, p. 47.

12. Sergei Parkhomenko, "'All Professors of Economics Will Be Against You': An Almost Official Statement by the Gaidar Team," *Nezavisimaya gazeta* (February 27, 1992), p. 5 in FBIS-USR-92-031, pp. 46–47.

13. Yury Makartsev, "Minds like Solomon, but Inordinate Retribution," *Rabochaya tribuna* (January 26, 1992), pp. 1–2 in FBIS-USR-92-009, p. 26.

14. V. Golovachev, "Mistakes Should Be Corrected," *Trud* (February 6, 1992), pp. 1–2 in FBIS-USR-92-028, p. 50.

15. Quoted in *Interflo*, November 1992, p. 7.

16. Moscow Russian Television Network (January 16, 1992) in FBIS-SOV-92-013, p. 57.

17. Moscow Russian Television Network (October 6, 1992) in FBIS-SOV-92-195, p. 26.

18. Peter Reddaway, "Russia on the Brink?" *The New York Review of Books*, January 13, 1993, pp. 32–33.

19. Marshall I. Goldman, "Yeltsin's Reforms: Gorbachev II?" *Foreign Policy*, no. 88 (Fall 1992): 77–80.

20. Moscow Russian Television Network (September 22, 1992) in FBIS-SOV-92-186, p. 25.

21. I. Ivanov, "Russia at the Foreign Economic Crossroads," *Ekonomicheskaya gazeta*, no. 31 (August 1992), pp. 1, 7 in FBIS-USR-92-111, p. 32.

22. *Izvestia*, January 28, 1992, p. 2.

23. Mark Kolesnikov, "Why Do Rivers of Raw Materials Flow to the West?" *Rossiyskiye vesti* (January 26, 1993), p. 3 in FBIS-USR-93-013, p. 86.

24. Like Leonid Gurevich of the parliamentary subcommittee on foreign economic activity. See Interfax (November 19, 1991) in FBIS-SOV-91-224, pp. 52–53.

25. *Financial Times*, September 23,1992, p. 30.

26. Presidential Decree No. 628, June 14, 1992, "On Procedures for Export of Strategically Important Raw Materials"; Presidential Decree No. 629, June 14, 1992, "On Partial Changes in Procedures for Mandatory Sale of Part of Hard Currency Earnings and Export Duty Exaction"; Presidential Decree No. 629, June 12, 1992, "On Payments and Settlements in Russian Foreign Economic Relations in 1992"; Presidential Decree No. 630, June 14, 1992, "On the Provisional Import Customs Tariff." Texts in *Commersant*, June 23, 1992, pp. 23–25.

27. *Commersant*, June 9, 1992, p. 4.

28. I. Savvateyeva, "Friends and Invoices," *Komsomolskaya pravda* (July 28, 1992, p. 2 in FBIS-SOV-92-147, pp. 24–26.

29. Vadim Bardin, Tatyana Korotkova, and Vasily Fyodorov, "New Package Aims To Prop up Ruble," *Commersant* (June 23, 1993), p. 26.

30. ITAR-TASS World Service (June 10, 1992) in FBIS-SOV-92-11⁴, p 47.

31. Tatyana Korotkova,"Export Monopolies to Continue under New System," *Commersant* (July 7, 1992), pp. 25–26.

32. Moscow Russian Television Network (October 6, 1992) in FBIS-SOV-92-194, pp. 29–30.

33. Russian Government Ordinance No. 854, November 6, 1992, "On Licensing of, and Setting Quotas on, Imports and Exports of Goods (Work, Services) on the Territory of the Russian Federation." Text in *Commersant*, November 17, 1992, pp. 22–24.

34. Moscow Russian Television Network (October 6, 1992) in FBIS-SOV-92-195, p. 26.

35. *Journal of Commerce*, September 19, 1991, p. 5A.

36. Vladislav Belyanov, "Russian Enterprises under Crisis Conditions: Results of Monthly Director Surveys," *Delovoy mir* (March 25, 1993), p. 7 in FBIS-USR-93-050, p. 14.

37. *Financial Times*, August 5, 1992, p. 10.

38. *Politics of Soviet Economic Reform*, January 15, 1993, pp. 5–6.

39. Moscow Russian Television Network (October 6, 1992) in FBIS-SOV-92-195, p. 24.

40. Quoted in *The Washington Post*, December 19, 1992, p. A10.

41. Viktor Serov, "Investment Incentives Drawn Up," *Commersant*, (January 26, 1993), p. 20.

42. Text of program in FBIS-USR-93-015, pp. 26–31.

43. V. Galitsky, Aris Zakharov and Aleksadr Frenkel, "The Depth of the Recession Is Decreasing," *Delovoy mir* (April 24, 1993), p. 6 in FBIS-USR-93-060, p. 52.

44. "Exports To Provide Debt Relief," *Commersant*, April 7, 1993, p. 4.

45. Vadim Bardin and Alexander Volynets, "Foreign Trade Still a Swamp of Subsidy and Privilege," *Commersant* (April 14, 1993), p. 24.

46. Vadim Bardin and Yevgeniya Shuvalova, "Tapping into New Profits," *Commersant*, April 7, 1993, pp. 26–27.

47. Kolesnikov, "Why Do Rivers of Raw Materials Flow to the West?" p. 87.

48. Bardin, "Preferences," p. 31.

49. Moscow Russian Television Network (April 16, 1993), in FBIS-SOV-93-073, p. 62.

50. Belyanov, "Russian Enterprises under Crisis Conditions: Results of Monthly Director Surveys," pp. 13–20.

51. Vladimir Gavrilenko, "What Does the Economic Reform Need?" *Krasnaya zvezda* (March 5, 1993), pp. 1–2 in FBIS-SOV-93-043, p. 29.

52. Lilia Lagutina, "Until Everything Has Been Lost, Nothing Has Been Lost," Interview with A. I. Volsky, *Rossiya*, no. 14 (March 31–April 6, 1993), p. 3 in FBIS-SOV-93-062, p 17.

53. Vasily Lipitsky, "Shock Deepens Split at the Top. The Power of Regional Elites Is Strengthening at Grass-Roots Level," *Rossiyskaya gazeta*, April 3, 1993, pp. 1, 3.

54. *International Herald Tribune*, March 8, 1993, p. 6.

55. Aleksandr Bekker, "Credits: Bankers Are Turning into Gentlemen. The IMF's Unusual Metamorphoses in Russia," *Sevodnya* (May 21,1993), p. 3 in *The Current Digest of the Post-Soviet Press* (hereafter CDPSP), vol. 45, no. 20 (1993): 7.

56. Irina Savvateyeva, "A 'Lobnoye Mesto' for Reforms? That's What the Ministry of Economics Could Become under Oleg Labov," *Komsomolskaya pravda* (May 14, 1993, p. 1 in CDPSP, vol. 45, no. 19 (1993): 6.

57. Sergei Glazyev, "On Industrial Policy in Russia," *Rossiyskiye vesti* (April 21, 1993), p. 4. in CDPSP, vol. 45, no. 18 (1993): 11.

58. Ibid., pp. 11–12.

59. Aleksandr Bekker, "The Government Is Putting Everything on the Altar of the Fatherland. The Evolution of Minister Sergei Glazyev," *Sevodnya* (May 12,1993), p. 3 in CDPSP, vol. 45, no. 19 (1993): 7.

60. Glazyev, , "On Industrial Policy in Russia," p. 12.

61. Lidia Malash, "Debates," *Megapolis-Express* (March 3, 1993), p. 13 in CDPSP, vol. 45, no. 9 (1993): 11.

62. Dmitry Oreshkin, "Regional Solitaire on the Eve of Constitution Day," *Sevodnya* (June 8, 1993), p. 3 in CDPSP, vol. 45, no. 23 (1993): 13.

63. Yelena Pestrukhina, *Megapolis-Express* (March 3, 1993), p. 13 in CDPSP, vol. 45, no. 9 (1993): 11.

64. Malash, "Debates," p. 11.

65. Vladimir Todres, "General Rutskoi Is Forming Himself a Voting Bloc," *Sevodnya* (May 25, 1993), p. 3 in CDPSP, vol. 45, no. 21 (1993): 17.

66. Sergei Glazyev, "There Are Forces Which Oppose the Creation of Currency and Export Controls," *Rossiyskaya gazeta* (June 25, 1993), p. 3 in FBIS-SOV-93-123, pp. 42–43.

67. *Financial Times*, August 23, 1993, p. 2.

68. *The Washington Post*, August 26, 1993, p. A22.

5

Breaking with Moscow:
The Rise of Trade and Economic
Activity in Former
Soviet Border Regions

James Clay Moltz

With the collapse of the former Soviet Union, an economy based on cen-trally-directed supplies and management has disintegrated. In its wake, a whole new system — or, more correctly, a collection of subsys-tems — is emerging. With the severing of traditional supply lines and the disruption of years of central planning, survival depends on the ability of the various regions to fend for themselves. When possible, these subeconomies are forging new market-based links with nearby foreign countries that can provide them with the capital, technology, and markets they need in order to survive the arduous transition from the old socialist economy to a new capitalist-inspired future that is struggling to be born in the various republics.

For those territories once favorably located close to Moscow or along central supply routes, the past advantages of their geography are rapidly losing their previous value. At the same time, less fortunate regions located at the end of old Soviet supply lines, but close to foreign capitalist economies, are discovering new and favorable economic opportunities. Imports are more readily available and export avenues for local products are both more accessible and more lucrative than old internal markets located across the expanses of the former Soviet Union.

The author thanks the Kearny Foundation for a grant that supported the research and writing of this study.

TRANSBORDER ECONOMIC TIES AND
THE POST-COMMUNIST ECONOMY

In terms of international relations, the end of communism and attempts by the new states of the former union to create beneficial commercial ties with foreign partners, and especially neighbors, have ended years of isolation from foreign contacts and returned Russia and the other Soviet successor states back into the world economy. In fact, as can already be seen from population shifts, construction projects, and new business development, border regions of the former Soviet Union are playing a very different role in their new republican economies than the one they played under communism, moving from peripheral status to central importance. The key reason is that close geographical proximity to foreign capital is a major impetus for economic development through investment, trade, and other types of economic contact. Such "transborder economic ties"[1] are helping to revitalize weakened border economies while promoting new forms of international cooperation among states long cut off from one another, in many cases since 1917.

Robert Scalapino's work on post–Cold War economic dynamics in East Asia has provided the useful term "natural economic territories" (NETs) to describe this phenomenon of previously-isolated but adjacent border regions reaching across international boundary lines to achieve collective economic gains from pooled capital, labor, and raw material markets.[2] As elsewhere in the international economy, synergistic effects materialize when foreign inputs can be drawn upon to overcome domestic inefficiencies. Not surprisingly, many such NETs are now forming around the former Soviet Union's border regions as economies previously isolated from one another by political constraints seek to establish mutually beneficial economic ties. In resource-rich border areas, the strategies of local leaders in Soviet successor states may include exchanges aimed at acquiring technology for semiprocessing industries, while also seeking foreign partners to invest in the local production of consumer goods and services. In other border areas with more developed industrial bases, newly-opened border trade may provide new markets for manufactured goods as well as access to the capital and technology required for enterprise modernization and environmental clean-up.

This study examines the growing importance of such transborder economic ties in the former Soviet Union. First, it categorizes the various types of new NETs forming in the border regions of Soviet successor states. Second, it discusses specific examples in northwest Russia, the Caucasus, Central Asia, and the Far East. Finally, it turns to a more in-depth analysis of the Russian Far East's southern territory and its growing integration into the greater Pacific Rim economy. Compared to other regions, the Russian Far East — a poor stepchild in the old

Moscow-centric Soviet economy — is in a unique position to benefit from the break-up of the old system through its establishment of new ties with its capital-rich neighbors. Moreover, with the influx of foreign ideas and under pressure to increase local living standards, such dynamic border regions as the Russian Far East may begin to put greater demands on their respective capitals for new forms of decision-making autonomy. In view of the administrative weakness of many new capitals, the rise of new transborder economic regions may, therefore, become an increasing source of tension as governments struggle between the conflicting dictates of political control and economic development.

REGIONAL NETS ALONG THE BORDERS OF THE FORMER SOVIET UNION

Two general trends appear in the development patterns of the new NETs now forming around the various Soviet successor states: cultur-ally- and historically-based NETs and economically-based ones.[3] In the first pattern, cultural similarities and historical ties across interna-tional borders are facilitating a renewal of economic ties. In the second pattern, economic ties are being formed for the first time despite cul-tural differences due to economic demand and compatible cross-border economic endowments.

Beginning with the first pattern, the large-scale renewal of econom-ic ties between local economies in Central Asia and adjacent Muslim states provides a good example. Here, the lifting of Communist era political obstacles and conditions of economic hardship have helped bring about the re-creation of centuries-old trade relations going back to the time of the Silk Road. In this least developed area of the former Soviet Union, shared Turkic- and Persian-based languages, the religion of Islam, and other ethnic similarities have made trade ties in Central Asia much easier to reestablish, compared to the task of creating new links to more distant capitalist countries in Europe, East Asia, or North America. Moreover, goods available from nearby Muslim countries are also more appropriate to local tastes and customs. Since the Soviet break-up, ties between Azerbaijan and Turkey, Turkmenistan and Iran, Kazakhstan and China, as well as Kyrgyzstan and China have been the most well-developed. Yet, years of political hostility and separation eco-nomically have left a legacy of separate infrastructures and severed rail and road links, thus hindering the rapid joining of these border regions. For example, the border between northeast Kazakhstan and China has only one narrow road, although the two sides, for economic reasons, are now working toward construction of a new rail line to facilitate border trade.[4] Further west, similar difficulties were the focus of talks during a visit by Turkmenistan's President Saparmurad Niyazov to Iran in August 1992. The two sides discussed the connection of area rail lines, considered joint banking arrangements, and signed an agreement (in coordination with Turkey) to build a gas pipeline linking the three bordering states.[5]

Moving from Central Asia to the Caucasus region, many of the same processes of re-creating historical NETs are at work, but in this case using traditional sea lanes instead of land routes. For example, whereas during the Cold War the Black Sea bristled with hostile weapons, today pre-Communist trading links across these waters are being reestablished with the aim of renewing commercial cooperation. In February 1992, a Turkish proposal led to the creation of the Black Sea Economic Cooperation Region, a new trading zone joining Turkey, Russia, Ukraine, Moldova, Romania, Bulgaria, Georgia, Armenia, and Azerbaijan. The Black Sea Pact aims at reducing barriers to trade, facilitating regional investment, and easing previous military tensions. It has already facilitated meetings between regional states, such as those between Russia and Turkey to discuss aid in the refitting of Russian ports and in converting its military factories in the region to civilian uses.[6] Further east, a similar Caspian Sea Pact, sponsored by Iran, now links Turkmenistan, Kazakhstan, Russia, and Azerbaijan to facilitate regional trade as well as energy and environmental cooperation.

With the establishment of Russia's post-Communist foreign economic policies, the most Western portion of the country, the region of Kaliningrad, is now seeking to develop new transborder economic channels with neighboring Poland and nearby Germany. This pattern fits the second, economically-driven, pattern more closely, given the overwhelmingly Russian population of present-day Kaliningrad and the lack of such ties previously. During Soviet rule, Kaliningrad was a closed region whose major industries served the Soviet Navy. Its economy depended heavily on internal supply lines to keep its factories running.[7] Since December 1991, however, Kaliningrad has been cut off from the rest of Russia by the independence of Lithuania and Belarus. Although existing bilateral treaties guarantee Russian access and rail routes to the region, Kaliningrad's government is actively seeking to develop more direct economic ties with the West, benefiting from its port and still-extant European-gauge railroads built by Germany before World War II. Toward this end, in 1991 the local population voted to create a free economic zone in the area to facilitate independent economic decision making as a means of attracting foreign investment and gaining control over local tax revenues for purposes of development. If local residents get their way, Kaliningrad may seek greater stability in the status of a "free" port, drawing on the historical models of Danzig or Hong Kong. With little hope of gaining significant new development funds from Moscow in today's deficit economy, local officials are turning increasingly to their neighbors, especially those further West, for ties that may soon outweigh those with Russia proper.[8]

Moving northeast into the forested region of Karelia, a similar, economically-based NET is being created. In this case, there are language and cultural differences as well as the additional problems caused, on the Russian side, by an economy with a weak technological base. Yet, across what used to be a militarized border with Finland, trade, communication, and investment are flourishing. The key commodities of exchange are Finnish technology, consumer goods, and business know-how for Russian-produced raw materials. Previously, this potentially profitable trade for Karelia fell under control of the central ministries, which channeled their resources to Moscow. But since the Soviet Union's break-up, Karelia's enterprises have begun selling their iron ore and timber directly to Finnish customers eager both for a new source of raw materials and for a chance to help clean up and modernize old Soviet factories, which have damaged the region's shared environment. The Finnish city of Kuhmo and the Russian city of Kostomuksha have become new regional centers for this cross-border trade, now linked by a newly-connected railroad between the two countries.[9] At the meeting point, a tax-free store brings together consumers from both sides seeking bargains on the other side's products.[10]

Moving from the Russian northwest across Siberia to Russia's even more harsh northeast, another new NET is being formed across the Bering Sea by the Kamchatka, Chukotka, and Magadan oblasts with the American and Canadian Pacific northwest. Despite some present economic incentives that are new, this NET seems to fit more closely with the cultural and historical pattern of development. Completely cut off from one another during the Cold War, the two sides now enjoy direct airline service between the Russian airports at Provid005ye and Magadan and various Alaskan cities, and there is considerable foreign economic activity in the formerly-closed naval base of Petropavlovsk. Indeed, Alaskan companies alone have started some 87 joint ventures in Siberia, ranging from exotic reindeer-meat sausage production to more traditional industries such as tourism and mining.[11] Benefiting from the similarities in climate and a shared interest in raw material extraction, American companies successful in Alaska, such as Caterpillar, are now beginning to move into northeast Russia with sales of advanced heavy machinery.[12] Meanwhile, the Rural Alaskan Television Network is now beaming programs to viewers in the Chukotka and Magadan regions,[13] helping native cultures reestablish ties broken by the coming of communism to Russia.[14] For both Russians and the various native peoples of the north, this Bering Sea NET signifies a renewal rather than a fundamentally new pattern of interconnection. Russian colonies (supported from Siberia) existed in Alaska and the Pacific northwest from the late 1700s to the mid-1800s, until the sale of Alaska to the United States in 1867.[15] Later in the nineteenth century when Russia gave up its American holdings and concentrated its attentions on the Amur and Ussuri regions, American ships from California and elsewhere made regular runs to northern Siberian coastal towns cut off from the mainstream of rerouted Russian supply lines.[16] Thus, while the volume of business between the two regions remains relatively modest, its historical and social significance to the two sides is very high.

Finally, moving to the very southernmost region of the Russian Far East (including Primorskiy krai, Khabarovsk krai, and Sakhalin oblast), we see one of the most active new NETs of all of those forming along the former Soviet periphery. Despite the lack of cross-border cultural ties between the now-dominant Russian population and its Chinese, Korean, and Japanese neighbors, new, economically-driven relations are developing in many industries and in great scale. Due to the region's relatively developed transportation infrastructure, especially rail lines, and maritime access to both the Pacific Ocean and the Sea of Japan, these ties are bringing large numbers of foreign investors interested in both export trade and the transit of goods into European Russia.[17] Like its northern cousin, the southern Far East's raw materials, particularly energy resources, fish products, and precious metals, fit a niche in the resource-poor but capital-rich northern Pacific Rim. But it is the southern region's better climate, skilled workforce, more developed industries, and closer geographical proximity to important Pacific Rim manufacturing centers that have made it more attractive to wealthy East Asian investors. Moreover, its much larger population has made it a focal point for foreign businesses seeking to introduce their products into the Russian market, such as Japanese cars and South Korean electronics. Finally, skilled labor in the major cities of Khabarovsk, Komsomolsk-na-Amure, and Vladivostok from Soviet military factories in the fields of shipbuilding, electronics, and aircraft construction are available for new high-technology ventures. These enterprises are now actively seeking out partners to help them in converting to civilian production, either as parts manufacturers, assemblers, or even end-product producers for East Asian companies. The southern Far East border region has been perhaps the most successful of the new NETs forming around the borders of the former Soviet Union and is, therefore, worthy of more detailed discussion. What factors are likely to shape its development as a region? What problems does it share with other border regions that may hold it back?

The next section of this chapter focuses on a series of related issues in examining the development of the southern Far East's international economic relations, including a brief history of the conditions of underdevelopment that characterized the region's position in the Soviet economy, a discussion of current foreign investment, and an analysis of the possible implications of the region's economic success.

CASE STUDY: THE RUSSIAN FAR
EAST'S SOUTHERN BORDER REGION

The Russian Far East has been a backward and neglected sector in the Soviet economy by virtually any measure.[18] Its reputation from the Stalinist era as the location of some of the worst forced labor camps did not endear it to potential settlers from the Western parts of the country, even after the camp system was broken up under Khrushchev. Despite considerably higher salaries, the local population totaled less than 8 million people in the late 1980s. Due to its vast resource endowments, Soviet planners chose to develop the area primarily as a raw materials exporter to the rest of the economy, rather than as a location for industry. This created a highly-skewed monoeconomy with harmful effects on the environment as well as local aspirations for a balanced regional economy.

Not surprisingly, living conditions in the Russian Far East lagged far behind those elsewhere in the country and the vast majority of migrants from European Russia returned home after only a few years.[19] The region remained a political and economic backwater, a "periphery" in every sense of the word, especially since the region's key ports had been all but completely shut off from foreign shipping after World War II. Due to Cold War tensions and the presence of both an American and later Chinese threat, the region was run by two major actors — the central economic industries and the Soviet military. The pattern of regional development — or rather, underdevelopment — was typically "colonial," and the population, much less the dispossessed native peoples, had no say on the direction of the economy.[20] Capital came into the region almost exclusively to improve the harvesting of raw materials or to bolster the region's military installations. Services, infrastructure, housing, and food remained abysmally poor.[21] The primary beneficiary was Moscow, which reaped the benefits of its hard currency exports, especially energy, timber, and fish. Ironically, estimates from the late-Soviet period show that over 50 percent of Soviet exports to the Organization for Economic Cooperation and Development countries (averaging over $10 billion a year) came from Siberia and the Far East, suggesting a massive outflow of capital from the region.[22]

Beginning with Gorbachev's dramatic speeches in Vladivostok in 1986 and Krasnoyarsk in 1987, a steady wave of pressure began to grow in the southern Russian Far East for the region to be opened to greater contacts with its Pacific Rim neighbors, especially in economic matters. The primary aim was to "normalize" the region's place both domestically and internationally and, by doing so, to elevate the region's deplorable living conditions.[23] Yet, despite a somewhat more ambitious Five Year Plan for the 1986–90 period, the region saw little improvement under Gorbachev, and, indeed, shared the absolute decline in living standards suffered by most of the country during 1991.

Internationally, Gorbachev had made major strides in normalizing relations with both China and South Korea, while seeing less auspicious results in his efforts to court Japan, largely due to his inability to deliver the Kurile islands. Nevertheless, the Russian Far East itself had benefited very little. While some foreign investment had trickled in, it had virtually no impact on the local economy, save occasional joint venture stores or restaurants priced well out of the range of average consumers. Large-scale deals, like the multibillion dollar timber agreement signed with South Korea's Hyundai corporation, benefited Moscow's coffers only while creating numerous local environmental problems.[24] Decision making remained almost exclusively in Moscow's hands. Indeed, despite all of the calls for a new start in the Pacific under Gorbachev, the key port city of Vladivostok remained closed to foreign investment.[25]

Opening the Region under Yeltsin

Following the failed August 1991 coup and Yeltsin's rise to unchallenged power in Russia, changes proceeded much more rapidly in the more populated and favorably located southern Russian Far East as decision making devolved to regional officials, especially over the economy. A rash of new deals was signed and foreign firms for the first time began to make their presence felt in the region. In early 1992, Vladivostok gained the status of an open city, creating a rush of new businesses as well as new diplomatic ties.

Although before 1937 it was a home for consulates from China and Japan, and during World War II a key point of distribution for American Lend-Lease aid, Vladivostok had withered diplomatically since 1945. Even in the last years of Communist rule the only Western diplomatic presence in the Far East was the Japanese consulate in Nakhodka. But already by the end of 1992 new consulates had been granted to a wide range of countries. The United States opened its consulate in August 1992,[26] while South Korea, India, and Japan announced their intention to open offices soon.[27] Meanwhile, Khabarovsk will be the site of an Australian trade mission and a second Japanese consulate in the southern Russian Far East, indicating a serious Japanese interest in this region of Russia close to their shores.

From their virtual absence during the Cold War, international airline routes to the Russian Far East have expanded dramatically since 1991. Indeed, the only international airport in the whole of the Russian Far East with direct flights to the non-Communist world was Khabarovsk, with a once-a-week flight to Niigata. During 1991, several more Aeroflot flights were added, including one via Anchorage to San Francisco. Moreover, that summer, Alaska Airlines began the first regular service from the United States, serving Magadan and Khabarovsk. In December 1991, an agreement also opened Sakhalin's capital of

Yuzhno-Sakhalinsk for international service.[28] Since then, Alaska Air has been approved to fly directly to Vladivostok,[29] something that would have resulted in a plane being shot down even a few years ago, as in the case of the ill-fated Korean Air Lines flight 007 in 1983. Indeed, talks have begun between Russian and American airport and airline officials about creating a new Pacific Rim air hub in Vladivostok. The city is closer to the American mainland than Tokyo or Seoul and, therefore, would save both fuel and time in trans-Pacific flights, particularly those involving transfers.[30] Among the project's advantages for the Russian side would be a tremendous surge in commercial development to service the new airport with aircraft maintenance facilities as well as hotels, restaurants, and duty-free shopping areas. Should plans be completed for a free enterprise zone in Vladivostok, manufacturing could be located near the airport as well.

The new Russian government has strongly favored foreign participation in the development of the southern Far East. During his first trip to South Korea since the Soviet break-up, President Yeltsin announced: "In a word, Russia is boldly opening its Far Eastern frontiers."[31] He spoke specifically of Russia's interest in creating a regional NET between the Russian Far East and the Pacific Rim, saying: "A zone of regional economic cooperation with Northeast Asia and the northern half of the Pacific as a whole could be created."[32] He rejected the secrecy of even the Gorbachev government regarding military establishments in the region and even opened the door for exchanges and coproduction deals between the Russian and South Korean militaries.

One of the most ambitious proposals for the opening of the region is the multinational project being considered for the Tyumen River region at the meeting point of China, North Korea, Russia, and the Sea of Japan. The inspiration for this idea is the hope of combining Chinese, and possibly North Korean, labor[33] with Russian raw materials and Japanese and South Korean technology and capital.[34] The region would be granted the status of a free enterprise zone and its factories would have direct access to a variety of customers across the Sea of Japan and the Pacific more generally. Planning for this project has been funded by the United Nations, which hopes the plan will promote not only economic development but also more peaceful political-military relations among its members.

A separate local development plan touted by Russia today is the Greater Vladivostok Project, which has similar aims but would be located on Russian territory, using the advantages of its already available factories, labor force, and infrastructure. It would also involve the creation of a free enterprise zone to attract foreign investment and develop trade with Pacific Rim countries. The project has elicited considerable foreign business and governmental support, especially in

Canada.[35] Finally, a more localized economic development scheme is also being promoted for the city of Nakhodka, the site of the Russian Far East's first established free enterprise zone. Details are still being worked out, but the South Koreans have already indicated that they will build a large industrial complex there.[36]

Although the Tyumen River and its sister projects have a long way to go, support for these concepts can already be seen in the flourishing border trade going on between China and Russia. A number of crossings are operating along the Amur and Ussuri Rivers. Moreover, Chinese laborers already number in the tens of thousands and have made positive contributions to the Russian Far East economy, especially in agriculture. Border trade typically involves Chinese clothing, food, and consumer electronics being bartered for Russian raw materials, consumer durables, cars, and heavy machinery. Similar trade and labor exchanges under the former Soviet Union with Vietnam and North Korea have notably been less successful and are being phased out.[37]

More significant for the successful transition of the region's industries toward marketization has been the growth of joint ventures with its Pacific Rim neighbors. One of the largest projects is the development of the Sakhalin oil shelf, currently being studied by the so-called MMM consortium, formed by Marathon Oil, Mitsui, and McDermott International, and recently joined by Royal Dutch Shell.[38] Once it moves past the research stage into production, it is expected that — besides increasing exports of oil and natural gas — the venture will provide jobs for thousands of Far Easterners. It is also expected to purchase millions of dollars in machinery from regional industries. For example, the recently-privatized ZLK shipbuilding factory in Komsomolsk-na-Amure has already won contracts for barges and rigs to serve the new venture.[39]

The general opening of Sakhalin Island and the Kuriles to foreign investment from Japan and elsewhere under radical pro-reform governor Valentin Fyodorov has helped stimulate other regions as well.[40] Ferry services have been reestablished between Hokkaido and Sakhalin, providing needed business for ZLK and other shipbuilders. On Sakhalin itself, there are dozens of evolving joint ventures, including one that provides Japanese television programming to the city of Yuzhno-Sakhalinsk. Even the ongoing Kurile Islands dispute and government pressure on Japanese businesses not to invest in Russia has failed to stem this interest. As the president of a Niigata-based bank comments: "The thinking of Japanese executives is that if they just wait around, then Russia's rich resources will all be spoken for by companies from other industrialized nations."[41] Some of these fears may be well founded, especially as eager South Korean and recent Taiwanese investors move into the area with their governments' encouragement. For example, in the rich fishing grounds surrounding the Kuriles, a new Taiwanese-Russian joint venture was formed in summer 1992. The rapid political changes in Moscow have made new economic relationships possible even between these two previous enemies under communism.[42]

Pressures for Regional Independence

The relative success thus far of the southern Russian Far East in attracting foreign investment, in combination with the continued dominance of Moscow-based ministries over many natural resources, has increased regional pressures for varying degrees of independence. Indeed, there have even been calls for a return to the period of complete independence under the short-lived Far Eastern Republic (1920–22), established while the Red Army consolidated power elsewhere and negotiated with Japan to end its military occupation of much of the territory. From 1990 to 1993, Sakhalin Governor Fyodorov made similar appeals as a means of pressuring Moscow to compromise and grant him greater economic independence, especially in his dealings with foreign investors and governments.[43]

Here and elsewhere, Moscow faces a dilemma: allow greater regional power over the economy or attempt to hold onto central powers and risk a slowdown in regional development combined with a rise in local pressures for political independence. Yet, the success of the region in developing transborder economic ties and thereby fostering development, providing jobs, and channeling investment into an expanding regional trading zones is providing leverage to regional decision makers, here and elsewhere in Russia.

One political organization that has led the way in pressing for increasing Far Eastern regional authority has been the Far Eastern Association for Economic Cooperation, a body organized by the heads of the oblast- and krai-level Councils of Peoples' Deputies in the Far East. The organization has sought to develop a coordinated regional strategy for development and consistent policies in regulations governing foreign investment. It has been only partially successful, however, due to internal divisions and pressure from the Yeltsin government not to step beyond certain limits. Yet, some reformers still press the issue. One supporter of the Far Eastern Association, Khabarovsk economist and deputy chief administrator Pavel Minakir, has also called for a separate financial system backed by a proposed Far Eastern Bank for Economic Development.[44] In light of these ideas, some central authorities see the organization as an attempt at complete economic autonomy, especially in regard to projects involving the use of the region's natural resources, and are likely to work toward its demise.

Most economists in the region, however, downplay the possibility of true independence because of the continued need for investment and social services provided by the Russian Federation government. Thus, particularly since the break-up of the Soviet Union, they have tended to focus more on the question of increasing their economic authority rather than seeking potentially self-defeating political independence.

PROBLEMS FACING FOREIGN
INVESTORS IN BORDER REGIONS

Several obstacles must be overcome by foreign investors interested in doing business in former Soviet border areas. Although some of the problems are common to the post-Soviet economy at large, they may affect border regions in different ways due to the distance of these areas from decision makers in Moscow and the absence of a recent history of dealing with foreigners. Other problems, especially in the area of infrastructure, are unique to these economic peripheries and relate to problems long neglected during the Soviet period.

One difficulty of conducting business in the Russian Far East is that deals settled in Moscow with the various state ministries often have not been effectively communicated or rendered acceptable to local officials. While under the Soviet system this type of activity led to resentment, today it may lead to outright sabotage of the agreements by local people and, possibly, even local officials. For example, Sakhalin's Governor Fyodorov opposed the oil and gas exploration contract given to the MMM consortium by officials in Moscow. He preferred an Exxon-Sodeco proposal that would have provided more jobs for the local population and funds for infrastructure development. He used every opportunity to give the consortium bad publicity and frequently made open statements highly critical of Moscow's high-handedness. Other examples include the mounting local opposition to the Hyundai timber concession by environmentalists and the minority Udegei people, whose ancestral lands and hunting grounds are being decimated by the company's logging. The Hyundai contract has been supported to date by Moscow and the Primorskiy krai administration,[45] but with the growth of democratic forces in the region, this situation may change.

A second area of concern for foreign businesses is the constantly shifting role of the state in governing joint ventures and other foreign economic activity. These factors affect Far Eastern ventures through inconsistent Moscow-based regulations, center-regional conflicts within state ministries, and outright corruption among local industrial officials. Even when companies know the situation in Moscow well, local problems can thwart the best plans because, as funds from the center have become increasingly scarce, local officials and state ministries alike tend to view foreign investors less as "partners in development" than as "deep pockets." Ironically, foreigners may become a substitute for Moscow, but without the threat of sanctions. However, the long-run effect of this targeting of foreigners may be a slowing of regional development. As one Japanese economist noted regarding the changing investment environment as he looked back on 1992, "Just this year alone, they must have changed the rules regarding joint ventures and foreign exchange two or three times."[46] The impact of these changes can be very damaging to a new joint venture. The experience of a San Francisco-based company in a joint venture with the local fishing processing industry in Khabarovsk during 1991 is typical.[47] After refitting a Russian factory at considerable cost and enduring a season of on-again, off-again problems with local ministry officials and the local workforce, the company finally succeeded in packaging four tons of the finished product — caviar from the Amur River — for export. But when the time came to take the product through customs at the airport, officials slapped on an unannounced 50 percent duty and confiscated two tons of the fully-packaged product.[48]

A third obstacle to successful investment in the region is the lack of business experience among Russian entrepreneurs. Since many of them are former Soviet officials and all are former Soviet citizens, there is a general lack of understanding of how to establish long-term contacts with Western businesses in a market-based setting. Moreover, a common mistrust of foreigners among a certain segment of the region's population is one of the lasting effects of the long isolation and heavy anti-Western propaganda typical in former Soviet border regions. Thus, not only was the Russian Far East's economy isolated from the surging capitalist development among its Pacific Rim neighbors during the 1970s and 1980s, but its population, many of whom were employed by the Soviet military, was encouraged to hold a suspicious attitude toward outsiders.[49] Today, this sentiment sometimes translates into counterproductive attitudes in their business dealings with foreigners. One common problem cited by foreign businesses is that Russia's new entrepreneurs may be reluctant to honor signed contracts and even believe that breaking contracts is justified, if they deem that the foreign partner is trying to "cheat" them by taking an "excessive profit." But what Russia's new entrepreneurs often do not take into account are the greater costs of doing business in the West and the substantial sunk costs incurred by the foreign partner in the initial stages of a joint venture. One such case of Russian mistrust and American missed signals involved a joint venture fishing operation in the Sea of Okhotsk in 1991. After having been provided with a ship and supplies by their American partner, the Russians suddenly sailed off and sold their catch to a Japanese vessel offering a higher price.[50] The Russians later justified breaking the contract by claiming that their American partners had set an unfair price and, moreover, were not taking steps to improve the living standards of their families and community — not on board ship, but in port. As one company executive lamented about the chaotic business environment in the new Russia: "I long for the Cold War when everything was run with an iron fist. Now it's a complete crapshoot over there."[51] Eventually, although the Russians confiscated the rest of the ship's supplies, the Americans did receive their vessel back. But the experience of this joint venture ended unhappily for both sides.

Thus, despite the great potential of many border regions, obstacles remain in the tenuous legal protection offered to foreigners and the sometimes unorthodox demands put upon foreign partners due to different understandings of the norms of capitalist business practices. This is not necessarily due to greed on the Russian's part, although in certain instances it may be. Often, it has more to do with the long legacy of planned economics under socialism and a different set of expectations by the Russian side. Until economic conditions improve, however, Russians are likely to use whatever opportunities they have in order to make up for the security they have lost in the transition to the new economy.

CONCLUDING REMARKS

The rise in the importance of former Soviet border regions is helping to redefine the direction of development in post-Soviet political economies. Yet, while these changes will undoubtedly improve the status of border regions and likely increase their political clout within their republics,[52] they are not necessarily the answer to all of the problems facing these former "peripheries." Other complex challenges exist, such as accomplishing more balanced economic development and safeguarding the local environment from excessive foreign operations. These issues and others will become crucial questions facing regional leaders as they move beyond the initial stages of their new contacts with foreigners into more extensive business and economic relationships.

One major finding of this research on transborder economic ties is the surprising impermanence of long-standing Soviet-era economic ties. Indeed, while a recent official document released by the Russian Foreign Ministry downplays the likelihood of the break-up of the economic portion of the Commonwealth of Independent States,[53] these transborder ties indicate a countertrend that is weakening the foundation of the Commonwealth of Independent States — the economic interdependence among the parts of the old Soviet system. But these new international ties are a positive sign for those who seek truly reformed economic systems in the Soviet successor states — ones that will look as much abroad for new investment, know-how, and technology as they do back to Moscow and to familiar practices from the Soviet-era.

In the long run, many of these formerly "peripheral" areas of the old Soviet economy may become new economic "centers" for their various republics. Interestingly, current trends suggest that the old Soviet political economy may be turning more and more in the direction of the post-industrial American political economy, where the coasts and border regions have become the source of new export-led growth, while central rust-belt cities have atrophied from the decline of old industries based on formerly-protected domestic markets. Similarly, these economic trends may well lead to considerable migrations of people to these profitable regions and a concomitant redistribution of political power away from traditional industrial centers.

As with China's prosperous Guangdong province, greater autonomy for these regions may be tolerated simply because, for the foreseeable future, they are likely to be the only areas in the post-Soviet economy where development is actually taking place.[54] If so, we should welcome this development, because a shift from centrally-directed economics to more diversified and market-based decision making will promote moves by these states away from economic autarky and toward more stable integration into regional trading relations and, consequently, into the world market. Furthermore, moves that increase the importance of trade are likely to provide further pressures on these successor states to follow policies that are consistent with the General Agreement on Tariffs and Trade and other international trading organizations. These trends should help ensure that a return to command-style economic policies and trade protectionism among the Commonwealth of Independent States does not occur.

Finally, in regard to regional independence, it is important to point out that new transborder economic ties and the creation of NETs will not in themselves result in the further disintegration of its constituent states. Indeed, in contrast to the situation in China, greater economic independence for former Soviet border regions may actually mollify demands for regional political independence, now that the old Soviet Union has broken up. Thus, the true road to success may lie in giving new freedoms to border regions while at the same time strengthening political unity through the electoral process and continued reforms. Although surely difficult, such a route will help ensure financial support from abroad while creating conditions for the creation of the economic base at home needed to make the transition to democracy succeed.

NOTES

1. For a previous use of this concept, see James Clay Moltz, "Transborder Economic Ties" (Panel on Patterns of Disintegration in the Former USSR), *Post-Soviet Geography*, 33, no. 6 (June 1992): 367–71.

2. See Robert A. Scalapino, "The United States and Asia: Future Prospects," *Foreign Affairs* 70, no. 5 (Winter 1991–92): 20–21.

3. These two categories are not mutually exclusive, as there may be elements of both patterns in a single area. However, one pattern usually predominates. This distinction is important because the underlying dynamics of the two patterns differ. Specifically, more economically-driven NETs are more likely to experience rapid growth and have more transformational effects upon their regions.

4. Interview with Amangel'dy I. Bektemisov, September 25, 1992.

5.   INTERFAX report published in Foreign Broadcast Information Service, *Daily Report: Central Eurasia* (hereafter, FBIS-SOV listed by number and date) FBIS-SOV-92-167 (27 August 1992), p. 64.

6.   *Hurriyet* (Turkey), August 30, 1992, p. 14 in FBIS-SOV-92-172 (3 September 1992), p. 13.

7.   For a history of the Soviet absorption of Kaliningrad after World War II, see Peter Worster, "From Germany's East Prussia to the Soviet Union's Kaliningrad Oblast: A Case of Sequent Occupance," *Soviet Geography* 27, no. 4 (April 1986).

8.   The continued presence of the Russian Navy, however, is likely to mitigate any serious pressures for political independence. In fact, the completion of the Baltic pullout means an increase in the military's presence, perhaps by as much as 35 ships and 350 aircraft as these weapons are transferred to Kaliningrad. See LETA (Riga) report, FBIS-SOV-92-225 (20 November 1992), p. 5.

9.   Interview with Dr. Alan Sweedler, September 1991.

10.   Ibid.

11.   See Yereth Rosen, "Alaskans Capitalize on Closeness to Russia," *The Christian Science Monitor*, May 11, 1992, p. 9.

12.   *Anchorage Times*, March 31, 1992, pp. E1, E6, cited in *SUPAR Report*, no. 13 (July 1992): 89.

13.   Yereth Rosen, "Renewing Old Cultural Ties across the Bering Strait," *The Christian Science Monitor*, May 11, 1992, p. 9.

14.   On these exchanges, see Nancy Shute, "From Unalaska to Petropavlovsk: Warm Welcomes amid Geysers and Snow," *Smithsonian* 22, no. 5 (August 1991).

15.   Long antedating these Russian-American ties were those established among the related native peoples across the Bering Strait and, before that, the land bridge that once linked the two continents.

16.   For more on the period, see Benson Bobrick, *East of the Sun: The Epic Conquest and Tragic History of Siberia* (New York: Poseidon Press, 1992), pp. 320–23.

17.   There are certain minority populations in the region with ties across borders here, but they are vastly overwhelmed by the Russian presence. Similarly, pre-1917 economic relations did exist between this territory and some of its Pacific neighbors, but the roles of the various parties were very different and the level of involvement considerably less.

18.   On the distinction between the northern and southern zones, and on the development of the Russian Far East in general, see F. V. D'yakonov, *Formirovaniye narodnokhozyaictvennogo kompleksa Dal'nego Vostoka* (Moscow: Nauka Press, 1990).

19.   For more on the relative position of Siberia and the Russian Far East in the old Soviet economy, see Robert N. Taaffe, "The Conceptual, Analytical, and Planning Framework of Siberian Development," in *Geographical Studies on the Soviet Union*, ed. George J. Demko and Roland J. Fuchs, Research Paper No. 211 (Chicago: University of Chicago Department of Geography, 1984).

20.   V. Vorontsov and A. Muradyan, "Dal'nevostochniy regionalizm" (Far East Regionalism), *Problemy Dal'nego Vostoka*, no. 6 (1991).

21.   For a detailed analysis of these issues in comparative perspective, see Rodger Swearingen, ed., *Siberia and the Soviet Far East: Strategic Dimensions in Multinational Perspective* (Stanford, Calif.: Hoover Institution Press, 1987).

22.   Michael Bradshaw, "Patterns of Economic Disintegration," *Post-Soviet Geography* 33, no. 6 (June 1992): 366. For longer range trends in Soviet-era trade from the Far East, see Gerald Segal, *The Soviet Union and the Pacific* (Boston: Unwin-Hyman, 1990), Chap. 6.

23.   It should be noted that a few enclaves run by the military, particularly Vladivostok, typically fared much better than the average Far Eastern city, although still far from standards enjoyed in Moscow.

24.   On these issues, see David Gordon and Antony Scott, "Russia's Timber Rush," *The Amicus Journal* (Natural Resources Defense Council) 14, no. 3 (Fall 1992).

25.   The city also remained technically closed to foreign visitors, although by 1991 those with official invitations could be granted special visas. The author visited Vladivostok in April-May 1991 under an invitation from the Institute of Economics and International Ocean Studies.

26.   The U.S. consul general in Vladivostok has already announced additional plans to open a U.S. publications library for the use of the citizens of Vladivostok, as an adjunct to the consulate. See L. Bryzgalina, "Budet amerikanskaya biblioteka," *Krasnoe znamya* (Vladivostok), February 6, 1993, p. 4.

27.   Japan will close its existing consulate in Nakhodka and also open a second consulate in Khabarovsk.

28.   To date, foreign charter services from the Pacific Rim serving business customers have dominated the airport's international traffic, with only a few Russian flights going out (largely due to costs). See "Redkiy rossiyskiy samolet doletit do serediny Khokkaydo," *Vostok Rossi* (Magadan), 72, no. 50 (December 1992): 3.

29.   "U.S. Approves Alaska Airlines' Flights," *New York Times*, October 20, 1992, p. D4.

30.   The first round of talks (called the "Airport Economic Conference") began in San Francisco in June 1991. See Richard G. O'Lone, "U.S. Soviet Push Cooperation to Build Transpacific Air Traffic," *Aviation Week and Space Technology*, June 17, 1991, p. 59.

31.   Cited in FBIS-SOV-92-224 (19 November 1992), p. 13.

32.   Ibid.

33.   North Korea plans to develop a "special economic zone" adjacent to the project. It has also opened the port city of Chongjin in support of the plan for a larger trading zone to facilitate North Korea's participation in the plan. See Clayton Jones, "Images, Sounds of North Korea," *Christian Science Monitor*, November 10, 1992, p. 14.

34.   On the Tyumen River project, Clayton Jones, "Asian Neighbors Plot New Hub," *Christian Science Monitor*, May 19, 1992, p. 4. Also Lincoln Kaye, "A Very Special Zone," *Far Eastern Economic Review*, May 14, 1992, p. 32; and Sam Jameson, "6 Nations Act to Create Asian Growth Center," *Los Angeles Times*, February 29, 1992, p. A8. Mongolia is another country interested in the project as a possible point of access for its products to the Sea of Japan via a proposed rail line.

35.   On the role of the city of Vancouver and Canadian business groups, see *Russian Far East Update* 2, no. 4 (April 1992): 6–7.

36.   See published text of Russo-Korean document signed at the Yeltsin-Roh summit in Seoul, November 1992 in FBIS-SOV-92-225 (20 November 1992), pp. 9–11.

37.   The problems stemmed largely from the apparently involuntary nature of the laborers' service and the high incidence of crimes against the Russian population committed by these impoverished workers.

38.   "Royal Dutch Joins Group to Study Sakhalin Fields," *New York Times*, October 1, 1992, p. D4.

39.   *Russian Far East Update* 2, no. 3 (March 1991): 11.

40.   Ironically, Fyodorov has recently been ousted from his position by local officials who opposed the fact that he was initially appointed in 1990 by the Russian government, rather than being elected from the region.

41.   Clayton Jones, "Russia's Resources Lure Japanese," *Christian Science Monitor*, December 15, 1992, p. 6.

42.   *Russian Far East Update* 2, no. 10 (November 1992).

43. On these movements toward Far Eastern independence, see Stanislav Glukhov, "Conflict and Political Blackmail," *Moscow News*, no. 46 (November 17–24, 1991).

44. See Pavel Minakir, "Ekonomika sovetskogo Dal'nego Vostoka: vyzov krizisy" (Economics of the Soviet Far East: Facing the Crisis) *Problemy Dal'nego Vostoka*, no. 5 (1991): 60.

45. *Tikhookeanskaya zvezda* (Vladivostok), August 26, 1992, p. 1 in *RA Report* no 14 (January 1993): 146.

46. Quoted by Clayton Jones, "Russia's Resources Lure Japanese," *Christian Science Monitor*, December 15, 1992, p. 6.

47. Interviews with company personnel as well as with Khabarovsk ministerial officials by the author. See also recent reporting on the joint venture by Matt Miller, "U.S. Investor Gets Cold Shoulder in Siberia," *San Diego Union-Tribune*, April 3, 1993, p. C-1.

48. Personal communication with Bob Lee, Portland, Oregon, businessman and president of Unik Business Center in Khabarovsk.

49. In Khabarovsk in 1991, for example, the author was called a *shpion* (spy) by a group of people on a train platform when he snapped an innocent tourist shot of the station. On the train to Vladivostok, fellow passengers were openly suspicious of the motives of a foreigner traveling to this then-closed city.

50. See "U.S. Seafood Companies Playing Russian Roulette," *Seafood Leader*, January–February 1992, pp. 46–47. Courtesy of Tony Allison.

51. Ibid.

52. In a small but telling development, the Yeltsin government agreed in late spring 1993 to an appeal by then-Primorskiy Governor Vladimir Kuznetsov to waive within the Far East region a new national law banning right-hand drive automobiles in Russia. The governor had argued that the presence of many right-hand drive Japanese vehicles in the region would cause an undue hardship for residents who had already purchased or were seeking Japanese automobiles. This recognition of the Far East's special place may be the harbinger of concessions from Moscow in other areas as well. On Kuznetsov's appeal, see "Administratsiya kraya vystupila v zashchitu avtomobiley c pravostoronnim rulevym upravleniem," *Vladivostok*, February 10, 1993, p. 3.

53. "Posle raspada v CCCR: Rossiya v novom mire" (After the Dissolution of the USSR: Russia in a New World), MGIMO, Russian Foreign Ministry, February 1992.

54. On the increasing political clout of Guangdong province, see Ann Scott Tyson, "China Grants Free-Market Autonomy to Guangdong," *Christian Science Monitor*, April 3, 1992, p. 8.

6

Commodity Exchanges and the Post-Soviet Market

Ariel Cohen

During 1990 and 1991, the economic climate in what was still the USSR remained in a state of winter chill. However, signs did emerge of a hopeful thaw in one area, the commodities exchange network, vital for the creation of price-forming mechanisms based on supply and demand and for the alleviation of supply bottlenecks, the legacy of the State Planning Committee (Gosplan). Unfortunately, several factors slowed the growth of the exchanges, including inflation, lack of regional cooperation among the Newly Independent States, and inadequate transportation and communications networks.

Despite their stunted growth, commodity exchanges served as the primary vehicle for new commercial structures seeking to circumvent existing governmental foreign trade bureaucracies and form direct links with foreign economic partners. In addition, the newly established bodies functioned as a breeding ground for nascent Russian entrepreneurs.

BACKGROUND

Pre-revolutionary Russia boasted several hundred flourishing commodities exchanges open to foreign firm participation. Russia played a prominent role in the grain, timber, metal, and petroleum markets.

After the 1917 October revolution, during Lenin's New Economic Policy, Soviet cooperative organizations, together with the Supreme Economic Council rebuilt the exchanges. The increasing involvement of the Bolshevik government in the economy initially transformed these institutions into economic-administrative state appendages and later eliminated them altogether. The exchanges became unnecessary as the government encouraged monopolistic production and stifled the role of the market in price-formation. With collectivization and rapid industrialization in the 1930s, the commodities exchanges were finally eliminated altogether by S. Ordzhonikidze, Stalin's Politburo member responsible for industry.

Under command economics in the Soviet Union, commodities were distributed by one gargantuan state supply bureaucracy, the State Committee for Supply (Gossnab). With time Gossnab increasingly failed to successfully perform this duty due to numerous factors, including the complexity of the national economy, corruption, inefficiencies inherent in central planning, and the lack of effective information and communication systems capable of assimilating a vast array of detailed economic data.

As part of the Gorbachev government's halfhearted marketization attempts, the creation of new private economic structures (cooperatives) was allowed, thus legalizing formerly underground economic activities such as Western consumer goods sales, private agriculture, and services. Soviet officials tolerated initiatives on the part of the country's businesspeople to create an alternative to the faltering government industrial and consumer goods distribution system. In 1990, private initiative was in the process of moving from small-scale enterprises selling Western-made consumer goods into the creation of major distribution channels, such as commodity exchanges.

A pioneer of this process, Vyacheslav A. Nikolayev, head of the training division of the Russian Commodities Exchange (*Rossiyskaya Tovarno-Syryevaya Birzha* or RTSB) and director of the Veles brokerage firm, states that from the summer of 1990 the appearance of commodities exchanges was the result of a bottom-up initiative by Russian entrepreneurs.[1] Instead of awaiting and following an *ukaz* (a government fiat), exchange promoters used the foundation of the legislation on shareholders' companies (*aktzionerniye obshchestva*) to establish these new market institutions as regular business ventures. This process required simple registration with the local city council, the gorispolkom. Only in late April 1991, more than six months post factum, did the Council of Ministers attempt to catch up by issuing a decree *(postanovleniye)* regarding exchanges. Thus, commodities exchanges, a prosperous and effective institution of both the Russian prerevolutionary and New Economic Policy era, reappeared as a nascent market institution in the midst of the decaying centrally planned economy literally "by popular demand."[2]

This chapter provides an overview of the growth of these early catalysts of market transformation and tools of Russia's integration into the world economy by focusing primarily on the period of their most active development, from 1991 to early 1992. It illustrates the role of exchanges as market institutions in an emerging Russian post-Soviet mixed economy and explores the weaknesses and promising aspects of this phenomenon.

EXCHANGES IN THE EARLY STAGE

By early 1991, several dozen Soviet exchanges had either opened their doors or announced their intention to start trade in the near future. A year and a half later, at the Sixth Convention of the Congress of Exchanges, which took place in Dushanbe, Tajikistan in June 1992, the 67 largest exchanges were named members of the Congress, while hundreds more were in existence.[3] The *oboronka* (military industry) undertook to assist the exchanges by setting up a space communications company, Kosmicheskaya Svyaz', that would connect the exchanges in the USSR and provide links with global financial centers. According to V. Nikolayev, as the exchanges developed, more and more specialization was required of the brokers as they acquired special knowledge, skill, and client bases and thus became more "industry-specific." The overall turnover of the exchanges was 120–150 million rubles in mid-1991, and 4–5 billion rubles in 1992.

The principal Russian commodity exchange, RTSB, was established in Moscow in mid-October 1990 by the dynamic businessman-turned-politician, Konstantin N. Borovoy, who served as its first general manager. Its starting capital was 50 million rubles, and consisted of 500 shares worth 100,000 rubles each.[4] At the time, it was a rather new type of Soviet enterprise, a publicly held company.

As of January 26, 1991, RTSB began trading on a daily basis after a period in which it had been open only two or three times a week. This modus operandi effectively returned the exchange to the pre-revolutionary mode of daily trade. RTSB activities were based on brokers bringing in offers from clients whom they signed upon a case-by-case basis or retained for periods of up to a year. When it opened, this largest Russian exchange boasted clients from all over the Soviet Union, including Lithuania, Latvia, and Estonia.

The brokers had to maintain the confidentiality of their deals, otherwise clients would transact with each other directly. In RTSB's first central hall in the main post office building,[5] an electronic tableau provided updated information on deals concluded, quoted local and international commodities prices, and informed the members of new offers as they flowed in. Customers were not allowed into the pit. Computerized trade was being planned, but was still a matter for the future.

In early 1991, Konstantin N. Borovoy estimated RTSB's daily sales volume as fluctuating between 1.5–400 million rubles. At that time, the exchange had 14 divisions. Twelve of these specialized in goods and raw materials such as wheat and metals (the latter was subsequently incorporated into a specialized Russian Metal exchange) as well as building materials, real estate, and so on. Products not fitting these classifications were sold in a division called *Auktzion* (the Auction). In addition, the exchange had a division that traded in surplus production lines and capital goods from the state-owned industry, as well as capital goods futures. A branch of RTSB to deal exclusively with clients from the military-industrial complex was set up in Kaliningrad (Moscow oblast).

As of early 1991, RTSB had 244 brokerage offices and 120 more ready for registration. Fourteen foreign firms had become members, investing $60,000 each. More than 100 participated in activities through their joint ventures in the USSR. The price of a place for a Soviet participant was only 150,000 rubles. The Council of Ministers of the Russian Republic was reported to have granted the exchange several general import-export licenses to allow it easier foreign trade operations. Borovoy indicated the intention of the exchange management to demand the right to unlimited foreign trade operations.[6]

With the appearance at the commodities exchanges of generic goods and raw materials, as well as foreign traders, Russian enterprises, through these market institutions, started to interact directly with foreign buyers. The commodity exchange brokers, some of the most sophisticated and aggressive business intermediaries in the former USSR, were much more efficient conduits of information from foreign clients to Russian producers than the Gosplan's bureaucrats. The latter had no personal incentive whatsoever to further the results of a foreign trade transaction. A broker, on the other hand, would do everything in his power to ensure the compliance of Russian suppliers with Western standards in order to consummate transactions and collect his commissions.

RTSB's main competitor was the Moscow Commodities Exchange (*Moskovskaya Tovarnaya Birzha* or MTB). Located at the former People's Economy Achievements Exhibition Park, it was established on May 19, 1990.

Unlike RTSB, which is proud of its entrepreneurial background, MTB evolved from the state and economic apparat of the former USSR. Its founders, including the Association of Young Managers, the Main Supply Directorate of the Moscow City Council and others, all have strong roots in the Komsomol and the old Soviet bureaucracy. It is important to understand, however, that MTB itself was never part of the established Soviet economic structure. Rather, this is a case of skilled entrepreneurial manpower transition from the state to the private sector — an important phenomenon in all transition economies. By 1989 it had become clear that private enterprise was no longer punishable, as it had been earlier. The potential economic rewards of entrepreneurship, despite the risks, led to an almost unstoppable exodus from the ranks of government, as the more enterprising among the elites abandoned it for the private sector.

By late 1991, MTB had four sections, including building materials and metal goods, computers and consumer electronics, industrial and consumer goods, and machine building equipment. According to exchange representative Yuri Zotov, the exchange was preparing to open two additional sections, agricultural goods and petrochemicals. Similar to RTSB, MTB had to continually struggle against its own customers' tendency to close deals outside of the exchange, a phenomenon that decreases broker commissions and exchange profitability.

As of 1991, a firm wishing to become an MTB member had to purchase a share worth 100,000 rubles and the right to open a brokerage firm. One share equalled one vote at the general meeting. Foreigners paid $20,000 to participate. In addition to one American firm specializing in construction, a number of Taiwanese consumer goods suppliers were interested in participating in MTB's activities.[7] Perhaps the most celebrated Western participant in the evolving commodity exchange sector was the law firm of Skadden, Arps, Meagher, Slate, and Flom, which served as MTB's U.S. representative. The oil and gas producers among MTB's membership and the burgeoning ranks of Western energy industry traders and investors in Moscow represent the potential for new business for this and other American firms.[8]

The two leading Moscow exchanges, RTSB and MTB, were fiercely competitive. For instance, RTSB planned for the creation of a congress of stock exchanges at a meeting held on September 2, 1992, while MTB devised a competing congress on September 8. The RTSB structure included the Congress of Stock Exchanges, International Brokers' Guild, Russian Financial Exchange, and the largest financial exchanges of Russia.[9] Further international cooperation was planned with the preparation of an Eastern European Forum of Financial Exchanges in Kiev (November 4–6, 1992).

The commodity exchanges spawned Russian financial and stock exchange sectors. In 1991, the Congress of Exchanges prepared guidelines for the creation of investment funds needed to trade vouchers and shares of privatized former government companies.[10] The installation of a modern communication system was expected to facilitate exchanges between members of the Congress and the directorate,[11] and other avenues of activity were planned.[12] These efforts, however, encountered difficulties and were criticized by members of the VI Exchanges Congress.[13] Due to the high inflation, starting in 1992, the morale of the brokerage firm managers and brokers plummeted as the economic situation in the country deteriorated.[14]

REGIONAL DEVELOPMENTS

The provinces in the USSR had a lot of catching up to do to ensure their fair share of the commodities market action. In addition to Siberian exchanges specializing in oil, the Asian Exchange, the second largest in Russia, is noteworthy. This exchange developed excellent ties to countries of the Pacific region, and played an important foreign trade role.[15]

The northernmost commodities exchange in the USSR opened in Vorkuta on January 19, 1991, for the purpose of trading in lumber, coal, and other raw materials. Founders of the exchange were the Vorkuta City Soviet, the Vorkuta Coal Combine (*Vorkutaugol'*), Northern Gas Combine (*Severgazprom*), Vorkuta Komsomol City Committee and others. Each founder invested 100,000 rubles up to a total capitalization cost of 1.4 million rubles. The plan was to allow up to 200 permanent participants to take part in trading, with a broker's slot at the exchange selling for 50,000 rubles. Other interested traders would have to go through brokerage firms.

Aside from the raw materials mentioned above, the Vorkuta exchange dealt in semiprecious stones, cement, cars and tractors, consumer goods, and fish. At its founding, it planned to establish a network of representatives throughout the USSR and to connect their offices in Moscow, the Baltics, and Kuban via telecommunication networks. Its chairman, Vladimir Goloborod'ko, appealed for the establishment of cooperative arrangements with other exchanges throughout the USSR as well as for the creation of an all-Union exchange association, and in the long term, a single exchange network.[16]

Another regional commodities exchange was created in 1991 in Barnaul, the Altai Commodities Exchange. Similar to its Russian predecessors, it was registered with the Barnaul City Council (*gorispolkom*). Due to the expansive chemical industry in the area, the main specializations of this exchange were chemicals and raw chemical materials. The Altai Commodities Exchange was capitalized at 10 million rubles. The cost of a share was 1,000 rubles. Vladimir Popov, manager of the exchange, declared that it would be part of the Altai free enterprise zone. Popov criticized the sales tax that had been introduced by Soviet presidential decree at the time and said that this tax would be counterproductive for the exchange trade.[17]

Meanwhile, the traditionally entrepreneurial south kept pace with the rest of the country. The Rostov exchange emerged as one of the nation's biggest grain-trading centers, and the advanced Germes organization attempted to start a grain futures trade.

The Southern Universal Exchange (Yu.U.B.) opened on January 31, 1991, in Nikolayev, Ukraine, with 30 Soviet and 20 foreign founders. Both Soviets and outsiders could capitalize in foreign currencies. The founders planned on an annual dividend of 10 percent, which was subsequently rendered meaningless because of exorbitant inflation rates. Participants paid 10,000 rubles, and one-time visitors 100 rubles, to engage in trade. The exchange planned to charge 3–7 percent per transaction, with the brokers receiving from 0.3–1 percent. The Southern Exchange developed a network of representatives in various regions, planning to create a long-distance, telecommunications-aided trade, negotiating cooperative arrangements with the exchanges of Moscow, Omsk, Novosibirsk, Nizhniy Novgorod, and other cities.[18]

Independence-seeking republics were also involved in setting up market mechanisms, as evidenced by the founding meeting of the Tbilisi Universal Exchange. This exchange capitalized at 20 million rubles, with shares costing 100,000 rubles each. The founders were cooperatives, commercial banks, and state structures.[19] However, wars raging in all three Transcaucasian republics prevented meaningful market development in this region endowed with metals and oil resources.

Additional commodities and goods exchanges were also created in Kiev, Gomel, Odessa, Perm, Ryazan, Kuzbass (Kemerovo), Volgograd, and Dnepropetrovsk.[20] There were 16 operating exchanges as of January 1991, while 22 more had applied for operating licenses and about 100 were in various stages of incorporation.

PERSONNEL CONSTRAINTS

Lack of education was a major obstacle in developing Russian commodity exchanges. After all, even the famed Plekhanov Institute of People's Economy lacked trained market-oriented specialists.

Some Russian scholars, such as Gorbachev's chief economic advisor, academician Leonid Abalkin, coined the derogatory Western-sounding term "ekonomiks" to contrast with "true," socialist "ekonomika." It is little wonder, then, that the first exchanges appealed for Western assistance. RTSB signed an agreement with the New York Mercantile Exchange to train Soviet oil brokers at a cost of $20,000 per year, while the St. Petersburg commodity exchange received some help from sister institutions in Europe and the United States. In addition, the Congress of Exchanges allocated funds to develop a Broker's Textbook and to establish an Institute for Commercial Research (*Institut Kommercheskikh Issledovaniy*).[21]

Further difficulties were encountered when the promoters of the stock exchanges found few, if any, qualified personnel to work in these emerging markets. For example, the Congress of Exchanges allocated funds to train brokers and develop model document packets that were made available to members interested in starting stock exchanges in the former Soviet Union (FSU).[22] While originally the exchange founders thought that 20 hours would suffice to prepare a broker, by 1992 it became clear that even 32 hours was not enough and plans were made to expand the training program even further.[23]

INTERNATIONALIZATION OF ALL-UNION TRADE

After December 1991, trade between commodity exchanges in different republics became complicated, as new barriers were erected by the newly independent states. Despite numerous attempts on the part of the exchange administrations to facilitate transactions, as well as the creation of an International Trading of the Congress of Exchanges (*Mezhdunarodnye Torgi Kongressa Birzhi*),[24] lack of collaboration from the government ministries made acquisition of the appropriate licenses all but impossible. Given the rampant corruption of the FSU, the unwillingness of these officials to allow lucrative foreign trade to pass out of their hands is understandable. Due to these difficulties, as well as other factors including the near collapse of the railroad transportation network, military conflicts in several republics, and weak communications and legal infrastructures in the provincial exchanges, the International Trading of the Congress of Exchanges was terminated in the summer of 1992.[25] Despite this initial defeat, the Congress of Exchanges continued to work on establishing new procedures for international trade.

Two factors, however, contributed to the potential integration of Soviet exchanges into the global economy. Specialization allowed the markets to increase the volume of transactions and facilitated the introduction of international industry-specific rules of trade.[26] In addition, in 1992 the Russian government started to sell export certificates (quotas) that allowed for exports outside Russia. The right to sell quotas was initially allocated to some of the leading Moscow commodity exchanges, such as the Timber Exchange, Moscow Non-Ferrous Metals Exchange, Inter-republican Universal Commodity Exchange, MTB, Nizhnevartovsk Oil Exchange, International Trade and Clearing Chamber, and others. These certificates were sold for commodities such as oil and energy products, ferrous and non-ferrous metals, fertilizers, and other goods. Large "floor" amounts of raw materials subject to licenses increased barriers to entry into the lucrative foreign trade market for small Russian firms.[27] A later step limiting export licenses to the leading 28 trade and industrial firms further concentrated foreign trade in the hands of the large business entities.

EMERGING FINANCIAL MARKETS:
THE CASE OF MOSCOW

In the developing post-Soviet markets, the borderline between the commodities and securities trade often blurred. In part this was due to the newly acquired economic freedom and the desire of fledgling Soviet businesspeople to experiment with new avenues of commercial activity. It was also the result of ill-defined or nonexistent regulations. By April 1991, the MTB started trading in futures credits. The standard financing contract was 100,000 rubles for three months. Trade in financing futures was conducted in the Interregional Financial Market, a division of MTB, which also began functioning in April 1991.[28] At that time, according to MTB's head of currency operations Vladimir Nosovich, the MFR dealers were primarily commercial banks. A securities division of MTB also started operations with Russian Republic government bonds and Soviet treasury promissory notes. Plans were in the works to issue stocks for Soviet municipal bonds and the KamAZ truck combine.[29]

Also in 1991, the Moscow International Stock Market Exchange (MMFB) began to sell brokers slots at 100,000 rubles per place. MMFB, capitalized at 10 million rubles, was originally established by the Ministries of Finance of the Russian Soviet Federated Socialist Republic (RSFSR) and the USSR, the RSFSR Savings Bank, and other state institutions. Meanwhile, the Moscow Stock Exchange also issued shares, priced at 10,000 rubles each. Foreigners were allowed to purchase the shares by paying in rubles or foreign currency according to the commercial exchange rate of the Soviet State Bank, or by donating computer hardware.[30] The leading role at MMFB belonged to Daiwa Securities, which provided massive assistance to the nascent institution.[31]

Major limiting factors for financial and stock market development included primitive processes of stock issuance and insufficient flows of assets available for investments. As of summer 1992, the initial stage of stock and financial market development in the FSU had drawn to a close. It was characterized by a feverishly high demand for shares, including the stocks of commodity and stock exchanges themselves. As the economic situation in the Commonwealth of Independent States deteriorated and inflation and hyperinflation developed, the markets stagnated due to lack of money in the hands of the population, and commercial and state structures. As a result, stock prices dropped in real terms, reflecting not only lack of trust in the nascent enterprises, but also the low real value of the firms themselves.[32] Despite the slowdown, the exchanges attempted to persevere, gearing up for privatization, voucher trade, and the appearance of new enterprises from which to sell their shares in the market.

The leading companies to develop stock and financial exchanges in Russia were *Finross* and *Rossiyskaya Fondovaya Birzha*. These two companies, connected with the RTSB, developed organizational technology for trade in shares and financial instruments, designed brokers' training, and set up insurance guidelines.

COMPETITION FROM LENINGRAD

As in other areas of Russian life for the last three centuries, rivalry between the two capitals is also reflected in economics. Business leaders in the former imperial capital of St. Petersburg (Leningrad) also developed a modern stock exchange.

The founding meeting of the Leningrad Stock Exchange (*Leningradskaya Fondovaya Brizha* or LFB) took place on February 28, 1991. The exchange capitalized at 28.5 million rubles. According to Igor Kluchnikov, chairman of the board, LFB planned to move from its current quarters in the Petrograd Raion Party Committee Building into the building of the old Russian exchange, the current Museum of Naval History. Thus, historical justice would be served and the symbolism of the act could hardly escape the notice of Russian observers.

From its inception, LFB planned to invest in the computerization of its operations, expansion of its infrastructure, the establishment of an insurance mechanism for its transactions, and initiation of an auditing corporation. At least 40 Leningrad companies stood ready to offer their shares for sale and became the exchange's first clients. Brokers from small Leningrad enterprises participated as founders of the exchange. LFB employees underwent a 20-hour course under American and Finnish supervision, which was deemed sufficient for their new duties. Executives of the International Federation of Stock Exchanges expressed willingness to provide the St. Petersburg exchange with expertise and guaranteed acceptance of LFB as members in their association. The New York Stock Exchange and the American Securities and Exchange Commission offered similar assistance.

As far as foreign participation was concerned, the promoters were interested in attracting foreign capital and expertise. Up to 40 percent of the exchange's shares were open for foreign bids. Numerous foreign firms had negotiated buying shares. The cost per share was 250,000 rubles, with foreigners either paying according to the official exchange rate of the USSR State Bank or contributing equipment.[33] It was part of the Russian post-Communist normalization that the second capital and major industrial center, Leningrad-St. Petersburg, was claiming its place under the economic sun.

INDUSTRY SPECIALIZATION

The parade of exchanges continued throughout 1991, including new organizations encompassing numerous sectors. With Russia's large energy sector, it was to be expected that oil, gas, and coal exchanges would spring up. The leading energy exchanges became those in the traditional Siberian centers of Tyumen, Surgut, Nizhnevartovsk, Noyabrsk as well as specialized markets in the capitals, such as MTB, RTSB, the Petersburg-Tyumen Exchange Planeta, and the Petersburg-Tyumen and Petersburg-Moscow exchanges Germes. The Tyumen and Moscow oil exchanges offered rental of the pipeline as a means to move oil supplies to the ports, while Germes pioneered futures and option oil trade.

Oil exchanges functioned against the background of the Russian oil industry's decline due to a crumbling production base and political instability in regions including Chechnia and Tatarstan, as well as the continuing instability and conflict in Azerbaijan. In addition, the Russian government decided to keep the price of oil and other energy artificially low, hence ensuring non-profitability in the oil business.

The main drawback of trade at these exchanges was the lack of Russian government export licensing, which hampered the export of oil to international markets. Quantities of oil sales were minimal, and prices were below world market averages. The largest transaction in January 1991 was for only 5,000 metric tons (MT) of oil, whereas international market transactions numbered 20,000 tons of crude per month for at least a year. The price was 2,220 rubles per ton in January 1992, whereas the going price in the economy was 3,351 rubles per ton. The highest volume transactions in February 1991 were for 50,000 MT in Moscow and 300,000 MT in Surgut.[34]

According to Russian experts, a revitalization of the oil trade required liberalization of energy prices and export licensing policy. This would increase Russian oil sector profitability and ensure a flow of Western investment. Once the licenses were sold as part of oil shipments offered at the exchanges, the price rose to 8,000 rubles per MT and oil prices inched toward world market levels.[35] With the establishment of official, as well as gray and black export, markets for Russian gasoline (A-76), its prices also showed a tendency to increase, as cheap gasoline became a lucrative commodity for sales to Europe and elsewhere, often commanding a mark-up of over 100 percent. Like oil, only price liberalization and the standardization of prices to world market norms could eliminate hidden subsidies and boost the Russian energy and petrochemical sectors.

The ferrous metals sector was also suffering from post-Communist structural readjustment. By June 1992, production had dropped by 3–7 percent compared with May, and by 7–12 percent compared with the same period in 1991. This drop in production occurred because of an unsatisfactory supply of raw materials and spare parts. With the slowdown of the transportation and secondary metal markets, metal scrap was not being delivered in sufficient quantities to producers,[36] thus hurting manufacturing. Due to the monopolistic status of many producers, consumer prices in the metal sector were held high, with corresponding cuts in production and high profit margins. The commodity exchange trade in ferrous metals grew in 1992 compared to 1991. Small transactions in ferrous metal goods registered at 5–15 tons, while the highest pig iron transaction was 2,300 tons. Construction steel was most in demand.

In 1992, trade volume in exchanges for non-ferrous metals had risen 300–500 percent from 1991, with the highest volume transaction for aluminum (4,000 MT) dominating the market. The market was characterized by a high level of fluctuation in volume and prices. With exchanges often selling surplus or old inventories, manufacturers' prices often were higher than the markets.[37]

The agricultural commodities exchange of Russia (*Rosagrobirzha*) started functioning on February 19, 1991, in Moscow. Its opening met with great success. Cut off from Ukrainian sugar, Russian exchanges began selling this commodity sourced from Latin America, the Philippines, and Southeast Asia. Western-origin animal feedstocks were also sold, thus encouraging international involvement in the Russian agribusiness market. Items in greatest demand included small production lines for meat, butter, and cheese processing, transportation for the countryside, and some building materials. The agricultural exchange later opened branches in Samara, Smolensk, Saratov, Sakhalin, and Dagestan.[38]

Another new exchange, the All-Russian Real Estate Exchange (Moscow), announced sales of its shares in 1991. The cost of one share was 250,000 rubles. Both Russian and foreign firms could become members, and foreigners could buy shares in rubles acquired at currency auctions.

A real estate exchange intended to provide its clients with appraisal and information services, as well as property market forecasting. Capitalized at 100 million rubles, its projected transactions were expected to be in hard currency or barter due to ruble inconvertibility. Investment in its shares was expected to be highly profitable.[39]

WANING GOVERNMENT SUPPORT

Since the inception of market development, RTSB and MTB engaged in an increasingly adversarial relationship. As noted earlier, while RTSB emerged due to private initiatives, MTB was the creation of former Communist bureaucrats. At one point, RTSB tried to lobby the Supreme Soviet of the Russian Federation to impose registration taxes for all exchange transactions throughout Russia to be paid to RTSB, contending that transactions not registered in this exchange should be considered null and void. Thus RTSB attempted to monopolize all exchange trade throughout the Russian Republic, a move that contravened the declared policy of the Russian Supreme Soviet. After this ploy failed, RTSB tried to merge with MTB, but the latter refused.

While infighting between the fledgling exchanges intensified, a new danger appeared, this time from the all-Union government of conservative Chairman of the Council of Ministers Valentine Pavlov (the last USSR Prime Minister).

Representatives of the All-Russian Exchange Center had warned that independent Russian exchange markets might be jeopardized when the central government transformed regional supply authorities (Gossnabs) into commodities exchanges. Twenty new Gossnabs were expecting "most favored status" from the Kremlin, which would have effectively destroyed the independent exchanges.[40] Regional or republican Gossnabs were members of the Inter-Republic Commodities Exchange (*Mezhrespublikanskaya Tovarnaya Birzha*) in Moscow, and were to be supplied with goods by state-owned enterprises. State-run exchanges in the major cities were intended to specialize in the commodities of their respective regions, such as timber, oil, and so on. The Gossnab representatives, in a last ditch attempt to "jump over the abyss in three steps," as the Russian saying goes, began establishing contacts with the Chicago Board of Trade, apparently planning an international debut.

Representatives of the independent exchanges were highly skeptical about the performance potential of former government bureaucrats as free marketeers. They pointed out that brokers would work with those exchanges that offered maximum freedom and incentive. "It is unlikely," said V. Nikolayev, "that the Gossnab will become a champion of free trade. But we welcome any competition. So far the development of the Gossnab market system proved to be slow."[41]

POST-SOCIALIST MARKET INSTITUTIONS

According to Russian analysts, commodities exchanges played an important role for both state and alternative economic structures as a distribution channel and a price-setting mechanism. With the collapse of the state-run distribution system, most commodities transactions were executed not by exchanges but rather directly between the supplying and buying agents of individual enterprises or in all-Union and regional trade fairs (*yarmarki*). Their yearly sales volume was over 170 billion rubles. While a huge barter economy began to develop, this trading activity still did not address needs for a short-term transaction forum and lacked the operational information necessary to effect continuous and responsive price formation.

To ensure thriving regional exchanges, the Soviet Union and Russia had to cope with the lack of appropriate legislation, a trained corps of securities and trade lawyers and accountants and other specialists necessary for the successful functioning of Western-style markets. Simpler commodities markets, requiring a less developed business infrastructure and enjoying a more highly visible (though less politically controversial) role due to the severe distribution bottlenecks they sought to circumvent, had a better chance of success than the stock markets.[42]

Exchange markets were subject to few government controls, with laws on trade and agency (*torgovo-posrednicheskaya deyatel'nost*) being the only legal foundation for regulation. As the market developed, more specific regulation was required, but economists warned that their government was traditionally prone to overregulation up to the point of choking. They emphasized a gradual strategy of building markets to a level where they would replace the old system. "Before one builds the Empire State Building, one learns how to build a wooden hut," maintained professor Anatoliy Zhuplev, a Moscow marketization expert. To facilitate this process, it was necessary to limit the categories of goods sold and to develop universal contract forms clearly specifying the rights and liabilities of the exchanges and their clients.[43]

The need for self-regulation, protection of buyers' and sellers' rights, delineation of liabilities, and standardization of contracts was understood by the parties involved. Russian traders attempted to follow the Anglo-Saxon path and regulate the exchanges themselves, as opposed to the German model where the state is deeply involved in regulation. This was laudable in view of the Soviet track record, which had been skewed toward overregulation of independent enterprise. As in other parts of the world, Soviet exchange operators would have preferred the do-it-yourself approach, as well as cooperative, rather than *dirigiste* initiatives from the government.

In an attempt to develop internal arbitration guidelines, the Congress of Exchanges supported the creation of Model Rules of Arbitration, the establishment of an arbitral court, and the planning of an arbitral appellate forum. Model contracts, especially important in interexchange and interrepublic trade, were written and distributed to members. The Congress also coordinated legal research to facilitate functioning of the exchanges.[44]

BARTER

When the exchanges opened in 1991, the demand was high for computers, consumer electronics, raw materials, autos, and chemicals. The RTSB emerged as the biggest exchange, implementing up to 116 transactions daily, with the highest daily sales volume in February 1991 at 54 million rubles.

A major deficiency of the emerging Soviet commodities market was the lack of on-line, real-time information systems to serve as a price-setting mechanism among various regional exchanges. To overcome this deficiency, RTSB planned to invest in two satellites manufactured by the Soviet military-industrial complex (which was desperately seeking civilian customers) to furnish this communications infrastructure. Meanwhile, prices in different exchanges may have fluctuated by more than 100 percent, providing great potential for personal enrichment. Thus, high-quality red brick in Nikolayev sold for 161 rubles/thousand, whereas in Moscow lower quality silicate brick sold for 200 rubles/thousand. Similarly, a cubic meter of lumber (in January 1991 at a black market price of 400 rubles) sold at MTB for 250 rubles, and at the RTSB for even less. Ironically, in this emerging market the estimate of barter equivalents, as in the case of the brokers' commissions, were often calculated using "state" prices.

While cash transactions were widespread, barter was common, especially involving autos, grain, sheet steel, and other commodities as a means of exchange. This pattern reflected the absence of established market prices, lack of confidence in the national currency, inflationary pressures, and widespread shortages. For example, in 1991, 22 tons of beef or 600 tons of grain were exchanged for a UAZ four-wheel drive car, or a VAZ-Niva; a Volga GAZ-24 was swapped for 800 tons of grain, while a KAMAZ truck was bartered for 1,000 tons.[45] The monetary value of the transactions for the purpose of commissions estimates was calculated in state prices, since they were stable and better understood than the constantly changing market prices. According to Nikolayev, as the economic crisis deepened, the use of short-term barter also grew.

Trade was not restricted solely to barter. Soviet and foreign enterprises also offered their equipment and commodities for convertible currency, including food processing equipment, autos, heavy machinery, grain, dried fruit, leather, and pelts. Hard currency was available to Soviet export enterprises that were allowed to keep some of their hard currency revenues. Use of convertible currencies increased as Soviet and foreign firms attained access to the Soviet State Bank currency auctions, and eventually to the Moscow International Currency Exchange (*Moskovskaya Mezhdunarodnaya Valyutnaya Birzha*).

BUSINESS ETHICS

According to a leading Russian observer of commodities exchanges, unreliability in business deals was then and remains today the single most distressing disincentive for transacting business at the exchanges. While sellers in 95 percent of the sale transactions demand upfront payment (*predoplata*), they do not deliver in 45–50 percent of the cases. Funds paid in advance are then returned belatedly, after a waiting period of up to three months, causing serious losses to buyers, especially under conditions of hyperinflation and providing unfair advantages to sellers.[46]

An outstanding weakness of the Soviet exchanges was and is the high volume of transactions concluded using the facilities of the institutions but not reported to them. This tendency denies the exchanges not only revenue, but *raison d'etre*. The brokers and administrations of MTB and RTSB were aware of this negative trend and implemented self-policing measures early on, such as conducting anonymous transactions, in an attempt to discourage it.[47]

Another drawback faced by the commodities markets was and remains the lack of specialization and focus, with one institution handling everything from sneakers to grain or computers. In essence, many of the first exchanges were giant wholesale operations, not Western-style commodity exchanges. According to Soviet specialists, this "infantile disorder" will eventually be overcome by increasing regional specialization, or through the emergence of specialized brokerage houses. Some justify the existence of "universal" exchanges as inevitable due to commodity shortages. These analysts argue that in the future the exchanges will evolve into industry-specific trade houses, specializing in construction materials, autos, office supplies, and so on.[48]

For the Soviet commodities exchanges to reach Western levels of activity, they needed to sign up at last 500 brokerage firms each. The only one faintly approaching this level in 1991 was RTSB, with approximately 300 brokers. MTB, as of March 1991, had only about 30. Within the following year, several markets achieved viability. Soviet-Russian experience is that with each broker firm signing in, the volume of trade activity grows as brokers bring in their connections and clientele.

The exchanges strived to become respectable, Western-style institutions. Their spokespersons, as well as independent observers, rejected claims that commodities exchanges were havens for *spekul'anty* (profiteers or speculators), contending that it was high time to understand that trade and commercial agencies are acceptable and perform socially useful activities. This was an important psychological breakthrough in a country where, until the 1960s, such "middlemen" were routinely shot, and "economic crimes" were treated with the same severity as high treason.[49] Only under Gorbachev was the death penalty for "economic crimes" finally dropped. State-run enterprises increasingly participated in trade on independent exchanges, with transaction volumes in the tens of millions of rubles. On the other hand, it was pointed out that the exchanges, as well as law enforcement organizations, had to take measures to prevent the sale of stolen goods or use of the exchanges as conduits for the illegal transfer of weapons, strategic raw materials, and nuclear technology.[50]

CONCLUDING REMARKS

Massive antimarket government intervention, anticipated by brokers in 1991, almost materialized during the August coup, when Konstantin Borovoy, founder of the RTSB, called for a Union-wide exchanges strike. But even when the government crackdown failed to materialize, the commodities exchanges did not become leading market institutions or "engines" of market transformation as other components of the market, primarily private property and appropriate legal and accounting systems, were still missing. They succeeded, nonetheless, in filling a necessary and useful economic niche, overcoming supply bottlenecks and accessing foreign markets on behalf of the nascent private sector in spite of the government bureaucracy.

Certainly, no single institution is capable of transforming an economy alone. Other building blocks of the market, such as investment and commercial banking, stock exchanges, a functioning system of business

and commercial law, a reliable court system, and a functioning entrepreneurial class, are indispensable to ensure the successful transition
from a centrally planned economy, and are in the process of being developed in Russia.[51]

Diversified commodity exchanges were the harbingers of the
market in Russia, and in a sense fell victim to their own success. As
enterprises realized their independence from the Gosplan-Gossnab
tutelage, they started to transact business in finished goods with each
other, bypassing the exchanges. The economic logic had dictated that
the exchanges will concentrate on standardized commodities only, as
their function had been in the West all along.

Despite their potential, the exchanges did not develop into market
distribution channels and price setting tools immediately following the
disintegration of the Soviet Union. They did serve as valuable "agents
of change" in the Soviet business world, since individuals who learned
from Western experience began to disseminate capitalist business practices beyond the world of the commodities markets themselves. The
exchanges became a breeding ground for fledgling Russian capitalists,
spawning financial markets, and commercial banking networks.

The development of Soviet commodities markets required sur-
mounting several formidable obstacles. First was the lack of market
know-how, legal frameworks, and the electronic hardware and software
needed to implement real-time exchange operations. These disadvantages created a demand for Western goods and expertise in the telecommunications, management, and financial sectors.[52] Second, the absence
of business ethics required for the successful functioning of such a complex market structure impeded the emergence of trusted and reliable
institutions. Third, a multi-billion ruble mechanism capable of sup-
planting Gossnab and handling large volumes of interrepublican and
international commerce was needed. Dealing in second-hand vehicles
and personal computers was not enough. Fourth, the exchanges failed
to create stocks of standardized goods and raw materials that could be
supplied to the customer if the seller did not deliver, thus undermining
their own reliability. Finally, the overall problem of ruble inconvertibility and government overregulation of licensing procedures prevented
Western businesses from participating in this revolutionary market
development.[53]

The August 1991 putsch undermined any chances that the USSR's
bureaucracy might have had to transform government trade and supply structures into Westernized market institutions gradually. The
Chinese experience indicates that such a transformation is, as a rule,
inefficient and requires tight government control and a lengthy time
frame. In order to develop effective market institutions in a formerly
centrally planned economy, one has to build from the bottom up and
around the government bureaucracy, not attempt to transform it. The
most competitive among the bureaucrats will see personal advantages

in the market structures and later find their place in these new commercial organizations, as occurred in the case of MTB. However, the stifling institutional culture of Communist bureaucracy needs to be rejected just as one would condemn a decrepit building.

In 1991, the Soviet centrally planned economy was in too much disrepair to be salvaged and could not proceed along the lines of Deng's China. The August 1991 coup had discredited the all-Union economic structures, which were rejected by the republics. Reformers, led by Yegor Gaidar, Boris Fedorov, and others came to power in Moscow aiming at total destruction of the old Communist distribution systems and creating the market from scratch. The old bureaucrats had a choice: to accept the reform (or at least pay lip service to it in the state sector), or to get out of the way.

In the transitional post-Communist economy, the commodities exchanges alone are not a panacea. However, as Russia develops its other market institutions, its civil law, and its legal foundations of private property, the exchanges will become what they are in the developed West — pillars of the market in which standardized commodities and not consumer goods or factory rejects are traded. In addition, the exchanges will be Russian "windows to the world," as by the early twenty-first century trade in Russian natural resources will become fully integrated into the global commercial flows.

NOTES

1. Personal interview with Vyacheslav A. Nikoayev, Director of Training, RTSB, February 1991.

2. Ibid.

3. *Protokol VI S'yezda Kongressa Birzh*, Dushanbe, June 20–21, 1992, p. 6, part 4.9. Unpublished.

4. In citation of Soviet and Russian sources in this chapter, most prices are given in rubles, despite rapidly fluctuating exchange rates. In 1992 alone, the ruble to dollar exchange rate plummeted 500 percent.

5. The exchange was later moved to the Polytechnical Institute in the center of Moscow.

6. Alexander Loktev, "Rossiyskaya birzha: s 26 yanvaria torgi budut yezhednevnimi, sovsem kak ran'she," *Commersant*, no. 4 (54) (1991): 7. As it turned out, the general export-import license was not granted as the Ministry of Foreign Trade retained control of the lucrative export trade.

7. Alexander Loktev, "Moskovskaya tovarnaya birzha otkryla postoyanniye torgi," *Commersant*, no. 3 (53) (1991): 10.

8. Alexander Loktev, "Vsled za klhebnymi korolyami na MTB prishli neftiyaniye. I ne tol'ko otechestvenniye," *Commersant*, no. 7 (57) (1991): 7.

9. "Finansovye Rynki," *Business Fact*, no. 163 (28 August 1992): 2.

10. *Protokol VI S'yezda Kongressa Birzh*, 1992, p. 13 (Protocol of the Sixth Congress of Exchanges), Moscow, unpublished.

11. Telecommunications problems for international exchanges trade were theoretically resolved and solutions presented by the company TEKOS. See *Poyasnitel'naya zapiska: Sistema Telekommunikatsii i obrabotki soobshchenii*

TEKOS, unpublished, July 1992 (Explanatory note: System of Telecommunications and message processing TEKOS), Moscow, unpublished (internal memo of Congress of Exchanges).

12.   *Programma deyatel' nosti Kongressa Birzh ot 1 iyl'a 1992*, pp. 1–2. Moscow, Congress of Exchanges, 1992. The program was published as an internal Congress document. The program included exchanges of information, maintenance of data bases, public relations with Congress, lobbying efforts, development of international trade protocols, education and training.

13.   *Protokol VI S'yezda Kongressa Birzh*, p. 12.

14.   *Polozheniye na rynke posrednicheskikh uslug v aprele 1992 (po rezul'tatam oprosa rukovoditeley brokerskikh firm*, Moscow Economic News Agency, 1992.

15.   "Tovarnye birzhi: proydennyi put 'i dal'neysheye razvitiye," *Business Pilot*, no. 1 (August 1992): 4 (hereafter "Tovarnye birzhi").

16.   "Zapolarnye birzheviki nachinayut torgi i prizyvayut ob'yedinyat'sa," *Commersant*, no. 2 (52) (1991): 9.

17.   Evgeniy Bagayev, "Altayskaya tovarnaya birzha: my s brokerov mnogo ne voz'mem," *Commersant*, no. 5 (55) (1991): 7.

18.   Valeriy Pesetzkiy, "Juzhnaya universal'naya byrzha operatziy ne nachala, no v sv'yzi uzhe vstupayet," *Commersant*, no. 5 (55) (1991): 7.

19.   *Commersant*, no. 5 (55) (1991): 7.

20.   "Birzhevye Novosti," *Commersant*, no. 8 (58) (1991): 5.

21.   *Protokol VI S'yezda Kongressa Birzh*, 1992, p. 10.

22.   Ibid., p. 11.

23.   Ibid., p. 13.

24.   "Technologiya MTKB — proyekt," *Protocols of the VI Congress of Exchanges*, July 9, 1992.

25.   *Protokol VI S'yezda Kongressa Birzh*, pp. 3–4.

26.   "Tovarnye birzhi," p. 4.

27.   Dimitrii Avkhimenko, "Birzhi nachinayut vneshneekonomicheskuyu deyatel'nost," *Business Pilot*, no. 1 (1992): 5.

28.   Alexander Loktev, "Na MTB budut prodavat'sya kredity," *Commersant*, no. 8 (58) (1991): 6.

29.   Pavel Andreev and Dimitrii Avkhimenko, "Rekford Fevralya — 116 sdelok v den," *Commersant*, no. 9 (59) (1991): 25.

30.   Nellie Shmakova, "MMFB nachala prodavat' brokerskiye mesta," *Commersant*, no. 9 (59) (1991): 7.

31.   Graciela Chichilnisky and Geoffrey Head, "The Opportunities in U.S.-Soviet Aid," *New York Times*, March 24, 1991, p. F9.

32.   *Protokol VI Kongressa Birzh*, 11.

33.   Andrey Koptyev, "V Leningrade poyavilas' fondovaya birzha," *Commersant*, no. 9 (59) (1991): 8.

34.   "Energy Carrier Markets," *Commercial Bulletin* (Moscow: Economic News Agency), no. 5 (March 1992): 2–3.

35.   Ibid., p. 3.

36.   "Birzhevoy rynok metallov," *Kommercheskii Bulletin* (Moscow: Agenstvo Ekonomicheskikh Novostey), No. 15 (August 1992): 1.

37.   Ibid., p. 5.

38.   Alexander Loktev, "Perviye torgi na rosagrobirzhe proshli uspeshno," *Commersant*, no. 8 (58) (1991): 6.

39.   Alexander Loktev, "Verossiyskaya birzha nedvizhimosti nachala prodazhu sovoikh aktzi," *Commersant*, no. 4 (54) (1991): 7.

40.   Alexander Loktev, "RTSB protiv MTB: Khronika boyevikh deystviy," *Commersant*, no. 9 (59) (1991): 9.

41.   Personal interview with Nikolayev, October 1991.

42.   Pavel Astakhov, "Birzhevaya torgovlya: defitzit prodavtzov i pokupateley," *Commersant*, no. 5 (55) (1991): 7.

43.   Personal interview with Nikolayev and Anatoli V. Zhuplev, department head, Moscow Personnel Center, Mosgorispolkom, a Soviet marketization expert, April 1991.

44.   *Protokol VI Kongressa Birzh*, p. 10.

45.   Pavel Andreev and Dimitri Avkhimenko, "Rekord Fevralya — 116 sdelok v den," *Commersant*, no. 9 (59) (1991): 24 (hereafter "Rekord Fevralya").

46.   Personal interview with Dimitrii Avkhimenko, Moscow, August 1992.

47.   Andreev and Avkhimenko, "Rekord Fevralya," p. 24.

48.   "Tovarnye birzhi," p. 4.

49.   Witness how far the evolution of business and political culture has progressed in post-Communist Russia: the commodity exchanges have already produced their businessmen-politicians, or a Russian version of Ross Perot. Konstantin N. Borovoy, the founder of RTSB, launched the militantly pro-free market Party of Economic Freedom, which was promoted at the sixth convention of the Congress Commodities Exchanges. Borovoy also serves as the vice-president of the Congress. Among the central players in the new party is the famous human rights activist and former dissident Vladimir Bukovsky.

50.   Personal interview with Nikolayev and Zhuplev, April 1991.

51.   For an interesting account of the problems experienced by an economy executing a more wholehearted transition to a free market, specifically, Poland, see Janusz A. Ordover, "International Perspective: Poland: Economy in Transition," *Business Economics*, vol. 26 (January 1991).

52.   John A. Quelch, Erich Joachimstaler and Jose Luis Nueno, "After the Wall: Marketing Guidelines for Eastern Europe," *Sloan Management Review*, vol. 33 (Winter 1991): 83–85.

53.   This problem might have been solved with the opening of currency auctions and eventually a currency exchange market at the State Bank of the USSR in 1991.

7

Monsanto's Operations in the Former Soviet Union: A Case Study

Paula M. Ross

Monsanto Company is a multinational corporation headquartered in St. Louis, Missouri, established in 1901 by John F. Queeny. From Monsanto Chemical Works, it expanded a producer of saccharin to Monsanto Company, a multibillion dollar corporation with a diverse portfolio of value-added products.[1] Chemicals and pharmaceuticals are two of Monsanto's larger, trade-positive industries, but the company makes and markets agricultural products; performance materials, including synthetic fibers, plastics, and specialty chemicals; food products, including NutraSweet brand low-calorie table top sweeteners. Monsanto is a global operation with major manufacturing plants in 10 countries; smaller plants in over 12 countries; sales offices or representatives in 65 nations; and customers in over 120 countries.[2] International business has been a key component of the company's strategy for over 50 years.

Monsanto became involved with the Soviet Union in the 1950s. The Soviet government was interested in purchasing a rubber chemical made by Monsanto for use in tire production, in order to increase vulcanization.[3] After contract talks were concluded, Monsanto's proposal for chemical sales was accepted and business began. The sale of rubber chemicals, however, was just the first building block in Monsanto's relationship with the USSR. In the four decades that followed this initial contact, Monsanto was able to expand its Soviet business relations and become a prominent feature of the former Soviet Union's (FSU) marketplace.

BUSINESS STRUCTURE

Monsanto diversified from a supplier of rubber chemicals, through the years, by "expanding [its] product mix to include other chemical products (plastics, specialty chemicals and resins) as well as agricultural herbicides and pharmaceuticals."[4] Business operations went so well that a Moscow sales office was established in 1980.[5] In 1982, Soyuchimexport, the Soviet Union's Chemical Trade Agency, signed an agreement with Monsanto Europe S.A., Monsanto's Belgian subsidiary, that covered the remainder of the then current Soviet five-year plan, which ran through 1985.[6] The pact called for overall trade among the participants to reach $300 million. Monsanto was to supply herbicides and resins to the Soviets, who in return would, according to the Tass news agency, "organize delivery from the U.S.S.R. of ammonia, methanol, aniline, and organic chemicals."[7]

TECHNOLOGY

In addition to sales of company products, Monsanto was approached by the Soviet government officials in search of advanced technology. They were interested in buying a Monsanto package (all of the relevant technology) for the operations and management of several of their manufacturing plants. Monsanto responded favorably. For startup jobs, Monsanto would send a team of technical experts to the plant site, where they would work until the factory was up and operational.[8]

Other arrangements were concluded whereby Monsanto helped the Soviets create new technologies and enter into new markets. One contract had originally been for phosphate. However, with Monsanto aid and know-how, the Soviets were able to both produce the phosphorus and use a spin-off product, diflourinated phosphate, to make chicken feed.[9] A license agreement was signed in 1974; and in 1980, Monsanto assisted C. E. Lummus with the startup of a acetic acid plant in Ukraine.[10] In addition, Monsanto helped two local Soviet phosphate facilities upgrade their physical plants: one from an environmental and the other from a quality standpoint.[11]

At this time, Monsanto does not have any manufacturing plants of its own in the FSU, but the company has several technology agreements. In these operations, Monsanto works to develop new technologies or improve upon existing ones. One such arrangement, pertaining to polycrystalline diamond and diamond-like coatings, is a three-part interfacing operation involving the National Technological Association, a private technological group from a Soviet university, and Diamonex, a new Monsanto subsidiary. Monsanto was involved in the research of proprietary technology in polymers and superhard surface coatings, and was looking for pockets of technology to aid in the development of diamond-like coatings. Monsanto had already established individual relationships with the two Soviet groups, but needed to create an initiative for the companies to work together. They were also in need of a manufacturer to produce the new product. For that reason, Diamonex, at the time a private venture capital firm, was added. Monsanto technology executives said, "Monsanto put the deal together, invested in a lot of the technology, and provided capital to the labs conducting the research." Monsanto also purchased Diamonex — transferring all Monsanto employees involved with the operation to Diamonex, letting Diamonex take over the management of the technical agreement between Monsanto and the Soviets, and placing responsibility for the entire project in the hands of the Diamonex managers. The project has so far been successful. Diamond-like coatings are used to provide a protective shield for optical devices like sunglasses and grocery store bar code scanners, and military operations. The polycrystalline diamonds are highly efficient thermal conductors and are increasingly being used by producers of electronic equipment to remove heat from miniaturized components.[12]

AGRICULTURE

For some time, Monsanto has been one of the world's leading producers of agrochemicals. This success was not lost on the Soviet Union. Sales of Monsanto's Roundup herbicide have been increasing since the late 1970s.[13] Monsanto has also been a part of the Soviet farming system since the 1980s, with demonstration farms in Russian and many Ukrainian oblasts.[14]

Trial farms and more direct contact with Soviet agriculturalists occurred because of democratization policies pursued in the late 1980s under Gorbachev. More direct contact with Soviet farmers not only allowed Monsanto to continue to import their agricultural technology to the FSU, but also enabled employees to train Soviet workers in proper product use.[15] By receiving Monsanto technology and a regular flow of information, the Soviets were able to increase their crop yields and raise farm production closer to world standards.

One of Monsanto's largest agricultural operations is located in Sumy, Ukraine.[16] In 1989, Monsanto and the State Agrochemical Association (Agrochim) initiated a project, the Sumy Agrocenter, that was to introduce agrochemistry, advanced farming technology, and progressive methods and systems of farming to Soviet farmers in order to achieve "high and stable yields."[17] Larger than other demonstration farms, Sumy was to encompass an area of 18,000 hectares. Agrochim, Monsanto and the local distributor, Selkhozimia, agreed that the cooperative program would involve the establishment of an Agrocenter similar to those in the United States. Its function would be to supply seeds, agrochemicals, and applications equipment, and also to train Soviet personnel in successful Western systems and techniques. The 18,000 hectares was divided into eight separate farms, and Monsanto's degree of involvement differed with each. For some farms, the Agrocenter was just a supplier, but for others, Monsanto acted as a crop manager, recommending what seeds to use, when to plant, or what herbicides to spray. In addition, on some farms, Monsanto provided incentives to farmers to use new technology and to increase the spray capacity of acreage.

The agreed upon target was an increase in crop yield by 15–20 percent. As a result of the cooperative program, Sumy farms increased their yields by as much as 63 percent. Because the targets were surpassed by such great margins, the area under the project's aegis was quickly expanded. The area Sumy now encompasses is 250,000 acres. The Sumy, Ukraine Agrocenter was so successful that Monsanto initiated a similar project (30,000 acres) in Dzhambul, Kazakhstan, and according to Brad Hill, "the concept has been so successful that [Monsanto] is rolling out smaller Agrocenters into most of the oblasts in Russia and Ukraine, [and] in Kazakhstan, [Monsanto] plans to roll out three new Agrocenters in the first quarter of 1993, each approximately 250,000 acres."[18]

RESEARCH AND DEVELOPMENT

According to Hill, "[Monsanto] has four different research and development collaborations that have been active for several years." The areas of research include plant genetics, polymer chemistry, superhard coatings, and pharmaceuticals.[19]

Pharmaceuticals, made by Monsanto's subsidiary G. D. Searle, were first seen as a new market prospect in the late 1980s, and have since grown steadily. Hill said, "[Monsanto] has benefitted from its R&D collaborations. Soviet science is very good in 'discovery' and Monsanto has helped to commercialize a new product and at least one new drug to date."

COMMUNICATIONS

Communications for any company in the FSU is difficult. However, the Monsanto Company took steps to ensure open lines of communication.

Monsanto dedicated international lines incorporated into their phone system. These business lines receive top priority for calls exiting the FSU. A telex system has also been in use for some time even though the methods are, according to James R. Savage, director of Technology, License and Acquisitions (Advanced Performance Materials), becoming outdated. Through its computer system, Monsanto also has e-mail. In addition to traditional methods of communications, Monsanto has a private mail pouch delivered from its Brussels office to its Moscow office every day. Finally, to ensure the flow of information among company personnel, technical meetings are held four times a year.[20]

Unfortunately, good communication lines do not extend beyond major cities, so when employees are posted to outlying regions for start-up purposes, operations can experience slowdowns. Because Monsanto has no way to improve existing communications, it tries its best to cope with these problems, said Mr. Savage, by sending good people in for the job, trying to stay in touch, depending on the people to handle any complications, and "treating the folks well when they return home."

EMPLOYEES

When the Moscow sales office opened in 1980, it was staffed with both Westerners and Soviets. Western employees were transferred to the USSR, but Monsanto had to hire its Soviet employees on a temporary basis from the Ministry of Foreign Trade.[21] Monsanto paid the ministry in dollars, but the ministry paid their workers in rubles, a big source of profit for the ministry.[22]

In 1989, Monsanto's employment system changed. It still employed both Western and Soviet workers, but unlike the temporary workers (that is, secretaries) that were hired from a central service organization, Monsanto could hire permanent Muscovite workers directly.[23] On January 3, 1989, Monsanto ran a small help-wanted ad for its Moscow office in the Soviet daily newspaper, *Izvestia*.[24] Michael A. Petrilli, International Sales Director (Fibers Division), said the ad "was just another way to advertise the job." At the same time, Muscovites employed by Monsanto found that their paychecks were different. Like their Western peers, Muscovites are Monsanto employees, not state workers, and they were paid in a combination of dollars and rubles with approximately 80 percent of the pay being in dollars.[25]

In addition to the staff in the Moscow office, Monsanto has a number of scientists working out of Moscow laboratories.[26] Through the Moscow office, an account has been set up that can provide U.S. dollars in cash for the lab employees to take care of financial problems they may have.[27]

The people Monsanto employs in the FSU may not always understand Western business, but the employees are treated like Monsanto employees worldwide. They go through intensive training sessions and are expected to be just as productive as elsewhere. "They may not understand Western reasoning or our system of accounting," said Robert A. Westoby, director of International Cash Management and Foreign Exchange, "but they are hard workers."

PAST CHANNELS OF OPERATIONS

The first business deals conducted between Monsanto and the USSR were done in conjunction with a Moscow foreign trade organization or trade company. Monsanto would channel its products and all other information through the trade company, which would relay the information to the appropriate Soviet ministry. After a few years, however, business was successful enough that Monsanto was able to drop the Moscow trade company and deal directly with the ministry. This is not to say that doing business with the Soviets was any less structured. The bureaucratic system of the Soviet government was extensive in and of itself.

All foreign (Western) products had to be channeled through *Soyuzkhimeksport*, the Soviet foreign trade association.[28] Soyuzkhimeksport was then subdivided into different sectors and departments. Therefore, for the sale of the rubber chemical used in tire production, Monsanto would have sold the product from their European headquarters in Brussels, Belgium, to the Ministry of Foreign Trade. The product would then have been processed through the Ministry of Transportation, the Ministry of Chemicals, the Ministry of Automotives, and the Agency for Tires.[29]

Although the Soviet system provided a framework for business within the country, the structure of that system created major inefficiencies. At the time Western businesses, Monsanto included, were not allowed direct contact with Soviet business. Monsanto would make contact with the low man at the ministry, who would send information up through the hierarchy, a tedious and time consuming process. To complete a deal, Monsanto representatives would work with a Ministry of Trade representative, who knew only that an order required fulfillment. For the person using the product, there was no direct transfer of information about the product or its uses. However, all that Monsanto was required to do was to provide the product and replace it if needed.

Even though the Soviet system was inefficient, the bureaucracy served as a catalyst for opportunity for Monsanto. According to Petrilli, Monsanto was able to increase trade with the Soviet Union by networking in the ministries. Because consistent business was conducted with one minister, a familiarity developed with other agents. By networking, Monsanto representatives could introduce new products and expand their business in the Soviet Union.[30]

PRESENT OPERATIONS

With democratization came more direct contact with Soviet businessmen and managers. Monsanto was no longer restricted to sales and repairs. Its employees could be hired as managers for startup projects at Soviet plant sites, and as consultants they would travel to farms and factories to train Soviet workers on the use of company products.[31]

Now, the identification of appropriate channels depends on the industries with which Monsanto is doing business.[32] Government ministers are no longer needed in many areas. Businessmen and factory managers are making many of their own decisions about purchasing, financing, and selling. However, some industries have remained with or returned to a more central structure at the discretion of factory managers.

Two examples of different operating channels are seen in Monsanto's transfer of technology and the company's agricultural education of Soviet farmers. Because of privatization in the agricultural industry, Monsanto employees were allowed to travel to farms, introduce products, and exchange information directly with farmers. They were also allowed to create demonstration farms and act as operations managers.

In the area of technology transfer, Monsanto works with a consultant, chosen by the Soviets. A consortium is created and a technical collaboration takes place between the members of the group: Monsanto, the consultant, and *Techmishimport*, the Russian ministry.[33] Thus, according to Brad Hill, "while Monsanto is cultivating new contacts, old relationships are being maintained in an effort to sustain effectiveness."

The collapse of the FSU has also created adverse effects on Monsanto's business there. There is no longer a clear-cut hierarchy of authority. No one is always sure who is in charge at the factory level.

Legal responsibility has not been a problem or stumbling block; Monsanto does business with whoever claims to have responsibility. Contracts already in place, instead of being rewritten under the new circumstances, are being extended, although Monsanto cannot be sure what will happen day-to-day because of the evolving Soviet laws.[34]

To ensure product delivery, Monsanto has hired a man based in Kiev who is in charge of getting Monsanto's products shipped out to their final destinations within a reasonable amount of time. If Monsanto relied on traditional channels and shipped its products directly to Scheremetyevo Airport, cargo could sit in holding areas for several months.[35]

EXTERNAL ISSUES

"The stagnant Soviet economy has had a profoundly negative effect on Monsanto's business," commented Hill. Countertrade has become the primary method of conducting business because lack of hard currency and ruble inconvertibility make anything else difficult. Loans and insurance are nearly impossible to receive and the banking system is extremely unstable.

FINANCES

When trade relations were first established between Monsanto and the Soviet Union all products were paid for with hard currency.[36] Petrilli described the Soviets as being extremely conservative and credit worthy. Bills were paid on time. "If there was no money, there was no purchase, and therefore no debt," said Petrilli. To gain the monetary base needed for trade, the Soviets would export oil, gas, other raw materials, chemicals, fertilizers, and ammonia to the West. Hard currency received was held on a centralized basis and then used to pay for the import of Western materials, including Monsanto products. Aside from their access to hard currency, the Soviets also had enormous gold reserves to back their purchases.

In the late 1980s, with the fall of oil and gas prices and the increasing inefficiency of Soviet oil production, problems mounted. Payments could not be met with hard currency, so Monsanto and the Soviet government established a barter system. Monsanto would agree to sell its products and simultaneously buy a Soviet product, thereby covering the cost of its product sales. Upon receiving the Soviet product, Monsanto would either use it as a raw material or turn around and sell it to consumers in Western Europe. Commodity chemicals, ammonia, and rubber were first used by the Soviets as countertrade items. Ammonia was used by Monsanto as a raw material for the production of other goods.[37]

According to Westoby, 1991 was when the situation began to noticeably deteriorate. Prior to then, Monsanto's growth curve for net sales had reached $150 million and was expected to keep rising up to the $200 million mark. But with the central government disintegration, coupled with diminished gold reserves, ruble inconvertibility, and crisis in the Soviet banking system, Monsanto's growth curve flattened out.[38]

Now, for Monsanto, a large percentage of business in the FSU is done in countertrade. Saflex interlayer, a plastic for laminated safety glass used in automobile windshields and other glazing processes, is one product that is still sold to the Russians for hard currency. This is because automobile exports to East and West Europe are still a major source of hard currency for the Russians, and they need Saflex for the production of their car windshields. Saflex is a required product and the Soviets will pay for it with hard currency.[39]

Countertrade is generally not a profitable enterprise. Bartering, from the Soviet side, is usually conducted with low profit, low quality products that Monsanto does not use. If it cannot use other Soviet products, then it endures the added cost of finding a prospective buyer for the materials. This all needs to be determined prior to signing any contracts. Additionally, as Soviet countertrade experts are aware, there is no guarantee the Soviets have not already sold the product to five other buyers. If this occurs, Monsanto becomes involved in a dispute over rightful ownership of materials.[40]

Westoby describes countertrade as a "messy business," but as long as Monsanto can maintain the price margin over that of the Russian export prices and continue to find consumers for Soviet products, the company will not lose money on the countertrade deals. One requirement is that Monsanto will only sell higher margin products for countertrade transactions.[41]

RUBLE CONVERTIBILITY

"Ruble convertibility is not a problem," said Westoby. The problem of getting financing for the FSU, he said, "lies in the fact that banks that had provided trade financing in the past are now saying no because too many claims are being made." One state run insurance company operating out of Brussels provides insurance policies to corporations shipping products around the world from Belgium. In July 1992, following the collapse of Vneshekonombank, claims on Soviet insurance policies escalated to the tens of millions. This company had to close its doors, and new business insurance for sales to the FSU practically came to a halt.

ExImBank also offers low-rate loans and insurance policies for business ventures in Russia and Ukraine, but according to Hill, "the Newly Independent State (NIS) banks have only lately been willing to offer a sufficient level of guarantee to satisfy ExIm and consequently this channel has not yet been useful."

Recently, ExImBank and other insurance issuers have softened policies concerning business in the FSU. One insurer told companies already having exposure in the FSU that if they receive overdue payments for products, the ceiling on their current insurance will be honored, and if payments are made, it will consider covering new business up to the ceiling in the FSU. Monsanto has six insurance applications in review by ExImBank.[42]

TRADE BARRIERS

According to Westoby, the neglect of intellectual property rights and potential for patent stealing pose a threat to Monsanto's trade with the FSU. One case occurred in 1980. The Moscow Institute for Plant Protection Chemicals appealed to the Soviet State Committee on Patents and Inventions to overturn Monsanto's rights for the herbicide *Roundup* — and won a favorable ruling. They alleged Monsanto's formula was too general to claim patent protection. Monsanto sent attorneys to Moscow and appealed in three separate hearings before the State Committee on Science and Technology, which manages scientific cooperation agreements granting Western companies the right to sell in the Soviet Union. After several months delay, Monsanto was informed of a favorable decision that confirmed the validity of the company's patent position in the USSR.[43] "The threat of patent stealing, or the stealing of information on a product's composition," said Westoby, "makes Monsanto wary about introducing priority products into the Soviet marketplace, and kept Monsanto from attempting to test or develop new products within the Soviet pharmaceuticals sector."

Patent protection-related problems began soon after the Carter Administration placed restrictions on Soviet trade. Because of the embargo, Monsanto was delayed in assisting the startup of a small organic chemicals plant in Uzbekistan, and was also forced to scrap a five-year agreement to supply silicon wafers for semiconductor manufacture.[44]

"The Soviets simply decided to strike back," said one businessman, accusing them of "waging a trade war against Monsanto to punish the company for cutting off previous projects." *Roundup* was caught in the middle of the dispute. C. E. Anagnostopoulos, retired vice-president and managing director (Europe-Africa) said the favorable ruling on the *Roundup* patent meant "the Soviets had evidenced a clear understanding that a change in government export policy may adversely impact a business transaction and that such events are beyond the control of individual companies."

As emphasized by the trade embargo imposed under President Carter, another barrier to trade between Monsanto and the FSU is cumbersome U.S. policy. For technology transfer to the FSU, Savage points out, "the U.S. government requires a set of documents be filled out describing the products, their uses, and possible alternate uses." Monsanto's products usually fall within the guidelines for acceptable exports to the USSR. However, occasionally the United States has stepped in and halted Monsanto's export operations, for example, polymer molecules, when they cited strategic reasons claiming that Monsanto's chemical materials can be used in the production of defense industry weapons.[45]

FUTURE PROSPECTS

The FSU for Monsanto represents a huge market (285 million plus consumers), with pent up demand, vast natural resources, and a well educated work force. According to Hill, "a market such as this provides Monsanto an opportunity to significantly increase our sales without having to invent new molecules or products, and there aren't a lot of markets such as this left to fuel the growth that companies need to thrive."

Besides Russia, Monsanto is actively pursuing business in Ukraine, Belarus, Kazakhstan, and Uzbekistan. According to Hill, Monsanto's agrochemicals are sold in each of these countries. Chemical products are sold primarily to Russia, Ukraine, and Belarus. Pharmaceuticals are sold primarily in Russia. Some sales are also made to the Baltic countries and Moldavia.

Sales offices were established in 1992 in Riga, Latvia; Vilnius, Lithuania; Minsk, Belarus; Kiev, Ukraine; and Alma-Ata, Kazakhstan. Two of the largest operations occurring in the NIS are Agrocenters in Sumy, Ukraine, and Dzhambul, Kazakhstan. Ukraine and Belarus have been designated top priority for defense conversion ventures. Also, Hill observed that although there are no immediate prospects, Monsanto hopes to develop business in Georgia, Armenia, and other former republics as they stabilize.

The former Soviet republics are now independent states, but Monsanto conducts business the same in these nations as in Russia. All deals, despite their origin, are done in either dollars, Belgian francs, Deutsch marks, or through countertrade.[46]

Future ventures for Monsanto will focus on approvals and registered sales for new agrochemicals and new pharmaceuticals. Finding appropriate new ventures in defense industry conversion is a top priority for Russia, Belarus, and Ukraine. Several joint ventures are being negotiated in the agricultural, chemical, and pharmaceutical sectors.

Monsanto began to sell NutraSweet in the FSU in early 1993. "However, unlike our marketing strategy in Western countries where we sell NutraSweet as a low-calorie sweetener," said Brad Hill, "in the NIS we are positioning the product as a sugar substitute." Monsanto is very optimistic about the potential niche for NutraSweet because of sugar shortages and the large number of diabetics in the FSU.[47]

Specifically for agriculture, John Lewis described Monsanto's long-term strategy as the desire to help the FSU develop a more prosperous agricultural system enabling them to trade on world markets. It would like to supply the FSU with an alternative market for their products, something other than purely governmental sales. Incorporated into the desire to help the FSU become members of the world marketplace are the objectives of greater technological transfer of Monsanto's products and materials, increased facilitation and support for the buying of products to maximize greater opportunities, and the possibility of getting involved in other ventures beyond normal business.

The FSU is a priority for Monsanto in the long-term. As Hill states, "Monsanto's long-term strategy is to be a major supplier to the industries we serve in the NIS such that the NIS represents a significant level of Monsanto's business." While Monsanto is already deeply involved in many areas in the FSU, new ventures are being pursued that should add to the company's growth and profits. Monsanto's strategy, says Hill, "calls for appropriate investment and joint ventures when the economic situation becomes more stable and our global supply and demand balance requires new capacity."

CONCLUSIONS

For the rest of the 1990s, business will be off from 1991's level, even though Monsanto has held up better than most of its competitors. According to Hill, the business decline "shouldn't be surprising considering [Soviet] imports are down some 30%, production has dropped about 20% in each of the last two years, they are cutting back on expenditures for the military, and they are operating with a 35+% [rate of] inflation per month." Monsanto executives say sales are expected to remain off until the infrastructure of trade and the economy of Russia and the NIS are revitalized. However, even with sagging sales, Monsanto Company provides the international economic community with a successful model for business operations in the FSU.

Unlike firms who want a quick in-and-out, Monsanto has invested time and capital in the FSU. Instead of pulling up stakes now that the chips are down for the FSU economy, Monsanto has chosen to seek out prudent and selective new business opportunities and develop new operations.

Although problems are many, Monsanto tries to seek appropriate solutions. Business is conducted with whoever claims to be in charge. Countertrade has replaced hard currency as a method of payment. A German bank with a Moscow branch is being used. Also, a nongovernment employee has been hired to ensure and expedite the delivery of goods through apt channels. By taking aggressive action in relation to problems, Monsanto does not waste time and money that could be invested in other areas.

Although Monsanto has over 40 years' experience in this market, it does not rely solely on past sales strength to support its base of trade in the FSU. It continues investing in new ventures and exporting new technology to the FSU to assist the development of FSU competitiveness in the world marketplace. Two examples of this strategy are the Agrocenters and diamond-like coatings.

Lessons to be learned from Monsanto's experience are numerous. Companies must be willing to engage in long-term investment. A solid base of trust should be established since a long-term commitment and relationship is of paramount value to FSU clients. Aggressive action must be taken to find a successful business. Training the Soviet side on how to manage their portions of the operation is essential. Finally, given the lack of available hard currency, businesses have to work with the Soviets to find alternative forms of payments in order to facilitate operations.

Business in the FSU is insecure and unstable. However, the Monsanto case demonstrates that with hard work, investment, and an ability to adapt to constantly changing factors, a business can succeed in the FSU. The key is to develop a long-term strategy and not expect immediate returns. With a commitment to the future in the FSU, companies can overcome present-day obstacles.

NOTES

1. Monsanto Company, *This is Monsanto* (St. Louis: Monsanto Company, 1991). For further information on the history of Monsanto Company, see Dan J. Forrestal, *Faith, Hope, and $5,000: The Story of Monsanto* (New York: Simon and Schuster, 1977).

2. "Going Global: An Interview with Earl H. Harbison, Jr., President and Chief Operating Officer of Monsanto Company, and 1992 Chairman of the Board of the St. Louis Regional Commerce and Growth Association," *St. Louis Commerce Magazine*, April 1991, p. 5. Monsanto Company is segmented into four geographic categories: Europe-Africa, Asia-Pacific, Canada, and Latin America. The countries in which Monsanto has major manufacturing plants are the United States, Canada, United Kingdom, Belgium, France, Japan, Mexico, Puerto Rico, Australia, and Brazil.

3. Michael A. Petrilli, International Sales Director, Fibers Division, The Chemical Group of Monsanto, phone interview by author, November 4, 1992, Denver, notes.

4. Bradley W. Hill, International Development Director, The Chemical Group of Monsanto, interview by author, November 10, 1992, questionnaire.

5. Petrilli interview.

6. "Soviet Transactions with Monsanto and Dow," *Chemical Week*, December 1, 1982, p. 19. See also, Matthew J. Sagers and Theodore Shabad, *The Chemical Industry in the U.S.S.R.: An Economic Geography* (Boulder, Colo.: Westview Press, 1990).

7. "Soviet Transactions with Monsanto and Dow," p. 19.

8. James R. Savage, Director of Technology, License, and Acquisitions, Advanced Placement Materials, Monsanto Company, interview by author, November 10, 1992, St. Louis, notes. A group of men were sent to Uzbekistan for six months and described the experience as the worst ordeal of their lives. Monsanto had trouble with communications and getting supplies to the men. Another man was sent to Kiev for a start-up operation, but had a much different experience. He bought a bike, went to the market every Sunday, and interacted with the local culture as much as possible.

9. Charles A. Ross, III, Vice-President Human Resources, The Chemical Group of Monsanto, interview by author, November 9, 1992, St. Louis, notes.

10. Frank Messer, "The Monsanto 'Jewel' Moscow May Snatch," *Business Week*, October 26, 1981, p. 86.

11. Hill interview. Ross said that in 1992 Soviet businessmen visited one of Monsanto's world-class phosphate plants in Soda Springs, Idaho, where they expressed interest in purchasing an environmental technology package for use in their phosphate plants.

12. Ross interview.

13. Hill interview.

14. Robert A. Westoby, Director of International Cash Management and Foreign Exchange, Monsanto Company, interview by author, November 10, 1992, St. Louis, notes. In 1988, Soviet Deputy Prime Minister Vladimir Gusev met with Monsanto President Richard Mahoney and toured a Monsanto demonstration farm in Chesterfield, Missouri.

15. In 1988, Monsanto Company, Coca-Cola Co., American Express, and Rubicam Inc. gave a one-day course in marketing at the opening of a meeting between

U.S. and Soviet officials to explore trade opportunities. "U.S. Ad Techniques Take Soviets by Surprise," *Chicago Tribune*, April 13, 1988, p. 5(C).

16.   John B. Lewis, Projects Director, Global Operations Division, The Agriculture Group of Monsanto, interview by author, November 10, 1992, St. Louis, notes.

17.   Ibid.

18.   Monsanto Company, Agricultural Division, "Agrocenter: Sumy, Ukraine" (St. Louis: Monsanto Company, 1992), p. 3. See also, Monsanto Company, *Annual Report: 1991* (St. Louis: Monsanto Company, 1992), p. 3; *This Is Monsanto*, p. 3.

19.   Hill interview.

20.   Savage interview.

21.   Westoby interview. Petrilli said that the ratio of Soviet to Western workers in Moscow is 4:1.

22.   Petrilli interview.

23.   Westoby interview.

24.   Sabrina Eaton, States News Service, January 4, 1989.

25.   Westoby interview.

26.   Savage interview. The fund is set up for a laboratory under the direction of Mr. Fedoseyev, scientist. Mr. Fedoseyev has also had the opportunity to visit operations in the United States.

27.   Hill interview.

28.   Petrilli interview.

29.   The paragraphs were a summary of information from Hill, Petrilli, and Ross interviews.

30.   Savage interview.

31.   Westoby interview.

32.   Hill interview.

33.   Westoby interview.

34.   Ibid.

35.   Monsanto executives, interview by author, November 10, 1992, St. Louis.

36.   Petrilli interview.

37.   Ross interview.

38.   Westoby interview.

39.   Ross interview.

40.   Westoby interview. Monsanto executives recall a legend about their countertrade business where a shipment of boots was delivered only to be opened and found to be all right-footed.

41.   Monsanto executives interview.

42.   Hill and Westoby interviews.

43.   C. B. Anagnostopoulos, "Monsanto's Patent," *Business Week*, December 7, 1981, p. 7.

44.   Messer, "The Monsanto 'Jewel' Moscow May Snatch," p. 7.

45.   Hill interview.

46.   Ibid.

47.   Lewis interview.

8

Marketization through Defense Conversion: A Policy Perspective on the Ukrainian Case

Margaret B. McLean and Deborah Anne Palmieri

A major challenge in the transition to a market economy for post-Communist countries is the creation from the ashes of the old command economy a productive and successful economic model that will lead these countries into the twenty-first century. While there are obvious obstacles to successful economic growth and development, post-Communist countries are uniquely positioned to rebuild their economies. No longer constrained by old Communist models and norms they are poised for a fresh start filled with unique, unconventional opportunities.

To develop futuristic perspectives, one needs to step back from stereotypical notions of socialism and communism, planned economies and free enterprise, democracy and dictatorship, and construct a hybrid economic model that, ideally, combines the best features of both market and command economic systems. Such a new hybrid model would focus not only on what was wrong with the old model of socialist economics but also on what worked successfully with the old system. By emphasizing the strong points of old economic experiences, the builders of the new economic regime can retain the most positive features and enhance them with innovative ideas from market economics, taking advantage of the lessons learned in the West through free enterprise and several hundred years experience of market-driven economics.

Among the first priorities of a successful transition should be economic stabilization, an increase in productivity, and the creation of national industrial and social well-being. Much of the industrial wealth of post-Communist countries is currently locked in the military-industrial complex. Unlocking this potential through the conversion process is a major challenge on the road to economic recovery and stabilization.

DEFENSE CONVERSION IN UKRAINE

The opportunities tied to conversion are especially compelling for Ukraine, because the defense sector has historically played a significant role in its economy. At present, Ukraine owns approximately 30 percent of the former Soviet military-industrial complex and up to 20 percent of its scientific centers.[1] As part of the old USSR, Ukrainian industrial production was heavily subsidized through supplies of artificially low-priced Soviet oil, certain metals, and other raw materials. The subsidies and the military focus of the manufacturing base created a fertile soil for technological development, making Ukraine into one of the most technologically advanced of the newly independent post-Communist countries. The development of advanced technologies is directly linked to the aviation and shipbuilding industries, production of high-grade metals, chemicals, pharmaceuticals, laser and optical technologies, and heavy machinery.

Endowed with technological expertise, a strong manufacturing base, and a highly educated population, Ukraine clearly possesses the potential to become one of the leading countries in Europe. Historically known as a bread basket of Europe, Ukraine accounted for 25 percent of all the grain and meat and 50 percent of the sugar produced in the former Soviet Union. Ukraine also contributed at least 20 percent of the former Soviet Union's industrial production, including 33 percent of steel, 50 percent of transportation-related production such as locomotives, ships, and airplanes, and a major share of high technology production.[2]

Yet despite its technological advantage and its strong agricultural base, Ukraine is not faring well on its road to post-Communist recovery. Ukrainian gross domestic product fell 25 percent in 1992 and is expected to fall by at least that much in 1993, and inflation could top 3,000 percent this year. The reasons behind Ukrainian difficulties are outdated energy-inefficient manufacturing equipment, lack of self-sufficiency stemming from the long-standing reliance on command-driven raw material supply networks, and stagnation of innovation due to archaic labor policies and lack of individual incentives. Conversion of the military-industrial complex should address these problems by providing avenues for technological upgrading of the manufacturing equipment, introducing new supply and distribution networks, and bringing innovation and increased productivity to the major sectors of the Ukrainian economy. Conversion, if properly implemented, can help solve housing shortages, accelerate development and implementation of information technologies, develop and improve transportation systems, re-equip health facilities, and achieve other currently elusive economic and social goals.[3]

The conversion process is not a simple task, however, and the implementation of any conversion strategy is complex and difficult. Until recently, the military-industrial complex earned one-third of all hard currency revenues for the former Soviet Union. This lucrative market still exists for Ukraine, although now it must be more cautious about to whom it sells its military might. It is generally recognized that the challenge is not to destroy the defense-related industry but to convert it to serve economic and political interests of Ukraine and its people. Successful conversion efforts would require massive retooling of the basic industrial infrastructure, retraining of the defense-oriented labor force, creation of new supply and distribution networks for raw materials and production output, and the establishment of markets for Ukrainian products in other countries of the former Soviet Union, Eastern Europe, and the West.

Such ambitious goals are not inexpensive and the architects of the conversion process must address the issue of how the expenses of conversion can be financed. At present, the Ukrainian government has insufficient funding and resources to promote wholesale conversion and to deal with its inevitable consequences, such as massive unemployment, a displaced workforce, and widespread enterprise bankruptcies and their politically destabilizing consequences. The debate among officials over how to proceed with conversion ranges from conventional bureaucratic lip service to radical, unworkable ideas, and the real solutions are by no means clear-cut. A successful conversion process requires creativity and careful consideration of alternatives that would abate unemployment, increase productivity, and create new growth and future jobs.

Regrettably, Ukraine is not in the position of Russia or some of the Central Asian republics, which can conceivably finance their conversion efforts through their abundance of natural resources. Ukraine's major natural resource is its bountiful farmland. The products of Ukrainian agriculture, which fed Europe for centuries, are now tainted by the Chernobyl catastrophe and alone are not sufficient to support conversion in Ukraine. Ukraine's other valuable resources are its highly educated labor force and its enviable technological base. While in need of reeducation and upgrading, the labor and technological wealth may be used effectively to revamp military enterprises, increase domestic production and, where needed, attract foreign capital to Ukraine. Foreign investment need not be viewed as inconsistent with the stated Ukrainian goal of self-sufficiency, instead it must be viewed as an opportunity to jump-start the conversion process and bring jobs, state-of-the-art technologies and know-how to Ukraine.[4]

CHALLENGES OF CONVERSION

Prerequisites: Controlling the Energy Crisis

Ukraine's government clearly understands that the key to balanced economic growth, industrial prosperity, and military conversion is the availability of inexpensive or, at least, moderately priced energy. The government's emphasis on energy alternatives underscores the two-year quest to reduce Ukraine's dependence on Russian oil through the development of regional and international alliances. In the last year alone, Ukraine signed agreements with Uzbekistan and Turkmenistan to provide technical assistance in exploring and modernizing its oil and gas resources. Similar agreements to develop oil and gas deposits have been forged with Kazakhstan. Armed with these important alliances, Ukraine will restart existing oil facilities in Mangistau and Aktubinsk, construct a new pipeline between Ukraine and Kazakhstan, and modernize and expand tanker ports on the Black Sea.[5]

At the same time, Ukraine pursues international partners. Agreements with Iran, Turkey, and several countries of the Persian Gulf should result in additional oil supplies to Ukraine. Negotiations with France, the largest nuclear energy user in Europe, may result in reevaluation of the use of nuclear energy in Ukraine, the politically unpopular, but practically essential, move necessary to achieve industrial prosperity in Ukraine. Cooperative work with American, German, and Japanese scientists resulted in and will continue to produce breakthroughs in alternative energy such as electrical-powered vehicles, wind-powered factories, and energy-efficient machine-building equipment.[6]

Ukraine is not the only former Soviet republic with energy problems, yet due to its dire need and aggressive search for energy alternatives, Ukraine is emerging as a leader among former Soviet republics in formulating creative solutions to its energy crisis. Not only has Ukraine acquired favorable agreements with former Soviet republics and foreign partners to supply crude oil and natural gas below world-market prices, Ukraine has been instrumental in forcing Russia to participate in the Interstate Council on Oil and Gas (dubbed the "Soviet OPEC"), an organization designed to ensure cooperation between former Soviet republics on the issues of oil and gas supplies and exploration.

Economic Revitalization: Conversion Strategy

The energy crisis notwithstanding, Ukraine pursues an aggressive goal of self-sufficiency by attempting to revitalize its industrial base and stabilize a downspiraling economy. Analysts indicate that Ukraine appears to target conversion as the process to lead it on its road to economic recovery.[7] To consolidate its conversion efforts, Ukraine formed the Ministry of Conversion, the only former Soviet republic to do so, and reorganized its enterprises so that all military-related complexes report to the ministry. The ministry is charged with the unenviable task of converting Ukrainian military enterprises without destroying the defense industry that currently brings significant hard currency proceeds to Ukrainian economy and assures its security and political independence.[8]

Several strategies have been identified as concurrent and alternative ways to achieve challenging goals of conversion. Among them are the so-called "domestic regrouping" strategy, the "joint efforts" strategy, the "compensation" strategy, the "public finance" strategy, the "Western credits" strategy, and the "foreign manufacturing" strategy.[9] These strategies have relative merits and shortcomings as discussed below.

The "domestic regrouping" strategy involves retooling factories and creating markets for new nonmilitary products through internal domestic efforts and without external help. This strategy has proven to be very difficult to implement in the hard-currency-strapped Ukraine. Through trial and error, some Ukrainian enterprises have tried to regroup on their own. Without aggressive guidance and assistance from the government, the strategy met with mixed results. The major obstacles to successful regrouping are lack of experience and financing, sluggish demand for products of converted enterprises, and problems with raw material supplies and distribution networks outside of Ukraine. The Ministry of Conversion is trying to breathe new life into this strategy by providing more guidance to fledgling enterprises, assisting with raw materials and distribution channels, and encouraging enterprises to share their experiences.

"Joint efforts" is a strategy designed to be used concurrently with the "domestic regrouping" strategy. Its aim is to promote conversion through joint ventures and joint stock companies between Ukrainian military enterprises and foreign companies. Over 300 of these joint enterprises currently exist in Ukraine. Most of them are trade-oriented, however, providing few jobs and offering little progress in the direction of conversion. The key to the success of this strategy is Ukrainian enterprises' ability to attract the right foreign partner interested in long-term growth and revenue potential and not just short-term profits. To achieve this goal, Ukraine must develop a foreign investment incentives program that would attract growth-minded enterprising partners.

After declaring independence in 1991, the new Ukrainian government enacted numerous ambitious foreign investment laws and a new tax system. The new laws provided for tax holidays, special incentives for joint enterprises, certain profit repatriation guarantees, and seemingly benign currency regulations.[10] These laws do not focus specifically on conversion incentives; however, they offer similar benefits to foreign capital involved in trade activities and investors who are involved in important and higher risk infrastructure and conversion projects. Further, these laws have been amended numerous times after the original enactment, giving potential long-term investors little security as to the future stability of the laws. The "joint efforts" strategy, combined with the "domestic regrouping" strategy, has the potential of being very effective, provided that proper tax and business incentives are in place.

The "compensation" strategy is often discussed, but not yet implemented on a large scale. As stated above, the key to Ukrainian conversion is the retooling of military factories for nonmilitary use. This process is expensive and Ukrainian enterprises do not have the necessary hard currency to purchase Western machine tools or to upgrade locally produced equipment to the level of Western specifications or quality demands. Under the compensation strategy, foreign firms could supply Ukrainian companies with equipment and machinery, using a proportion of the resulting production as payment-in-kind.

This strategy is not new in principle. Natural resource enterprises have used it for years to finance exploration in the oil fields and mines with known substantial deposits. The market for natural resources such as petroleum, precious stones, and metals is clear and, therefore, the compensation for initial investment through production sharing in a natural resource exploration context is relatively simple. But, the market for the products of conversion is not always apparent and foreign firms are naturally more reluctant to invest. To overcome this reluctance, the Ukrainian government should introduce proper incentives designed to encourage investment in the retooling of Ukrainian military enterprises. Favorable export and tax regulations, combined with provisions for some control by the foreign investors on what the newly retooled enterprises can produce to generate profits, should produce a necessary stimulus to attract investment. This strategy is similar to the "joint efforts" strategy because foreign investors would bring in not only hard currency investment but also technologies and marketing know-how to develop markets for Ukrainian products outside of Ukraine. It is different in one important aspect, however. Under this strategy, foreign firms would not own equity interest in the converted Ukrainian enterprise.

The so-called "public finance" strategy involves the use of proceeds from Ukrainian foreign trade to reinvest into the retooling of defense-oriented factories. This reinvestment strategy can and should be used concurrently with several others outlined above. This is a very promising approach because it promotes the overall goal of Ukrainian self-sufficiency, while encouraging Ukrainian participation in the world market. As currently conceived, this strategy would entail an easing of export regulations to promote Ukrainian exports and hard currency earnings. The Ukrainian companies would then sell back 50 percent of their hard currency proceeds to the government for *Korbovantcies*, as is currently required by Ukrainian currency regulations. The collected funds would be reinvested by the Ukrainian government for the conversion of the military-industrial sector.

The major drawback of this approach is that it causes significant disincentives for Ukrainian business to return their hard currency earnings to Ukraine. While the easing of export restrictions and reduced tariffs are a surefire way to stimulate outbound trade and generate hard currency, the mandatory sale of hard currency earnings has the unfortunate side effect of producing capital flight in inflationary economies like that of Ukraine. Entrepreneurs are naturally reluctant to hold their profits in korbovantcies, that today loses its value at the hyperinflation rate of up to 25 percent per month. Entrepreneurs, therefore, have incentives to try to avoid mandatory currency sale-back regulations and try to keep their hard currency earnings abroad by reinvesting outside of Ukraine, thus "capital flight."

To avoid this "capital flight" phenomenon and to achieve the reinvestment of hard currency earnings into Ukrainian conversion, the government may consider providing tax and general business incentives for Ukrainian entrepreneurs to reinvest in Ukraine. If projected returns on investment in Ukrainian conversion projects are equal to or better than those available elsewhere, Ukrainian entrepreneurs would much rather reinvest in Ukraine and see their local economy prosper through their investment in the conversion process.

Another conversion strategy that is often mentioned is the use of "Western credits" to retool factories and convert defense enterprises. Western credits in excess of several billion dollars are available to Ukraine through the International Monetary Fund, World Bank, European Bank for Reconstruction and Development, and other multilateral financial organizations.[11] Further, certain money is available through the Export-Import Bank of the United States and through the Overseas Private Investment Corporation to provide financing to American companies interested in exporting their technology and products, including manufacturing equipment, to the republics of the former Soviet Union. Ukrainian enterprises, directly or through their American partners, should aggressively pursue these opportunities and use the funds to outfit the military-related enterprises with state-of-the-art technology and machine tools for domestic production. One critical point is that Ukraine should use its Western credits wisely, because, as with any debt, it eventually needs to be repaid. The use of Western credits, therefore, is most appropriate for investment in enterprises with revenue potential sufficient to repay the investment.

Finally, another conversion strategy that warrants consideration is the use of existing Ukrainian factories for production of foreign goods for export worldwide, the "foreign manufacturing" strategy. Western companies have used inexpensive labor in Southeast Asia and Latin America for years to produce sophisticated products. Ukraine possesses a labor force that is very inexpensive by the world market standards. Ukraine can and should compete successfully to attract the manufacturing companies of Western Europe and North America to its now idling defense factories. Foreign manufacturing would provide jobs to the labor force and new equipment and facilities to defense factories. Again, tax incentives, export regulations, and income repatriation concessions are the keys to successful implementation of this conversion strategy.

The strategies outlined above address the issue of retooling of the enterprises but must also consider the important companion issue of labor retraining. The Ukrainian labor force is one of the most educated, literate, and technically sophisticated in the world, yet it lacks expertise in Western technologies and industrial know-how. Computer literacy, for example, is low. A successful conversion strategy would have to include retraining of personnel in the use of modern technology as well as in new industrial skills in general.[12]

Retooling and upgrades in industrial processes will necessarily lead to the displacement of workers. To avoid massive unemployment, the workers will have to be retrained to do different jobs in the new post-conversion era. The retraining, just as retooling, is an expensive exercise that must be planned for and budgeted. The added challenge to retraining is the likely resistance from a complacent workforce, especially older workers reluctant to change and fearful of learning new skills. Yet despite its obvious difficulties and costs, retraining is essential for successful conversion.

IMPLEMENTATION OF CONVERSION STRATEGIES THROUGH ECONOMIC AND LEGAL INCENTIVES

Unquestionably, Ukraine needs to convert its military-industrial sector to increase productivity in the economy, to generate jobs and the demand for its products and services, and to transition successfully to a market economy. While much can be done through the strategies of "domestic regrouping" and "public finance," which include no foreign investment, foreign investment is still needed to jump-start an economy that for so long relied on the military-industrial complex as a source of employment and growth.

There are four critical steps that Ukraine must undertake to succeed in the conversion process. First, it must convince the world that it is a good investment.[13]

Its tax system must be pegged to allow for attractive returns on investment. It is important to remember that in its search for foreign investment Ukraine is competing for Western dollars with Russia, Kazakhstan, Poland, and other countries of Eastern Europe. A stable tax regime that encourages long-term investment, technology transfer, and employment is essential. While the current profit tax is pegged at a moderate 30 percent, the value-added tax is at a high 28 percent and repatriation withholdings are high. Export duties for manufacturing products that hover between 15 percent and 35 percent make manufacturing in Ukraine for export abroad unprofitable for most enterprises. Existing tax incentives are unfavorable for conversion projects and provide little incentive to pursue conversion-related business opportunities.

Another obstacle to foreign investment in Ukrainian conversion is that tax and business laws change too often, with new legislation often contradicting previous laws. This makes it difficult to plan for the future. Ukraine's attempt to deal with this problem through a grandfathering provision in the 1992 tax legislation — a provision that allowed businesses, for several years after the change in the law, to continue operating under the previous tax laws in effect at the time of the business formation, if the old tax regime was more favorable — was marred recently when the Ukrainian Parliament decided to override the grandfathering provision for the increase in the value-added tax. Focusing on the revenue-generating aspects of taxation, the Ukrainian government decidedly ignored the role of the tax system as an investment-attracting mechanism. This unfortunate event undermined the trust foreign business people had in the reliability of Ukrainian business law and the government's commitment to market reforms. Consequently, taxes should be pegged to attract foreign investment to the high priority industry sectors of Ukraine and the tax and business legal systems need to be stabilized to allow for long-range planning.

The second important step is that the legal and administrative framework should be modernized and streamlined to make it easier to do business in Ukraine. The government should encourage the dissemination of information on how to do business and how to participate in the conversion process. Ukrainian companies, when working with Western partners, should become more sensitive to Western business culture — this includes speeding up the negotiation process, standing by the commitments made, honoring contracts, and recognizing the importance of executing transactions, not just talking about them. Attorneys representing the interests of Ukrainian firms need to become more sophisticated, more familiar with international law, and more skilled in Western negotiation and dispute resolution techniques.

Third, Ukraine must address the problem of double taxation, often a stumbling block for foreign investment. In 1992 Ukraine started negotiations on the tax convention for avoidance of double taxation between Ukraine and the United States. Unfortunately, the process stalled and no progress occurred in the last six months. In the meantime, both Russia and Kazakhstan have negotiated similar treaties with the United States and several other foreign countries. The possibility of double taxation on profits generated in Ukraine makes it very difficult to attract serious foreign investors who are willing to make significant investments in the infrastructure and conversion process in Ukraine.

Fourth, as a final measure, Ukraine must develop and implement a workable framework for intellectual property protection. Protection for trademarks, copyrights, patents, trade secrets, and industrial know-how essentially does not exist in Ukraine today. Enactment and vigorous enforcement of intellectual property legislation is essential to attract conversion-related technology transfer projects and to make Ukraine a desirable site for foreign manufacturing.

Because the effective use of foreign capital in defense conversion projects requires a delicate balancing act of complex international and domestic economic, legal, financial, and political issues, the short-term outlook for the Ukrainian defense conversion is not necessarily clear-cut or even optimistic. One possible way to navigate effectively through these multiple obstacles is to create an advisory panel under the auspices of the Ukrainian Ministry of Conversion. The panel would combine the representatives from the ministry-selected defense enterprises, the Parliament, foreign and domestic lawyers, tax specialists, economists, and bankers who would offer multifaceted expertise and consulting to the ministry and the enterprises on an as-needed basis.

While the above observations and recommendations provide some solutions, they do not offer answers to all the questions. Even if implemented, they do not necessarily guarantee an immediate success in conversion, but they can be useful to stimulate the Ukraine economy on its way in the aggressive pursuit of its conversion strategies.

CONCLUDING REMARKS

In this turbulent period of transition from old command economies to new economic models, it is critical to realize that a market economy is not a panacea. As many capitalist countries discovered over the last several hundred years, the invisible hand of the market so eloquently immortalized by Adam Smith in *Wealth of Nations*, needs a slight push and a little guidance and planning to work efficiently for the benefit of society. The architects of post-Communist restructuring must realistically focus on what market economics can and cannot do to reverse the present malaise of declining gross domestic product, plunging national income, and sluggish labor productivity. Economists, government officials, technological experts, and the intelligentsia are charged with the development of a clear and realistic picture of how the operating principles of market economics can be specifically applied to the unique scenario of transition from centralized command-economy to a new hybrid model. Left with a legacy of economic growth fueled by the military-industrial complex and the completely neglected consumer sector, the transitioning economies must pay special attention to conversion from the defense-based economic machine to the more balanced and diverse industrial sectors.

Legal and economic incentives are probably the fastest and most efficient way to promote defense conversion and growth. The key to success lies in a combination of Western investment in critical sectors such as defense conversion and government initiatives to develop a well-balanced economy. Those post-Communist countries that can covert their military-driven economies into consumer-driven economies will likely succeed in conquering inflation and unemployment and will stand a better chance of transforming into robust economies that can compete successfully domestically and in the global economy.

NOTES

The authors acknowledge the research and editing assistance of A. Zuccarelli, an international analyst with Holme Roberts & Owen *LLC*. A version of this chapter appeared in the August 1993 issue of *Politichna Dumka*, a Ukrainian political economy publication.

1. Interview conducted with the former Ukrainian Minister for Machine-Building, Military Industry and Conversion Victor Antonov in *Krasnaya Zvezda*, Moscow: ITAR-TASS, World Service (1455 GMT, February 26, 1993). Anatoly Dokuchaev, "'Oboronka' Ukrainy vybiraem svoi put'," *Krasnaya Zvezda*, February 26, 1993, pp. 1, 2.

2. Report prepared for the U.S. Department of Commerce, Washington, D.C., "Country Profile: Commercial Overview of Ukraine," March 1993.

3. William J. Perry, "Demilitarization in Russia and the United States," *Russian, Ukraine and the U.S. Response*, vol. 8, no. 1 (1993): 31–42. Perry delivered this paper at the Twelfth Conference of the Aspen Institute, Queenstown, Maryland, January 9–14, 1993.

4. Iuri Serbin, "Ne nadeyatsia na dobrogo diadyu," *Holos Ukrainy,* no. 181 (September 23, 1992): 3.

5. See *Interfax* (Via Kyodo) (February 23, 1993) in FBIS-SOV (February 24, 1993), 64:2 and *Nezavisimaya Gazeta*, (February 27, 1993) in FBIS-VSR (March 18, 1993): 85:2.

6. See Viktor Rozsokha, "The International Atomic Energy Praises Us. Our Own People Condemn Us. Is This Justified?" *Holos Ukrainy*, May 15, 1993, p. 4; Anatoly Sychkov, "Sredstvo ot anemii," *Delovoi Mir*, no. 206 (October 24, 1992): 5; Viktar Volodin, "Ukraina, Armeniya i gosudarstva Srednei Azii v poiskakh soyuznikov," *Izvestia*, April 27, 1992, p. 4. Note also that France and Ukraine have agreed to cooperate in the development of nuclear technologies, Kiev Ukrainskii Radio in Ukrainian, 1855 GMT, July 1, 1992.

7. Dokuchaev, "'Oboronka' Ukrainy vybiraem svoi put'," pp. 1, 2. See also Andrey Kokoshin, "Forward March," *Delovoi Lyudi*, no. 32 (April 1993): 4. See also, "'Voennie Zavodi Ukrainy budut vypuskat' grazhdanskiu produktsiu," *Delovoi Mir*, December 11, 1992, p. 7.

8. Yuri Kornev, "O Konversii, o vremeni, o sebe," *Pravda Ukrainy*, June 23, 1992: 2. See also Victor I. Antonov, "Conversion of the Military Industries in Ukraine," in *The Role of the Military Sector in the Economics of Russia and Ukraine: Proceedings of the RAND-Hoover Symposium*, ed. C. Wolf (Santa Monica, Calif.: Rand, November 1992, pp. 139–51.

9.   See Antonov, *Krasnaya Zvezda*. See another interview with Antonov, "Vragu ne sdayiotsia nash gordii 'Variag'," *Promyshlennii Vestnik*, May 7, 1993, p. 5. Antonov discusses different conversion strategies, citing the economies of South Korea and Japan as ideal models in Victor Antonov, *Ekonomicheskaya gazeta*, no. 27 (July 1992): 6.

10.   See "Law on Foreign Investment," *Holos Ukrainy*, (April 25, 1992), pp. 6–8; "Law of Taxation on Enterprise, Organization Incomes," *Holos Ukrainy*, (March 19, 1992), pp. 2–3; "Law on the Privatization of State Enterprise Property," *Rabochaya gazeta*, (May 6, 199)2, p. 1. A good summary of these laws appears in a report titled "The Agriculture Storage and Transport Facilities Market in Ukraine," prepared by Yuri Polomev at the American Embassy-Kiev, December 1992.

11.   U.S. Department of Commerce, "Country Profile: Commercial Overview of Ukraine" (Washington, D.C.: U.S. Department of Commerce, 1993), p. 7. See also, announcement of opening of IMF office in Kiev, Kiev Radio Ukraine World Service, 2200 GMT, July 3, 1992.

12.   For more background, see editorial report, "The West on Russian-Style Conversion," Moscow Russian Television Network, 1945 GMT, May 18, 1993; Valery Baberdin, "The Defense Complex Is Russia's Asset. It Must Not Be Squandered!" *Krasnaya Zvezda*, December 12, 1992, p. 1.

13.   For more on Ukrainian economic reform and Western attitude toward Ukraine, see interview with Volodymyr Ryzhov, economic advisor to Leonid Kuchma in *Uryadovyy Kuryer* (March 23, 1993) in FBIS-SOV (March 31, 1993), 63:1.

APPENDIX

Chronology of Major Soviet and Post-Soviet Decrees and Developments Pertaining to Foreign Economic Relations with the West, August 1991 to July 1993

10/91 President Mikhail Gorbachev and the presidents of eight republics sign an economic union treaty in Moscow declaring that private ownership and competition is key to economic recovery. Republics not signing included Azerbaijan, Georgia, Moldova, and Ukraine.

USSR joins IMF as special associate member. USSR President Gorbachev and IMF Managing Director Michael Camdessus exchange letters.

Twelve Soviet republics sign memorandum to collectively assume responsibility for Soviet foreign debt, estimated to be about $60 billion.

11/91 USSR State Council abolishes 36 Union ministries and 37 other Union agencies. Ministry of Foreign Affairs and Ministry of Economic Relations merged into new Ministry of Foreign Relations.

Ukraine and Moldova sign Soviet economic union treaty.

Parts of this chronology are derived from Paul R. Surovell, *Interflo: A Soviet Trade News Monitor* (Maplewood, N.J.), various issues. It continues as a sequence from the chronology in Deborah Anne Palmieri, ed., *The USSR in the World Economy* (Westport, Conn.: Praeger, 1992), Appendix. That chronology ran from March 1985 to August 1991. All Interflo materials used with permission from Paul Surovell. Some information derived from the *World Almanac 1993* (New York: Pharos Books, 1992).

11/91   Seven Soviet republics reach a preliminary agreement on a loose confederation, "Union of Sovereign States."

Decree passed on USSR Trade Missions abroad.

Russian President Boris Yeltsin granted broad powers to initiate radical economic reforms.

Decree passed on Liberalization of Foreign Economic Activity in RSFSR, signed November 15.

World Bank President Lewis Preston and USSR President Gorbachev sign major agreements on technical cooperation. World Bank will provide technical advice on a range of topics, including macroeconomics, foreign investment, and the development of a legal framework.

G-7 agrees to reschedule Soviet debt through end of 1992 if Soviets meet numerous conditions, including timely interest payments and adherence to IMF recommendations on economic reform.

New organization, East European Cooperation and Trade, formed to revive economic relations among former COMECON countries. Includes Russia, Bulgaria, Poland, Czechoslovakia, Kazakhstan, Hungary, and Ukraine.

12/91   Soviet Union disbanded and replaced by Commonwealth of Independent States with 12 of the 15 republics participating. President Mikhail Gorbachev resigns, and Russian President Boris Yeltsin becomes dominant personality in the Commonwealth.

Text of Basic Provisions of Program for Privatization of State and Municipal Enterprises in Russian Federation for 1992 approved by Russian Government. Program also implements Russian Law on Privatization of State and Municipal Enterprises of July 1991.

IMF creates new department for former Soviet republics.

1/92   Numerous regions in FSU begin establishing free economic zones.

Russian Supreme Soviet Decree on USSR Bank for Foreign Economic Affairs.

Paris Club of 17 creditor governments agrees to allow 8 former Soviet republics to defer principal loan payments on $3.2 billion.

2/92   Russian Central Bank assumes control over USSR Bank for Foreign Economic Affairs per earlier decree by Russian Supreme Soviet Presidium.

Decree by President Yeltsin transforms Committee on Foreign Economic Relations into Ministry of Foreign Economic Relations, to be led by Petr Aven. Yeltsin creates his own Ministry of Economy, led by Andrei Nechayev, and Ministry of Finance, led by Yegor Gaidar.

4/92   Yeltsin Decree No. 388 to create Export Control System to protect Russia's exports, particularly in the areas of raw materials, technology, scientific information, and military weapons.

IMF approves membership for 14 of 15 former Soviet republics.

G-7 approves $24 billion aid package for Russia.

5/92   Russian Government Decree No. 360 issued on Statute on Plenipotentiaries of Russian Ministry of Foreign Economic Relations in Russian Federation republics, krais, oblasts, autonomous, and individual regions. Primary tasks of plenipotentiaries are to assist in development of regions' foreign economic relations and to implement state control and regulations in accordance with legislation.

6/92   President Bush and President Yeltsin hold first ever United States-Russia Business Summit. Outcome of the conference is MFN tariff treatment for Russia; Bilateral Investment Treaty, which allows for the free transfer of profits, a guarantee of non-expropriation of United States investments and international arbitration to settle business disputes; Treaty for the Avoidance of Double Taxation of Income; a United States-Russian Business Development committee, and numerous other joint agreements and declarations.

Russia becomes member of IMF.

7/92   Russian Central Bank issues instructions on Procedures for Mandatory Sale of Percentage of Hard Currency through Authorized Banks. Includes Procedures for Purchasing Foreign Exchange on Domestic Hard Currency Market.

Russian Government Decree No. 443 on Foreign Exchange and Economic Commission of Russian Government.

President Yeltsin adopts additional package of legislative acts and decrees to liberalize foreign economic activity and guarantee private investment.

Russian government appoints Deputy Prime Minister Aleksandr Shokhin to head Foreign Exchange and Economics Commission that replaces Foreign Exchange and Economics Council.

UN Commission for Europe reports number of joint ventures registered in FSU rose to 6,600 in April 1992 from 5,600 in January 1992, but many may not be operational.

President Yeltsin appoints Deputy Prime Minister Aleksandr Shokhin as Russian representative to IMF and IBRD.

8/92 IMF approves $1 billion credit line and World Bank approves $600 million credit line to Russia.

President Yeltsin disbands Ministry of Finance Foreign Investment Committee, and transfers its functions to Russian International Collaboration and Development Agency, headed by Deputy Prime Minister Aleksandr Shokhin.

Russian representative to international financial institutions, Konstantin Kagabvsky, is named Russian executive director at IMF.

9/92 Russia retracts previous commitment to assume liability for entire debt of FSU; complicates Russian debt talks with IMF and Western creditors.

European Commission launches tender to select consortium of European banks to assist new Russian Project Finance Bank.

Western credits promised to Russia delayed or suspended because of loan defaults and concerns over whether Russia can repay new loans.

10/92 Paris Club meeting of creditors of FSU unable to reach decision on postponement of debt.

11/92 Russia defaults on grain credits from United States, Canada, and France.

Russian Government Decree No. 848 on Use of Foreign Credits Granted to Russia on Basis of Intergovernment Agreements.

Russian Government Decree No. 854 on Licensing and Setting Quotas on Export and Import of Goods (Work, Services) in Russia.

12/92 World Bank approves $90 million loan for Russian privatization program.

Western creditors agree to defer Russian foreign debt payments until March 1993.

Russia warns that it can afford to pay only $2.5 billion of its foreign debt in 1993, according to Russian Foreign Economic Relations Ministry.

Prime Minister Yegor Gaidar is forced to resign following parliamentary pressure against his economic reforms. He is replaced by a conservative, Viktor Chernomyrdin.

Foreign Economic Relations Minister Petr Aven replaced by his former deputy, Sergei Glazyov.

1/93 Russia, Norway, Sweden, and Finland agree to set up a joint council to promote Arctic cooperation in trade, environmental protection, and other areas.

New Russian export duties introduced on commodities including crude oil, rare earth metals, anthracite, lumber, copper scrap, aluminum, and others.

2/93 United States Export-Import Bank approves $86.2 million to GAZPROM, its first direct loan to Russia.

3/93 Western commercial bank creditors agree to defer for three months former Soviet debt payments due 31 March 1993. Deferral is the sixth since December 1991.

IMF temporarily stops granting loans to Russia.

GATT reports that Russia did not rank among top 25 trading nations in 1992 (although USSR ranked in top 20 in 1991).

3/93   Russian exports to West were down 25 percent in 1992 to $27.6 billion, while imports fell 22 percent to $25.6 billion.

Russian Government Decree No. 406 on Review of Concessions (Privileges) in Foreign Economic Activity. Concessions will be confirmed and renewed by ruling of Government Monetary and Economic Commission.

4/93   Paris Club of 19 Western creditor governments agrees to reschedule more than $15 billion of $20 billion of former USSR debt payments owed in 1993. Agreement provides six-year grace period, after which repayment will be spread over ten semi-annual installments.

G-7 agrees on $28.4 billion aid package for Russia at Tokyo meeting (does not include $15 billion Paris Club debt rescheduling agreement). Package includes $12.4 billion in loans from IMF, World Bank, and IBRD; $6 billion IMF sponsored ruble stabilization fund; $10 billion in loans and loan guarantees from national export-import banks.
Boris Yeltsin obtains a majority on the referendum related to presidential confidence and economic reforms.

5/93   Russian Central Bank Statute on Procedure for Importing into Russia and Exporting from Russia Foreign Currency and Securities in Foreign Currency by Authorized Banks.

President Clinton and Russian President Boris Yeltsin meet at summit talks in Vancouver, Canada. Clinton announces $1.6 billion aid package to Russia.

7/93   G-7 grants $3 billion to Russia to help privatize big state enterprises, including export credits, loans from international financial institutions, grants, and technical assistance.

IMF approves $1.5 billion loan to Russia.

Selected Bibliography

Aganbegyan, Abel. *The Economic Challenge of Perestroika*. Bloomington: Indiana University Press, 1988.

Aslund, Anders, ed. *The Post-Soviet Economy: Soviet and Western Perspectives*. New York: St. Martin's Press, 1992.

Assetto, Valerie J. *The Soviet Bloc in the IMF and the IBRD*. Boulder, Colo.: Westview Press, 1988.

Bergson, Abraham and Herbert S. Levine, eds. *The Soviet Economy: Toward the Year 2000*. London: George Allen & Unwin, 1983.

Bertsch, Gary. *East-West Strategic Trade: CoCom and the Atlantic Alliance*. Paris: Atlantic Institute for International Affairs, 1983.

Blasier, Cole. *The Giant's Rival: The U.S.S.R. and Latin America*. Pittsburgh: University of Pittsburgh Press, 1983.

Boettke, Peter J. *Why Perestroika Failed: The Politics and Economics of Socialist Transformation*. New York: Routledge, 1993.

Bornstein, M., et al., eds. *East-West Relations and the Future of Eastern Europe: Politics and Economics*. London: Allen & Unwin, 1981.

Bradshaw, Michael. *The Effects of Soviet Dissolution*. London: Royal Institute of International Affairs, 1993.

Brykina, V. A. and B. S. Vaganova, eds. *Vnesheekonomicheskie sviazi sovetskogo soiuza no novom etape*. Moscow: Mezhdunarodnye otnosheniia, 1977.

Clemens, Walter C. *Can Russia Change?: The USSR Confronts Global Interdependence*. New York: Routledge, 1993.

Collins, Susan M. and Dani Rodrik. *Eastern Europe and the Soviet Union in the World Economy*. Washington, D.C.: Institute for International Economics, 1991.

Colton, Timothy J. and Robert Legvold. *After the Soviet Union: From Empire to Nations*. New York: W. W. Norton and Co., 1992.

Desai, Padma. *Perestroika in Perspective: The Design and Dilemmas of Soviet Reform*. Princeton, N.J.: Princeton University Press, 1990.

Edwards, Geoffrey and Elfriede Regelsberger, eds. *Europe's Global Links: The European Community and Inter-Regional Cooperation*. New York: St. Martin's Press, 1990.

Fallenbuchl, Zbigniew M., ed. *Partners in East-West Economic Relations: The Determinants of Choice.* Ontario: University of Windsor and H. McMillan, 1980.

Friedlander, Michael, ed. *Foreign Trade in Eastern Europe and the Soviet Union.* The Vienna Institute for Comparative Economic Studies Yearbook II. Boulder, Colo.: Westview Press, 1990.

Frieson, Connie M. *The Political Economy of East-West Trade.* New York: Praeger, 1976.

Fukuyama, Francis. *Gorbachev and the New Soviet Agenda in the Third World.* R-3634-A. Santa Monica, Calif.: The Rand Corporation, 1989.

Geron, Leonard. *Soviet Foreign Economic Relations under Perestroika.* New York: Council on Foreign Relations Press, 1990.

Gorbachev, Mikhail S. *Perestroika: New Thinking for Our Country and the World.* New York: Harper & Row, 1987.

Hasegawa, Tsuyoshi and Alex Pravda, eds. *Perestroika: Soviet Domestic and Foreign Policies.* London: Royal Institute of International Affairs, 1990.

Havrylyshyn, Oleh and John Williamson. *From Soviet disUnion to Eastern Economic Community?* Washington, D.C.: Institute for International Economics, 1991.

Hecht, John L., ed. *Rubles and Dollars: Strategies for Doing Business in the Soviet Union.* New York: HarperCollins, 1991.

Hewett, Ed A. *Reforming the Soviet Economy: Equality vs. Efficiency.* Washington, D.C.: Brookings Institution, 1988.

Hewett, Ed A. with Clifford G. Gaddy. *Open for Business: Russia's Return to the Global Economy.* Washington, D.C.: Brookings Institution, 1992.

Hewett, Ed A. and Victor H. Winston, eds. *Milestones in Glasnost and Perestroika.* Washington, D.C.: Brookings Institution, 1991.

Holzman, F. D. *International Trade under Communism: Politics and Economics.* New York: Macmillan, 1976.

Hough, Jerry F. *Opening up the Soviet Economy.* Washington, D.C.: Brookings Institution, 1988.

____. *Russia and the West: Gorbachev and the Politics of Reform.* 2d ed. New York: Simon and Schuster, 1990.

IMF, IBRD, OECD, EBRD. *A Study of the Soviet Economy.* Paris, February 1991.

Institute for East-West Security Studies. *Managing the Transition: Integrating the Reforming Socialist Countries into the World Economy.* First-Year Report by Working Group on International Economic Change, Restructuring, and East-West Security. New York: Institute for East-West Security Studies, 1989.

Islam, Shafiquil and Michael Mandelbaum, eds. *Making Markets: Economic Transformation in Eastern Europe and the Post-Soviet States.* New York: Council on Foreign Relations Press, 1993.

Joint Economic Committee. *Gorbachev's Economic Plans.* Vol. 2. Study Papers submitted to the JEC Congress of the United States. Washington, D.C.: U.S. Government Printing Office, 1987.

Jones, Anthony and William Moskoff. *The Great Market Debate in Soviet Economics.* New York: M. E. Sharpe, 1991.

Kemme, David M. and Claire E. Gordon, eds. *The End of Central Planning? Socialist Economies in Transition: The Cases of Czechoslovakia, Hungary, China, and the Soviet Union.* New York: Institute for East-West Security Studies and Hellenic Foundation for Defense and Foreign Policy, 1990.

Kostecki, M. M. *East-West Trade and the GATT System.* New York: St. Martin's Press, 1978.

Kraus, Michael and Ronald D. Lebowitz, eds. *Perestroika and East-West Economic Relations.* New York: New York University Press, 1990.

Kulbalkova, V. and A. A. Cruickshank. *Thinking New about Soviet New Thinking.* Berkeley: University of California, Institute of International Studies, 1989.

Lang, Laszlo. *International Regimes and the Political Economy of East-West Relations.* Occasional Paper 13. New York: Institute for East-West Security Studies, 1989.

Lavigne, Marie. *International Political Economy and Socialism.* New York: Cambridge University Press, 1990.

Lawrence, Paul R. and Charlambos A. Vlachoutsicos, eds. *Behind the Factory Walls: Decision Making in Soviet and U.S. Enterprises.* Boston: Harvard Business School Press, 1990.

Levcik, F. and Jan Stankovsky. *Industrial Cooperation Between East and West.* New York: M. E. Sharpe, 1979.

Levinson, Charles. *Vodka-Cola.* 2d ed. Essex, England: Anchor Press, 1980.

Liebowitz, Ronald, ed. *Gorbachev's New Thinking.* Cambridge: Ballinger, 1988.

Lynch, Allen. *The Soviet Study of International Relations.* Cambridge: Cambridge University Press, 1987.

Milanovic, Branko. *Liberalization and Entrepreneurship: Dynamics of Reform in Socialism and Capitalism.* New York: M. E. Sharpe, 1989.

Milner, Boris Z. and Dimitry S. Lvov. *Soviet Market Economy: Challenges and Reality.* Amsterdam: North Holland, 1991.

Moskoff, William. *Hard Times: Impoverishment and Protest in the Perestroika Years.* New York: M. E. Sharpe, 1993.

Naylor, Thomas H. *The Gorbachev Strategy: Opening the Closed Society.* Lexington, Mass.: Lexington Books, D. C. Heath, 1988.

Neu, C. R. and John Lund. *Toward a Profile of Soviet Behavior in International Financial Markets.* R-3524-USDP. Santa Monica, Calif.: The Rand Corporation, August 1987.

Neuberger, Egon and Laura D. Andrea Tyson, eds. *The Impact of International Economic Disturbances on the Soviet Union and Eastern Europe Transmission and Responsibility.* New York: Pergamon Press, 1980.

Nove, Alec. *East-West Trade: Problems, Prospects, Issues.* Beverly Hills, Calif.: Sage, 1978.

Palmieri, Deborah Anne. *The USSR and the World Economy: Challenges for the Global Integration of Soviet Markets under Perestroika.* Westport, Conn.: Praeger, 1992.

Puffer, Sheila M., ed. *The Russian Management Revolution: Preparing Managers for the Market Economy.* New York: M. E. Sharpe, 1992.

Saunders, Carl T., ed. *Money and Finance in East and West.* Vol. 4. The East-West European Economic Interaction Workshop Papers, The Vienna Institute for Comparative Economic Studies. New York: Springer-Verlag, 1978.

Scherr, Alan. *Foreign Direct Investment in the Soviet Union: Status and Trends.* Briefing Paper No. 5, Project on Soviet Foreign Economic Policy and Economic Security. Providence, R.I.: Brown University, Center for Foreign Policy Development, 1991.

Schiffer, Jonathan. *Soviet Regional Economic Policy.* New York: Macmillan and St. Martin's Press, 1989.

Shiryayev, Y. and A. Sokolov. *CMEA and European Economic Cooperation.* Moscow: Novosti, 1976.

Smith, Alan. *Russia and the World Economy.* New York: Routledge, 1993.

Surovell, Paul R. *Soviet Trade and Investment under Mikhail Gorbachev: A Chronology, 1985–1990.* Maplewood, N.J.: Interflo, 1991.

Tedstrom, John, ed. *Perestroika and the Dilemma of Soviet Economic Reform.* Boulder, Colo.: Westview Press, 1990.

Theberge, James D. *The Soviet Presence in Latin America*. New York: Crane Russack, 1974.

Ticktin, Hillel. *Origins of the Crisis in the USSR: Essays on the Political Economy of a Disintegrating System*. New York: M. E. Sharpe, 1992.

van Brabant, Jozef M. *The Planned Economies and International Economic Organizations*. New York: Cambridge University Press, 1991.

____. *Privatizing Eastern Europe: The Role of Markets and Ownership in the Transition*. The Netherlands: Kluwer Academic Publishers, 1992.

Weichhardt, Reiner, ed. *The Soviet Economy under Gorbachev*. Brussels: NATO Economics Directorate and Office of Information and Press, 1991.

Wilczynski, Jozef. *The Economics and Politics of East-West Trade*. New York: Praeger, 1969.

____. *The Multinationals and East-West Relations: Towards Transideological Collaboration*. Boulder, Colo.: Westview Press, 1976.

Williamson, John. *The Economic Opening of Eastern Europe*. Washington, D.C.: Institute for International Economics, 1991.

____. *Trade and Payments after Soviet Disintegration*. Washington, D.C.: Institute for International Economics, 1992.

____. *Economic Consequences of Soviet Disintegration*. Washington, D.C.: Institute for International Economics, 1993.

Woolcock, Stephen. *Western Policies on East-West Trade*. London: Royal Institute for International Affairs, 1982.

Index

About the Editor and Contributors

DEBORAH ANNE PALMIERI is President of the Russian-American Chamber of Commerce and an Adjunct Professor at the University of Denver specializing in economic and business relations between Russia and the West. She is the author of *The USSR and the World Economy* (1992) and co-author of *The Dynamics of Soviet Foreign Policy* (1989) in addition to numerous business writings and academic articles. She is the recipient of over 12 major academic honors, including MacArthur Scholar Fellow at Duke University; Columbia Presidential Fellow; and Visiting Scholar at the London School of Economics.

ARIEL COHEN is Salvatori Fellow in Russian and Eurasian Studies at the Heritage Foundation, a Washington, D.C., public policy research institute, where he writes extensively for the national and international press. He has written extensively on Soviet and Russian politics and business.

EILEEN M. CRUMM is an Assistant Professor at the University of Southern California, School of International Relations. She is currently working on a book comparing theories on how positive and negative incentives function in international politics. She has also written on privatization plans in the FSU republics, the U.S.-Soviet relationship, and emerging patterns of aid in the post–Cold War.

MARGARET B. MCLEAN is an Associate at the Denver law office of Holme Roberts & Owen. Her practice focuses on international business and tax law, with special emphasis on Eastern and Western Europe.

JAMES CLAY MOLTZ is Senior Researcher and Assistant Director of the Monterey Institute of International Studies, Program for Nonproliferation Studies. He has published widely on Russian economic and security issues, including in *Soviet Economy*, *Post-Soviet Geography*, and *World Politics*.

PAULA M. ROSS is a graduate student at the University of Denver, Graduate School of International Studies specializing in technology and economics in the former Soviet Union.

WILLIAM E. SCHMICKLE is Chair of the Political Science Department at Guilford College where he specializes in Russian foreign and domestic policy and the reform of the Russian foreign trade system. He has published numerous articles on Soviet and post-Soviet trade policy in *Crossroads* and *Russian Far East News*.

ERIC A. STUBBS is a Manager with the Price Waterhouse Financial and Economic Analysis Group in Washington, D.C. He was a member of the first U.S. delegation to testify before a committee of the Supreme Soviet and has authored 3 books and over 20 articles on Russian fiscal policy, financial institutions, East-West business, currency convertibility and reform.